T0287983

Onoto Watanna

THE ASIAN AMERICAN EXPERIENCE

Series Editor
Roger Daniels, University of Cincinnati

A list of books in the series appears at the end of this book.

Onoto Watanna

The Story of Winnifred Eaton

DIANA BIRCHALL

University of Illinois Press
URBANA AND CHICAGO

Manufactured in the United States of America
C 5 4 3 2 1
♾ This book is printed on acid-free paper.

Library of Congress Cataloging-in-Publication Data
Birchall, Diana, 1945–
Onoto Watanna : the story of Winnifred Eaton / Diana Birchall.
p. cm. — (The Asian American experience)
Includes bibliographical references and index.
ISBN 0-252-02607-1 (acid-free paper)
1. Eaton, Winnifred, 1875–1954. 2. Novelists, Canadian—20th century—Biography. 3. Eurasians—United States—Biography.
4. Chinese—Canada—Ethnic identity. 5. Asian American women—Biography. 6. Eurasians—Canada—Biography. 7. Japan—In literature.
I. Title. II. Series.
PR9199.3.W3689Z58 2001
813'.52—dc21 00-012167

For my son, Paul Birchall,
Winnifred's great-grandson
"1/16 Chinois"

It gives food for thought—the fact that a couple of centuries from now, the great grand children of the Chinese woman who married an American will be Americans and nothing else, whilst the descendants of her sister, who married a Chinaman and probably followed her husband to his own country will be Chinamen, pure and simple.

—Sui Sin Far (Edith Eaton)

Ideals are luxuries that few of us could afford to have.

—Onoto Watanna (Winnifred Eaton)

Contents

Acknowledgments

> I am myself quite excited over the prospect. Would not any one be who had worked as hard as I have—and waited as long as I have—for a book!
>
> —Sui Sin Far

I HAVE HAD AN enormous amount of help from many people, some of whom have become part of an extraordinary network of what we whimsically came to call "Winniers," stretching from the United States and Canada to Poland and Japan, who generously shared their discoveries and insights with me. We have conducted our "Winnying" largely by e-mail, and this has been a project that has drawn a far-flung family together and made many friendships of people living thousands of miles apart but linked by their interest and enthusiasm.

First and foremost I want to acknowledge the contribution of my first cousin Paul G. ("Tim") Rooney. He generously shared private family papers and photographs with me, and he and his wife, Mary, gave me the warmest hospitality on several visits to their home in Toronto, where I followed Tim around with a notebook to record all his personal reminiscences about our remarkable grandmother. Of no less importance was the help of his daughter Elizabeth Rooney, a library technician in Toronto, with whom I have spent three years in nearly constant e-mail communication. We started out almost strangers and are now the friendliest of cousins, who have shared all the excitement and joy of working on a project of mutual and absorbing interest. Elizabeth has patiently and promptly answered scores of family questions; has spent long hours in library research, unearthing long-lost stories by and articles about Winnifred; has copied photographs and documents; has shrewdly speculated about Winnifred and her life; and has excitedly run around Montreal, New York, and Banff with me in the pursuit of discoveries. We have grown to know Winnie together.

The third in the triumvirate of my greatest helpers has been Dominika Ferens, a graduate student at the University of California at Los Angeles who is now an assistant professor at Wrocław University, Poland, and who I learned by chance (a mutual acquaintance in a coffeehouse) was doing ethnological work on the Eaton sisters. Our e-mail acquaintance grew into friendly and fascinating weekly study sessions, and Dominika did nothing less than take me by the hand and teach me how to do academic research. I knew when I started this project that I, a nonacademic with nothing but an ancient and forgotten bachelor's in history, had to have help—"a researcher," I thought—but Dominika taught me how to help myself, in a process that at times seemed like getting a Ph.D. in midlife. In the midst of her own pressing scholarly concerns, she obtained books for me by routes to which I had no access; she was the one who discovered Edith Eaton's Jamaican writings; she arranged the screening of several of Winnifred's Hollywood films; and she helped and encouraged me in ways too numerous to list.

I am grateful to the late Amy Ling of the University of Wisconsin, who really put Winnifred Eaton on the scholarly map in the first place. From the start, she offered enthusiastic encouragement to a novice biographer. She generously shared her papers, pointed me in right directions, remained an authoritative sounding board for me in spite of her illness, and read an early draft of the manuscript. She is missed by all who knew her.

The work of another pioneering scholar, Annette White-Parks, was of the greatest importance to me; her seminal biography of Sui Sin Far, Winnifred's sister, was a model and an inspiration.

Special thanks to Jean Lee Cole, a doctoral candidate at the University of Texas at Austin who joined Dominika and me in many exciting and fulfilling hours of the research and discovery and was always there for me with intelligent, judicious advice. Thanks to Linda Moser of the Southwest Missouri State University for crucial early encouragement, for sharing her research papers, and for finding "Winnie" stories. Thanks to Eve Oishi of Long Beach State University for useful criticism that helped me reshape the book through several drafts. Thanks to James Doyle, Lisa Botshon, and Edward Marx for sharing key findings.

I am grateful to the wonderful staff at the University of Calgary Library, especially Apollonia Steele, for kind help far beyond the call of duty (or library hours). And to the staff at L'Atelier d'Histoire Hochelaga-Maissonneuve for assisting Elizabeth Rooney and me and for enduring my halting non-French questions. Warm thanks to my cousin L. Charles Laferrière and his wife, Celine, for welcoming me to their Montreal home and sharing family papers. And to my English cousins Bertie, Amalia, and Ted Lewis for kindly showing me Winnifred's ancestral home in Macclesfield and for helping me with library research there. Thanks to Roger Lewis for unearthing much family background information and to John Mann for providing me with fascinating information about the Home and Colonial Schools in England. Thanks to Frank K. Lorenz, curator of Special Collections at Hamilton College, for material about Bertrand Babcock that was a revelation to our family. Thanks to my editors, Karen Hewitt, Ann Lowry, and Jane Mohraz. Thanks to my mother, Helen Reeve, for her reminiscences about Winnifred and Paul Reeve. And thanks to my dear husband, Peter Birchall, for all the love and poetry in my life.

Introduction

IT WAS A CENTURY ago, in the spring of 1901, that Winnifred Eaton, an ambitious young woman writer of twenty-five, arrived, as so many hopeful young men and women did, in New York City. She had been taking aim at the big time for as long as she could remember, and her goal was now in her grasp. She had already published one novel, under the invented Japanese pen name Onoto Watanna, and dozens of stories. Like someone out of one of her own romantic tales, she carried in her valise the manuscript that was to bring her fame and fortune—*A Japanese Nightingale* would sell some 200,000 copies, would one day be made into a Broadway play and a silent film, and would make her famous.

The path to Winnifred's success was anything but a familiar formulaic tale; it was a do-or-die enterprise involving her whole being, during which she took not only a new name but also a new identity, a new age, even a fake ethnicity. Winnifred came from an extraordinary background. Growing up in Montreal as one of the fourteen half-caste children of an English artist and his Chinese wife, she had to contend with poverty and prejudice. Nonetheless, she possessed natural optimism and vitality, as well as a powerful, yet disarming egotism: for all the discouragement of her surroundings, she had a sublime self-confidence and firmly believed she was a wonderful girl, a singular girl. She voiced this feeling in her autobiographical novel (immodestly entitled *Me* but published anonymously): "Down in my heart there was the deep-rooted conviction, which nothing in the world could shake, that I was one of the exceptional human beings of the world, that I was destined to do things worth while. People were going to hear of *me* some day. I was not one of the commonplace creatures of the earth, and I intended to prove that vividly to the world."[1] These expressions of boundless confidence were tempered in her memoir with her rueful comment, "You perceive I had an excellent opinion of my ability at that time. I wish I had it now. It was more a conviction then—a conviction that I was destined to do something worth while as a writer."[2]

If she was not the divine writer who could stun the world with the éclat of her prose, she was a canny marketer, a desperate poseur, and an adventurer, a young woman who embodied the early-twentieth-century Horatio Alger attributes of pluck and spunk, because she had nothing to lose. Through any and all means open to her—deception, cleverness, manipulative wiles, bold independence, feminine seductiveness—Winnifred won the early commercial success and fame she craved. She experimented and postured her way through life, with the result that she led a very interesting one. She ultimately achieved a different renown, acknowledged years after her death, as a pioneer Asian American writer—very possibly the first Asian American novelist.

What she would have made of this distinction is an open question. Doubtless she would have been thrilled beyond measure to know that she had been rediscovered as a writer, beginning in the 1970s, twenty years after her death, and eventually resulting in the reissue of four of her novels (*Me, Miss Numè of Japan, The Heart of Hyacinth,* and *A Japanese Nightingale*). What would she have thought of the panels of academics who regularly meet at national conferences, ranging from the American Studies Association to the Association for Asian American Studies, to ponder the significance of her life and writing, her pose, her cultural heritage, her place in the Asian American literary canon, her significance as a cultural anomaly? Perhaps even the notion that her granddaughter, only glimpsed at the age of three, would write her biography half a century later would have made her smile. Like so much that happened in her life, these events were surprising. If Winnifred's fiction was both original and peculiar, her life was even more so.

As a young girl, Winnifred always had an example before her in her determination to shape herself as a literary woman and a cultural phenomenon. Her oldest sister, Edith Eaton, pointed the way. Under the pen name Sui Sin Far, Edith achieved only modest success in her short lifetime, but today she is respected, anthologized, and lauded as the mother of Asian American fiction, the writer of stories that present a humanized and sympathetic view of Chinese immigrants and the half-Chinese. Edith, a person of purpose and direction, wanted to be a champion of her people, through her writing, from as early as the age of eight. She was always a painfully sensitive girl, who took things harder than her rough-and-tumble younger siblings, and memories of her youth as a "half-caste" child formed her themes. She described the searing intensity of her feelings when she first recognized herself as Chinese, and how she responded to taunts by screaming, "I'd rather be Chinese than anything else in the world!" These feelings grew in her. "Why is my mother's race despised?" she asked. "I look into the faces of my father and mother. Is she not every bit as dear and good as he is?"[3]

Winnifred shared many of her older sister's feelings. She loved and felt protective of her Chinese mother ("poor little mama").[4] However, the legend and mystique of her mother's country did not cast its spell over her as it did over Edith. Winnifred never strongly identified herself as Chinese or championed their cause, though she admired Edith for doing so.

The young Winnifred, perhaps initially inspired by her father's travel tales, became passionately interested in the mystique of Japan. Edith could declare, "Behold, how great and glorious and noble are the Chinese people!"[5] But oddly, Winnifred, in her young days, seems to have felt that way about the Japanese—even though they were not her own race. Hers was an intriguing, perplexing obsession. It delighted her to write about this unknown, unseen country, a magical, mystical fairyland, and to play-act a Japanese role. With a knack for conveying her enthusiasm, she spun her way to popularity and fame. Boldly, she chose to lie about her ethnicity—to "become" a Japanese author and aristocrat—reasoning, perhaps, that it was not much of a shift: to her white audience, after all, Chinese and Japanese were much the same.

Winnifred was not ashamed of being Chinese and was known to speak proudly about her ancestry in private, but this was something she could never do publicly, lest she blow her Japanese "cover." When she eventually abandoned what had become a tiresome pose, her ethnic status was a topic to be avoided out of embarrassment at having practiced a deception in the first place. That, later in life, was her real shame—not her ethnicity but the lie—and despite the many interviews she gave in her life and her numerous confessional writings, she never once spoke about her past pretense.

Perhaps it was partly from not wanting to tread on the "Chinese" territory Edith had taken for her own that Winnifred ingeniously concocted her Japanese identity, at a time when "Japonisme" was all the rage but to be "Chinoise" was not. Only much later did she conclude that it was a "cheap device,"[6] not the real and enduring fame she had planned for herself.

Winnifred has been taken to task by some scholars and academics who disapprove of her elaborate deception in her bid to succeed and who approvingly embrace her older sister. It is true that she did not display a sense of morality and altruism as strongly as Edith did. That would have been a tall order, for Edith was an unusually unselfish, idealistic woman, to the point of being self-righteous and irritating at times. With her strong sense of family responsibility, fierce independence, and lifelong ill health, Edith remained unmarried and devoted herself to her high-minded goals. Winnifred, however, did not sacrifice a personal life. Although she took her responsibilities seriously and proved it by helping her family members during every stage and condition of her life, her principal aim was to get ahead, to succeed.

"Almost hysterically alive," is how a reviewer once described Winnifred,[7] and it was so. Blessed with self-assurance, bounding with vigor and life, Winnifred had the health and energy that her older writing sister lacked. The physical ills that Edith struggled against hampered her career and ended it early. But Winnifred was cut of different cloth. She had the energy to carve her way with more vitality than Edith did, and she was spurred on rather than held back by family ties. She traveled in a direction much different from her sister's, and she was successful far earlier and to a much greater commercial extent. Her output included at least fifteen published novels and some unpublished ones, an enormous assortment of screenplays and film treatments, and literally hundreds of short stories and articles.

Which sister was the better writer? There is no question which was the more prolific. When Edith died at forty-nine, she had published only one book of collected short stories, *Mrs. Spring Fragrance.* Today she is seen as more serious and enlightened, with views of cultural matters that were ahead of her time. Winnifred, by contrast, is a fascinating creature of subterfuge and contradictions, who perhaps had more natural writing talent—a facile use of words and a genuine gift for storytelling. But she wrote primarily for money, and although some writers have achieved greatness by doing so, she never rose to such heights. Her work is vivid and vital, however, and particularly in her autobiographical writing she displays freshness and urgency in delineating the life of a young working woman at the turn of the century that is informing and beguiling.

In addition to her fascination with Japanese culture and her perennial enjoyment in writing about herself, there was another touchstone in Winnifred's writing, something to which she returned again and again: her focus on the "half-caste" experience. Winnifred was as interested in such characters as Edith was, but she did not write solely about the half-Chinese or half-Japanese. Her characters are half-Mexican, half-French, half-Gypsy, half-black, half-Indian, half every brand of exotic background—and they are also, always, half-white. As a general rule, her characters are torn between their mother's people and their father's, and they possess contradictory qualities that are at war with one another. Not surprisingly, these qualities reflect the social attitudes of the time they were written: the typical "white" characteristic was refinement, while the nonwhite qualities were passion and artistic ability. In Winnifred's fiction, it is the two warring types of "blood" that make the Eurasian a unique, gifted individual, worthy of respect and possessing an innate nobility. Her stories are reworked, revived, repeated, and patched into other stories, with ethnicities switched around—but throughout the body of work, the half-caste theme is marked. It was always in Winnifred's mind, and she never stopped writing about it.

By presenting a wide spectrum of "half-caste" characters, as well as fully Japanese and fully white ones, Winnifred was doing something not so far removed from what Edith did, though her methods were more disguised, less straightforward: she personalized such minorities to a public that knew little of them beyond racial stereotypes and prejudices. It was not Winnifred's primary purpose to teach lessons combating racism. Her books were, first and foremost, romances and melodramas, intended to entertain, to enchant, sometimes to shock, with such frivolous titles as *The Wooing of Wistaria* and *The Heart of Hyacinth.* They were written, one and all, out of commercial motives, but the subtext is there.

As Amy Ling says, "Edith's response to racism was a frontal assault, direct and confrontational. Winnifred's response, however, was indirect, covert, and subversive—like the Trojan Horse, an ambush from within the walls. . . . What Edith in her writing asserted—the Chinese are human and assimilable—Winnifred in her life demonstrated."[8] That each sister chose to assert an Asian identity gave them the "ethnic authenticity to support writing careers based in large part on ethnic themes."[9] But as Ling points out, Winnifred's success "was not due to her knowledge of the Japanese, the Irish, the English/Canadian, but to her understanding of the human condition. Whether her protagonist is a Japanese geisha, an Irish cook, or an orphan raped by a Canadian cattle baron, they are all, like Winnifred Eaton herself, survivors in a harsh world."[10]

Some scholars have been baffled about where to place such a contradictory "trickster" creature as Winnifred. Samina Najmi, in her introduction to the reissued *The Heart of Hyacinth,* discusses Winnifred's anomalous situation: "[Watanna] slips through the cracks of contemporary multicultural agendas. . . . feminist and Asian American literary critics often simply ignore Watanna, not knowing what else to do with her . . . most Chinese Americans do not acknowledge her because she is not avowedly Chinese in her identification or her literary concerns. To most Japanese Americans, her biological heritage makes her a fake Japanese."[11] This, however, is changing. She is increasingly being recognized as a literary pioneer. Eve Oishi, in her introduction to the reissue of *Miss Numè of Japan*, says simply, "Winnifred Eaton still remains arguably Asian America's most prolific and best-selling author."[12]

Whatever Winnifred's status, she is undeniably a fascinating, glittering, exotic creature of the fin de siècle, with a psychological modus operandi all her own. A self-supporting "working girl" who typed in offices in the Chicago stockyards by day and churned out stories at night, she elevated herself from a world that might have been depicted by Theodore Dreiser in *Sister Carrie* to a fashionable New York literary world inhabited by such figures as Edith Wharton. Winnifred's flexible shifting between such worlds was in the end perhaps her most singular characteristic.

"There are times in my life when I have been whipped and scorched, and nothing has healed me save to get away quickly from the place where I have suffered," Winnifred wrote.[13] This is a revealing summation of the way in which Winnifred, by nature, operated and made her decisions and choices in life. Her entire career may be seen as a history of bolting from one situation to the next. Hers was not a life of cunningly thought-out strategy, of prudently planned steps. Neither deliberate nor passive, she was given to impulsive action, and, since this trait was accompanied by a lifetime habit of hard work and perseverance and a shrewd eye for marketability, the result was a career not only commercially successful but also rich in piquant contrasts and startling changes. At different times in her life, she saw and presented herself in such varying incarnations as a Japanese poet, a reporter in Jamaica, a theatrical New York personality, a Canadian rancher's wife, and a Hollywood screenwriter.

Winnifred's whole life was marked by the dramatic gesture and drastic, abrupt, total change. Her reaction when in untenable circumstances was not merely to leave the scene physically but to do more: to reinvent herself, to become someone else. In addition to producing a kaleidoscopic variety of highly colored tales, she actually lived them.

At all ages and stages, Winnifred was very much of her period. Amy Ling has aptly described her as a chameleon who changed her attitudes according to whatever the prevailing ones were.[14] With her inventive imagination, brashness, and love of adventure, Winnifred enacted truly sweeping and dramatic changes, almost like the stuff of fiction. Winnifred's real life constantly imitated fiction and is as puzzling, picaresque, and compelling a story as any she ever told.

Although I was her only granddaughter, I did not grow up knowing that story or very much about her at all. My father—her poet son, Paul Eaton Reeve—and mother were separated, and I grew up in New York City with my mother's family, a universe away from my all-but-unknown Canadian relatives. I knew that my grandmother had been a writer, but her Japanese romantic novels and the little I had heard about her theatrical personality seemed outlandishly dated, hard to relate to. I thought her a dead issue, like her books in libraries. Whenever I visited a library for the first time, curious habit made me glance through the *W*'s, and her books were always doing the same thing: gathering dust, with the last check-out dates ten and twenty years earlier. No one had ever heard of Winnifred or Edith.

But then there began, unexpectedly, a stirring of scholarly interest. My cousin Tim Rooney wrote me to report that a professor named Amy Ling had come to see him, to ask questions. She wrote essays about Winnifred and coauthored a collection of Edith Eaton's short fiction with Annette White-Parks. Annette White-Parks also visited our Eaton cousin in Montreal, Charles Laferrière, and wrote a full-length biography of Sui Sin Far. The works of the Eaton sisters began to appear in college courses, and people were writing dissertations about them. The library books were always checked out now. I was surprised, but Tim, an academic himself, was not. At his mother's death, he had donated most of our grandmother's papers to the Glenbow Archives (later they were moved to the University of Calgary Library's Department of Special Collections), because, he said calmly, "I knew the academic world would get around to Winnie one day."[15]

But even he could not have foreseen the extent of the reawakening of interest in these two sisters. When *Me* was republished, it occurred to me that since there had been a biography of Edith, it was high time for a biography of Winnifred, who had lived nearly twice as long and had a far more dramatic and mesmerizing life. Why, then, should I not write it and go on a journey of discovery of the woman I once called my "bad grandmother" but with whom I have since learned to feel a grateful kinship?

Becoming acquainted with Winnifred Eaton, trying to conjure up what she was really like, has been a constant source of surprises, revelations, shocks, and laughter. I have explored her ancestral home in England and the poor Montreal neighborhood where she grew up; I had the bizarre experience, for a writer and story analyst who has spent her own working life in the movie business, of reading my own grandmother's screenplays and screening several of her films; I talked to a few people who had actually known her; I explored an enormous archive full of her clippings, publicity puffs, and scrawled letters; I pored over every one of her books and stories; I read numerous Ph.D.

dissertations and scholarly articles on theories of her ethnic mysteries; and I have become acquainted with an impressive network of scholars and distant relatives, many of whom have become dear friends. So, for all the joy, the challenges, and the detective thrills of this extraordinary adventure, and most of all for my mystical yet satisfying feeling of connection to a unique personality, I thank her.

Onoto Watanna

Prologue

A JOLLY, LAUGHING LADY, dark, dressed like all well-to-do older ladies in New York in 1950, in hat, furs, and pearls, smiled widely down at me, a tiny, pretty, dark-haired child with vaguely Asian features, sitting on the floor.

"This is your grandmother, too," the grown-ups said in a bright artificial tone. "Isn't that funny? This lady is your grandma—just like Grandma is!"

"No," I responded, at once. She wasn't. My grandma was my whole world, the one who loved me, cuddled me, comforted me, took care of me. There couldn't be another one.

"Yes, she's your grandma, too—your other grandma."

Impossible. Uncertainly, I toddled over to the warm, familiar presence. "You're my *good* grandma," I declared.

There was much laughter, and the lady whom everybody now agreed was the Bad Grandma, laughed the loudest of all, but I could tell that she was profoundly hurt and embarrassed. The other grown-ups apologized profusely. "She doesn't mean it—she doesn't know what she's saying. Denny, you shouldn't say she's bad, she's just as good as—"

The Bad Grandma smiled on. "No, no, it's perfectly all right. I understand. She doesn't remember ever seeing me before. She doesn't know me. Of course, Naomi is your real grandma, your good grandma. That's fine." She was all kindness and reasonableness, doing her best to reassure me that it didn't matter, and still valiantly smiling; but with a child's sure instinct I knew that she was cut to the heart.

That was the only time I ever remember seeing my paternal grandmother, Winnifred Eaton Reeve. When her visit to New York City was over and she went back to her home in Calgary, with her kind, rich husband, Frank

Reeve, it was as if she had never been there at all. Three or four years later, we learned that she had died of a heart attack. Still later, her daughter, Doris, came for a visit and brought me two tokens: a copy of one of the many novels Winnifred had written, with the unpromising title of *Cattle,* and a photograph of Winnifred, still fairly young, kneeling on a lawn, oddly dressed in a kimono, with that same jolly, wide grin.

1. A Half-Caste Child

"Half-breeds are either cynics, or they are philosophers or geniuses. They are seldom ordinary—seldom normal."
—Onoto Watanna, "The Half Caste"

"SINCE I WAS first able to think I have had intense longings for wealth. To have money, to have honor, greatness, grandeur and splendour, to have all this, was to live. Money, to me, was everything." Those were the first words of the first story that the young Winnie Eaton ever published. According to her own account, she was just fourteen when "A Poor Devil" was accepted by Montreal's *Metropolitan Magazine.*[1] This may be open to question, as accuracy in dates and facts in general was not something Winnifred ever put a great deal of store in. And it is true that in this story, she was not writing directly about herself but creating a character. Nevertheless, these opening words are unusual for a young person's first published effort, and they do reflect Winnifred's own feelings, for she always did want to be rich. A self-made woman to the core, she did all she could to achieve this end.

Not only did she want to be rich, but she longed to be famous as well—a singular, courted individual, distinguished for her genius, her éclat. Growing up in Montreal in the 1870s and 1880s, racially different from those around her, she firmly believed she was special. In her first autobiographical novel, *Me,* published in 1915, she wrote, "I had always secretly believed there were the strains of genius somewhere hidden in me; I had always lived in a little dream world of my own, wherein, beautiful and courted I moved among the elect of the earth" (4).

Whence came her early and enduring ambition? From poverty, of course. And from an inborn egotism and strength of will and purpose that was shared by several of her many brothers and sisters. Winnifred was separated by ten years in birth, and a decade's different experiences, from her oldest sister, Edith, yet Winnifred's self-assessment in *Me,* "I think I had the most acute, inquiring and eager mind of any girl of my age in the world" (6), is a blood relative to Edith's declaration, "At eighteen years of age what troubles me is not that I am who I am, but that others are ignorant of my superiority. I am small, but my feelings are big—and great is my vanity."[2]

Characteristically, it was Edith who showed insight into the nature of that vanity; Winnifred never bothered her head about whether she was vain or not. Not much given to contemplation, she poured herself out in her stories, letters, and diaries, barely stopping to think as she recorded her dreamed-up tales and her experiences. She pushed on eagerly with the job of creating the person she intended to be. But the emphatically strong and determined personality, the sense of self-importance, is evident in both sisters, the two in their family who became writers.

Both were born into a remarkable and remarkably poor family, headed by an English father and a Chinese mother. This was a circumstance then so uncommon as to be almost unique, and this sense of uniqueness, of being set apart from everyone else, was something both sisters felt deeply. The enormous Eaton family—twelve of the fourteen children survived past infancy—was unlike any other family living in Montreal at that time. No one else had a mother like theirs—for Grace Eaton may have been the first Chinese woman to reside in that city.

The little Eaton children were "half-caste," or "half-breeds," a matter of some discomfort and even shame to them, in a time and place where it was normal and natural to be either French or English but never half-Chinese. "Why should we always be pointed out . . . and made to feel conspicuous and freaky?" Winnifred asked in her second autobiographical novel, *Marion*, published in 1916.[3]

Each of the siblings dealt with this background in his or her own way. Some, like Edith, were defiantly proud of it, some accepted it, and some—like Winnifred—went to various lengths to disguise it. But there is no doubt that the sisters did share a distinct sense of singularity. We may wonder how a girl, not an only child but one of fourteen, could manage to feel unique and uniquely gifted, but both Edith and Winnifred surely did. The feeling of being somehow set apart and wanting to prove her own worthiness and all the attendant strands of talent, desire, and ego were manifest in the younger sister, as well as the elder one, from an early age.

In that enormous family, with few amusements and much drudgery, Winnifred, a middle child, was a gifted storyteller who used her tales to entertain the little ones to whom she was assigned the job of nursemaid. In *Marion,* Winnifred describes the character who is her own alter ego, Nora, as "a wonderful story-teller" whom the children would listen to by the hour (58).

In another passage, she paints a vivid picture of the storytelling that went on in the Eaton household, seventy years before television was in every home. The little girls would peel potatoes, or shell peas, or sew together and invent long tales with such titles as "The Princess Who Used Diamonds as Pebbles and Made Bonfires out of One-Hundred Dollar Bills" and "The Queen Who Tamed Lions and Tigers with a Smile" (37).

A born romancer and fabricator, Winnifred began when very young to fashion an image for herself, a striking and glamorous image, very different from the plain, apple-cheeked Winnie Eaton of Montreal. Her natural myth-making abilities were so strong that it is hardly surprising that a cheerful propensity to mold facts to suit her—an indifference to dull truth—became one of her most characteristic features. In later life, a dear friend one day clapped her hands to her ears and exclaimed, "Winnie, black is white with you! If you tell one more lie, I am going to walk out of this house!"[4]

A biographer must occasionally share this feeling of exasperation and amusement. Such a fictionalizing tendency was not uncommon in career women who were Winnifred's peers. In her biography of the screenwriter Frances Marion, Winnifred's professional contemporary and friend, Cari Beauchamp quotes Marion's reaction to being accused of telling false stories: "But the real story isn't dramatically correct!" Beauchamp's amused comment is, "I love these women, but they are hell on historians."[5] Or as Amy Ling puts it, "Winnifred's talent for fiction was so pervasive that the boundary between fact and fiction is not at all clear."[6]

Even the facts of Winnifred's birth are surrounded by fabrication and mystique. She usually gave her birthdate as 1879, and so it appears in most contemporary articles about her; but she was actually born on August 21, 1875, a fact she preferred to conceal. Concealing one's age almost amounted to standard practice for professional women of her generation,[7] and what may have begun as an attempt to make her early writing career sound even more precocious and prodigious may have continued because her second husband was slightly younger than she was. She also liked to describe herself as a seventh child, which sounded attractively mystical, but she was in fact the eighth. A five-year-old boy, Ernest, the actual seventh, died the year before Winnifred was born. And on her baptismal certificate (she was baptized with two older sisters, May and Christina Agnes, at Montreal's American Presbyterian Church),[8] she is listed, for the first and last time in her life, as "Lillie Winifred." The Lillie quickly vanished, and she ever afterward wrote her name with two *n*'s: Winnifred.

The strange marriage between Edward Eaton, a young Englishman from a silk-manufacturing family in Macclesfield, and his Chinese bride, Grace

Trefusis, took place in Shanghai on November 7, 1863. Edward, then twenty-three, and his seventeen-year-old bride were married in a Church of England ceremony at Trinity Church. Grace's parents are listed on the marriage certificate as "unknown."[9] The marriage register shows that the couple was married earlier in a Roman Catholic ceremony that took place aboard a ship.

The Eatons were not of the fabulously wealthy nobility about which the poor girls growing up in Montreal loved to fantasize. They were, however, a respectable family. For generations there had been Eatons in the silk-manufacturing business in and around the Midlands town of Macclesfield. Upton Cottage near Prestbury, where Edward's father and grandfather lived, still stands, a handsome red-brick house with its own carriage house, which looks out over the rolling green hills bordering the Peak District.

Edward's grandfather, Isaac Eaton, was born in Macclesfield in 1783 and was schoolmaster and organist at nearby Pott Shrigley, a shaded, quiet little village (*shrigley* is a word pleasingly derived from *shriggel* or *shriggeleg,* meaning a wood frequented by shrikes). He retained those offices until 1815, when he became clerk of the Old Church, Macclesfield, duties he discharged for nearly half a century. For almost as long a period, he was the actuary of the Savings Bank of Park Green, Macclesfield. In 1807, he married Ellen Unwin of Pott Shrigley. Graves of the Unwin family are still to be seen in the small, pretty country church of St. Christopher's in the village.

Isaac made his last will and testament in 1858, bequeathing most of his property to his sons, Edward and George. Edward—Winnifred's grandfather—was justice of the peace of Tower Beach Hall, as well as justice of the Court of Common Pleas of Chester County. Appointed by Queen Victoria, he sat on the bench for twenty years. In 1860, he purchased a chemical manufacturing business,[10] and in census records, his profession is listed as dry salter (a dealer in dye materials and colors) and dry goods merchant employing two or three men.[11]

Winnifred, growing up hearing legends of her father's fine English relatives, enthusiastically invested them with importance and glamour. The storybook world of England, the English aristocracy, appealed to her romantic strain. She wrote in *Me,* "My father's an Oxford man, and a descendant of the family of Sir Isaac Newton . . . the greatness of my father's people had been a sort of fairy-story with us all, and we knew that it was his marriage with mama that had cut him off from his kindred" (26).

Other legends she liked to embellish were that an ancestor was head of the Bank of England and that "great-grandpapa was Squire of Macclesfield, and was knighted [in the] Jubilee year."[12] Although these colorful stories were largely myths, some of them, like most good myths, contained a germ of truth. Certainly Isaac Eaton's actuary job with the local savings bank was not with the Bank of England, but his nephew became mayor of Macclesfield and was knighted. The Newton link is unproved (though there is an Ayton among Newton's family connections). But Winnifred herself firmly believed the Isaac Newton story; she told it time and again and named her alter ego in her autobiographical works *Me* and *Marion*, Nora Ascough, which may be a reference to Newton's mother, Hannah Ayscough.

Such was the English grandeur, the noble glory of her paternal ancestors, that Winnifred so cherished and romanticized. She called her grandfather, proudly and inaccurately, "One of England's greatest merchant princes."[13] But she never saw the family home in England, as Edith did. Winnifred never traveled to England or to Europe at all, any more than to Japan or China.

Edward's stories about his home must have contained a full measure of the snobbish attitudes of the period, filtered through an understandable nostalgia for better times. Some of his children imbibed these attitudes; even the high-minded Edith was not above some old-fashioned English snobbery. In *Marion*, Winnifred paints a lively portrait of her oldest sister and in one scene describes her lecturing the younger ones: "Since we are obliged to live in a neighborhood with people who are not our equals, I think it is a good plan to keep to ourselves. That's the only way to be exclusive" (41). Perhaps the sentiments should be attributed to their actual author, Winnifred; but Edith undoubtedly did have her "English" standards of behavior and relished imposing them on her younger siblings.

Winnifred knew just how far removed a half-caste girl living in poverty in Quebec was from an imaginary ideal of the English aristocracy. Despite her admiration of this ideal and her love of romancing, she had a healthy sense of realism about what she really was and what she had to do. She was never afraid of work but embraced it with energy, and she was a phenomenally hard worker: her actions belied her romance about aristocracy, for she never for a moment aspired to a life of idleness and leisure for herself. She liked to be doing.

Among the more powerful dreams that Winnifred nurtured was the pervasive American rags-to-riches one, about achieving success through hard work. In her own home, what she observed was a case of riches to rags, rather than the reverse. There was precious little romance in the life of her parents, apart from their initial coming together. Winnifred's mother loved to dwell on this period in her life. "She tells us over and over again of her meeting with my father in Shanghai and the romance of their marriage," Edith wrote.[14]

Little is known about how Edward and Grace met and how they came to marry. The few known facts are soon told. When Grace died in 1922 at the age of seventy-five (on her death certificate her color is listed as "Yellow"), her father's name was given as A. Trefusis, her mother's as Ah Chuen, and both were said to have been born in China. One version of the family tradition holds that Grace Trefusis was the youngest child of a Mandarin lord: "She was kidnapped by circus performers at the age of three. Too scared to ask for ransom, they put her to work in the circus. One year later the Mathesons (Sir Hugh Matheson), Scottish missionaries, rescued her and brought her to England as their ward."[15] Whether this story can be taken at face value, it is what family members believed.

Sir Hugh Matheson was a member of one of the two families that created Jardine-Matheson, a major trading enterprise associated with Mathesons Bank in London, which traded mainly in tea and opium. Following the Opium War of 1839–42 and the Treaty of Nanking in 1842, which opened Shanghai and other Chinese ports to English traders, they were among the first merchants to gain entry to the China market.

Perhaps the likeliest Matheson candidate to have been Grace's benefactor is not Sir Hugh (though the family would "love a lord" in the retelling) but Donald Matheson, who came to China as a merchant for Jardine-Matheson and in 1849 resigned from the firm on moral grounds, disapproving of the opium traffic. This would have been when Grace was three years old, which is about the time she was supposedly taken to England. Donald Matheson became chairman of the committee of the Society for the Suppression of the Opium Trade.[16] When he returned to England to train as a missionary, it is not far-fetched to think he may have brought home a Chinese foundling.

However she got to England, Grace was certainly educated there. Although no records exist of her at the Home and Colonial School in London, where she was supposed to have trained as a missionary, a good deal is known about the school itself. The Home and Colonial Society was founded in 1837 by a group of Evangelical gentlemen who were in sympathy with the views of the Clapham Sect (which included William Wilberforce and other well-known reformers). The first college established in Britain with the aim of training teachers to work with children, it was housed at the northern end of Gray's Inn Road, near King's Cross Station. By midcentury, the government gave grants to train teachers, and courses were run for nurses, for women to teach in the army schools for soldiers' children, and for the preparation of young women to work as missionaries. Many graduates were sent abroad to work.[17]

Winnifred wrote in *Me,* "My mother had been a tight-rope dancer in her early youth. She was an excitable, temperamental creature from whose life all romance had been squeezed by the torturing experience of bearing sixteen [*sic*] children. Moreover, she was a native of a far-distant land, and I do not think she ever got over the feeling of being a stranger in Canada" (3). That the experience was torturing is confirmed by Edith's account. The earnest and responsible "big sister" later wrote about the anguish she felt when her mother delivered another baby: "My mother's screams of agony when a baby is born almost drive me wild, and long after her pains have subsided I feel them in my own body."[18] Winnifred was one of those babies whose birth tormented Edith, and it was probably not the last pang she was to give her big sister in her life.

Grace did not, as might reasonably have been expected, die in childbirth but sturdily survived to an old age. Her obituary calls her, with truth, "one of the best known and most picturesque characters in Montreal . . . a woman of considerable intellectual and literary attainments, [who] will be remembered by a serial story she wrote in the *Montreal Witness* which depicted the life of China as she knew it, the principal scene being laid in her native city of Shanghai. She was an active church-worker, being an Anglican."[19]

Many years later, in her own old age, Winnifred's daughter, Doris, wrote to a Japanese correspondent, "I remember my grandmother quite vividly, as a very pretty woman, beautifully mannered and very intelligent." But, Doris added to this, "My mother was not particularly proud of the fact that she was partly Chinese. As a child she had suffered from racial prejudice in Montreal, and I think would have preferred to be all Chinese or all English."[20]

Winnifred seldom wrote about her mother, and when she did, she carefully refrained from mentioning her race and the name of her home country. In one passage from a 1908 story about gardens, she referred to Grace in a wistful strain:

> I often think of my mother, and her pathetic attempts to recall the bloom of the flowering land of Japan [*sic*] which had been her home. The first time she made the long journey to this country, she carried with her a dozen or more boxes in which seeds and slips were planted, and even at sea she had her little green growth always with her. Here in America she was never without her own bit of a garden, her "flowering spot," as she named it, and often it consisted only of an ugly hotel window ledge, or the roof of some city house.[21]

Typically Winnifred had more to say about her father, whose early exploits in life she admired and took courage from: "Was I not the daughter of a man who had been back and forth to China no fewer than eighteen times, and that during the perilous period of the Tai-Ping Rebellion? . . . What could not his daughter do?" she demanded rhetorically in *Me* (5). When her father died in Montreal in 1915, she may have had a hand in writing his obituary, which describes his "romantic career" and how he was sent to the Far East to establish a branch of his father's business: "There he lived while the country passed through the Tai-Ping rebellion, and there he became acquainted with the late Gen. Gordon. He was the trusted friend, too, of many of the natives, being known by the Chinese as 'the one honest white man.'"[22]

Another obituary mentions his brother Isaac's marriage to a Japanese woman.[23] According to family tradition, Isaac traveled to China and Japan with Edward and married a Japanese bride. Winnifred once described the brothers as "two young and ardent adventurers dispatched to the Far East, there to extend the trade of my grandfather."[24]

The obituary tells of Edward's migration to the New World: "Mr. Eaton came to America toward the close of the Civil War and established a wholesale drug and dye firm in Pine Street, New York, but he lost his fortune to speculation in Wall Street. He was noted for his generosity in the days of his affluence, and was one of the chief subscribers toward the building of Grace Church parsonage in New York. . . . He came to Montreal forty-one years ago, after the loss of his fortune, and at last took up the profession of an artist."[25]

On the subject of her artist father, Winnifred once told an interviewer, "He had a great deal of artistic ability and as a young man had taken a gold medal at an exhibition at the Paris salon. Grandfather, however, insisted that 'no son of his should follow the beggarly profession of an artist.' His paintings became well known to Canadians, some of them being bought by the Duke of Argyle and the late Lord Strathcona."[26]

Shortly after the birth of the Eatons' first son, Edward Charles, in China in 1864,[27] the family returned to England, perhaps leaving China because of war conditions. Winnifred claimed that her parents sailed to England in a sailing ship that took a year to make the journey.[28]

Whenever and however they traveled, a tantalizing snippet of family tradition holds that Grace, all dressed up in Mandarin robes, was driven in a carriage through the town of Macclesfield for her first introduction to her husband's family. Ordinarily she wore proper English Victorian dress. A photograph of her as a young woman shows her in a high-necked gown with a bustle, but certainly Edward was making no secret of his Chinese wife if he paraded her in exotic costume. "Behold, my new daughter-in-law!" his father is supposed to have shouted.[29] We can only imagine the sensation this must have caused in stolid Victorian Macclesfield. How the family received her is unknown, but the young Eatons were still resident in the family home in Prestbury when Edith Maude, their first daughter, was born on March 15, 1865.[30]

By family accounts, Edward was a "remittance man" and was turned out of his ancestral home for bringing home a "yellow" bride; but if this was so, he was not turned out immediately, for the Eatons did not migrate to North America until 1867, where their third child, Grace, was born in Jersey City. *Trow's New York City Directory* lists Edward Eaton as a merchant living in Jersey City in 1868 and then as an owner of a wholesale drug business in New York City. Within a year, however, Edward had lost whatever capital he had and returned to Macclesfield.[31]

About 1872, Edward left England again and moved his growing family to their permanent home in Montreal. Montreal may have been chosen because a branch of his wife's church was established there, but another advantage was that it was across the Canadian border, where Edward's debtors could not pursue him. By that time the string of children included Edward, then eight; Edith, seven; Grace, five; Sara, four; Ernest George, three; and Christina Agnes, two.[32] The first child born in Montreal was May Darling, born in 1874 and named after a kind neighbor who gave Edith French and music lessons.[33]

Both Edith and Winnifred have left us lively descriptions of their family's arrival in the city. Edith recounted in her "Leaves from the Mental Portfolio of an Eurasian":

> The sleigh which has carried us from the station stops in front of a little French Canadian hotel. Immediately we are surrounded by a number of villagers, who stare curiously at my mother as my father assists her to alight from the sleigh. Their curiosity, however, is tempered by kindness, as they watch, one after another, the little black heads of my brothers and sisters and myself emerge out of the buffalo robe. . . . "Les pauvres enfants," the inhabitants murmur, as they help to carry us into the hotel. Then in lower tones, "Chinoise, Chinoise." (220)

To this day, L. Charles Laferrière of Montreal, the grandson of Christina Agnes, the child who was then the baby of the family, signs himself proudly "1/8 Chinois."

Winnifred's own description of the family's early days in Montreal is in her book *Marion:* "'In dat familee ere are eleven cheeldren, and more—they come! . . . De father he come from Eengland about ten year ago. He was joost young man, mebbe twenty-seven or twenty-eight year ol', and he have one leetle foreign wife and six leetle children. They were all so cold. They were not use to dis climate of Canada. My wife and I, we keep leetle 'otel at Hochelaga, and she . . . make for dem the good French pea-soup'" (1). The speaker in this passage is Monsieur Thebeau, the grocer, a real-life neighbor of the Eatons in Hochelaga, their French working-class neighborhood in Montreal.[34] The narrator of *Marion* is pained by his commentary: "It was horrid that the size of our family and our mother's nationality should be told to everyone by that corner grocer" (2).

The ineffectual father could do little for his brood. "My father was an artist, and we were very poor," Winnifred wrote in *Me* (3). In *Marion,* she depicts him sitting at his easel, with his blue eyes fixed absently on his canvas: "Papa, with the heart and soul of a great artist, 'painting, painting,' as he would say with a grim smile, 'potboilers to feed my hungry children'" (5). One day Winnifred would write potboilers to feed hers. Another line from *Marion* that rings true to life is when the father advises his aspiring artist daughter, "'Better be a dressmaker or a plumber or a butcher or a policeman. There is no money in art!'" (6).

The family's need was acute, for Edward earned next to nothing from his paintings, and his occasional jobs as clerk and bookkeeper at the cotton mills brought in very little.[35] In desperation, he made another trip back "home" to England to try to get help for his brood. Winnifred describes this in *Marion:*

> Papa was going to England to try to induce grandpa—that grandfather we had never seen—to help us. We clung about mama's skirts, poor little mama, who was half distraught and we all kept waving to papa. . . . Suppose his people, who were rich and grand, should induce our father never to return to us! . . . But papa did return! He could have stayed in England, and, as my sister Ada [Edith] extravagantly put it, "lived in the lap of luxury," but he came back to his noisy, ragged little 'heathens.'" (15–16)

It is not known if he received aid, but this may have been the last trip Edward took to England; he remained settled in Montreal for the rest of his life. The family lived in the center of a textile manufacturing district that was not very different from what Edward had known back home in Macclesfield. There were the same kind of enormous factory mills, the largest being Victor Hudon's cotton mill, which was constructed in 1874, the same year the Eatons' address first appears in Hochelaga.[36]

During the 1870s, the family moved from one poor lodging to another in the workers' quarters, sometimes living in the section set aside for English-speaking employees, sometimes in the French section, which was cheaper. From 1873 to 1891, the Montreal city directories reveal that the Eaton family moved nine times, and it is possible that some of these moves were caused by evictions.[37] However traumatic this may have been for the children, the frequent moving set a pattern in both Winnifred's and Edith's lives. Edith was so peripatetic and difficult to follow in her movements that her biographer, Annette White-Parks, calls her "a bird on the wing," and Winnifred, even when encumbered with a household that included four small children, also constantly and casually kept changing residences. Until late in life, she would move at the drop of a hat, not only because she was in some dire financial crisis but also because she felt that one house or another was "not ideal." Moving was an accustomed way of life for the Eatons.

The type of row houses that the Eatons inhabited were three-story affairs with rows of corniced windows under the eaves. Working people had a floor per family; only better-off families had access to all three stories.[38] However, by the mid-1880s the Eatons may have lived in a house that boasted both upstairs and downstairs, judging by Winnifred's descriptions in *Marion*. The book is set in 1884, when the heroine (Winnifred's sister Sara) was sixteen and Winnifred was nine. By this time, the older children were working, and Edward was able to give up his mill jobs and work solely as an artist. The family had attained a slightly higher degree of comfort, though the household was still crowded and chaotic. Winnifred describes how her father used to paint in the kitchen with the children all about him because that was the only warm room in the house.

There was only fireplace heating ("Our Canadian houses did not have furnaces in those days," she noted in *Marion* [59]), and the narrator of *Me* laments that she had to sleep "in a room with four of my little brothers and sisters. I hate to think of that room. As fast as I picked up the scattering clothes, others seemed to accumulate. *Why* do children soil clothes so quickly!" (114).

Typical Hochelaga working-class houses had no indoor plumbing at that time but featured a "backhouse" in the garden. White-Parks notes, "Poor sanitation, mixed with overcrowding, was largely responsible for one of the highest infant mortality rates in the world in St. Mary's of Hochelaga."[39] In 1885, a smallpox epidemic swept through Montreal. In *Marion,* Winnifred calls it a "veritable plague" and points out that the French Canadians, not the English Canadians, were the ones chiefly afflicted, for they resisted vaccination; there were antivaccination riots all over the French quarter. Her father is depicted as being shaken out of his normal passivity by the emergency: "Ours was the only house on our block (or for that matter the surrounding blocks), where the hideous, yellow sign, 'PICOTTE' (smallpox) was not conspicuously nailed upon the front door, and this despite the fact that we were a large family of children. Papa hung sheets all over the house, completely saturated with disinfectants. Every one of us children was vaccinated, and we were not allowed to leave the premises. Papa himself went upon all the messages, even doing the marketing" (13–14).

Old photographs of Montreal reveal the world the Eaton family lived in, tenements with gayly painted staircases winding in curlicues outside the fronts of the houses, decorated with strings of laundry. Family life was lived out on the balcony in the summer months, while in the deep freeze of winter Montrealers were enlivened by a world of snowplay—sledding, ice hockey, and races up and down the snowy slopes of Mount Royal, the city's "mountain." For winter's centerpiece, there were the wondrous, sparkling ice palaces, a glorious late-nineteenth-century phenomenon. These fantastic structures were built in central squares in cities of the frozen north, and their glittering beauty captured the imagination of the young Winnifred as well as Edith, who both mentioned them in their writings.

In their descriptions of this family, an image of the parents begins to emerge. Edward Eaton, a fair, blue-eyed man with delicate hands, was gentle and liked to stay out of arguments. He would read his paper and pretend not to be listening when anything uncomfortable was going on. He failed to fully support his family as either wage earner or artist, but where their health was concerned, he could take a strong stance. He admired his bustling, bright, emotional, overburdened Chinese wife and was bitter about his own lack of fame and success. A few of his "potboilers" survive; they are very attractive sea and landscapes, though hardly works of genius.

Family tradition holds that Grace was the stricter parent. When Grace sent a child out to the woodshed, where Edward would be painting, for a whipping, Edward was too kind-hearted and would only pretend to carry out her instructions.

Grace, though she was like a well-bred Englishwoman in her speech, manners, and dress, passed on to her children Chinese stories, songs, and superstitions. Edith described her mother as "very bright and interested in every little detail of practical life." Edward once told Edith that she "will never make half the woman her mother is, or her sister [Grace] will be."[40]

This sister, Grace, next in age to Edith, was another exceptional woman. Though not a writer herself, she married a promising young essayist, Walter Blackburn Harte, and after his early death she forged her own remarkable career as the first Chinese American woman lawyer in Chicago. A woman of great energy and resolve, she went to her law practice daily until her death at eighty-nine. In health and spirits, she resembled Winnifred rather than the frail Edith; she surely possessed the same brave and enterprising drive as her writing sisters.

The Eaton family was one of strong women. Most of the children shared a powerful desire not only to make something of themselves despite their lack of a formal education but also to help their parents, brothers, and sisters. Like the large, poor Bertram family in Jane Austen's *Mansfield Park,* they were "born to struggle and to endure." In large measure, they succeeded. None of the sisters ever forgot the large, struggling family at home, and they sent what money they could to those in need. It was a habit they never outgrew; Winnifred was helping her younger sisters financially until the day she died.

The children all went to work early, the older ones earliest of all. Edward Charles, who was called by the neighbors "Le Petit Père" for his protective ways with his sisters, was "entered in an office," as Edith put it.[41] He grew up to be a business success, becoming managing director of the firm of Frothingham and Workman. Edith was ten when she was first sent out to work. She later described her experience: "My sisters are apprenticed to a dressmaker. . . . I tramp around and sell my father's pictures, also some lace which I make myself. My nationality, if I had only known it at that time, helps me make sales. The ladies who are my customers call me 'The Little Chinese Lace Girl.'"[42]

The big, impoverished, noisy, artistic Eaton household had a raffish, bohemian atmosphere. In *Me,* the heroine's friend declares, "I'm a bohemian. Ever hear that word?" The girl nods. "Mama used to call papa that when she was angry with him" (133).

Much formal education was something the Eatons were not able to provide for their numerous progeny. The children's schooling was sketchy. Edith attracted the notice of a "lovely old lady," Mrs. Darling, a neighbor of the Eatons on St. Mary Street, who taught her music and French and encouraged her to learn about her mother's people.[43] Winnifred, of course, never came under the influence of this remarkable teacher, but as a later child, she was able to stay in school longer than Edward Charles and Edith and went to work at fifteen.[44] Yet there were opportunities for work earlier in her childhood, and she remembered selling lemonade in the summer at a circus and singing the verse, "Lemonade, in the shade, made by a little maid."[45]

For all their lack of schooling, the Eatons did not grow up uneducated. They all loved to read. When Nora, Winnifred's alter ego in *Me,* arrives in Jamaica as a young girl and her new employer gruffly asks her if she has ever read anything, she readily replies, "Yes, Dickens, George Eliot, and Sir Walter Scott; and I've read Huxley and Darwin, and lots of books on astronomy to my father, who is very fond of the subject" (26). The family loved poetry, and in *Marion* Winnifred describes the girls reading Tennyson and making up poems about subjects ranging from God to a wicked hen that could crow like a cock.

Winnifred's recollections of the Hochelaga days reflect her mingled pity for her parents and impatience with their poverty, as well as her ardent determination to better her situation and escape the degradation in which she lived. Yet poor as the family was, they may have kept at least one servant.

Winnifred mentions a servant several times in her work. In *Me* she relates that "we had only one servant that I can ever remember, a woman named Sung-Sung whom papa brought from China; but she was more like one of our family, a sort of slave" (18). She describes woolen underwear and knitted stockings "that Sung-Sung had made for an older brother, and which had descended to me after two sisters had them!" (30). In *Marion,* Sung-Sung changes sex: "Mama was sick and the doctor said she could have chicken broth. Well, there was no one home to kill the chicken, for that was the time papa went to England. . . . Sung Sung, our old servant, believed it would be unlucky to kill one with the master away—one of his everlasting superstitions" (38).

Was there really a Sung-Sung? Edith said that the first Chinese she ever saw apart from her mother was in New York, when she was seven, and if Edward brought Sung-Sung from China, she would have been part of the family already. Edith also described how her mother "tells us tales of China. Tho a child when she left her native land she remembers it well, and I am never tired of listening to the story of how she was stolen from her home."[46] In her own writing, however, Winnifred refrained from mentioning any Chinese knowledge coming from her mother. Could she have invented Sung-Sung as a kind of stand-in for her mother, painting her unflatteringly as a kind of Chinese bonne?[47]

Both Winnifred and Edith were given a great deal of responsibility for their younger siblings. Edith was the eldest, while Winnifred, as a middle child, was so positioned that when her older sisters went out to work, the duties of nursemaid devolved on her as more children came. She loathed child care, as is reflected in *Me:* "This is my conception of hell: a place full of howling, roaring, fighting, shouting children and babies. It is a supreme torture to a sensitive soul to live in such a Bedlam" (113). In *Marion,* she paints herself as a young girl carrying babies (59), while other little ones clung to her hands and skirts. There is much more in a similar pitiful mode.

Despite her dislike of child minding as a girl, Winnifred grew up to be the affectionate mother of four children of her own. By the time she was a mother, however, she was a successful enough writer to afford servants, so that she never had to perform nursemaid duties.

Winnifred's attitude toward her enforced task of caring for her little brothers and sisters is hardly unnatural. It was unwanted drudge work and could be frightening, as it must have been when her younger brother, Lawrence, born in 1882 when Winnifred was seven, died two years later. This would have been the first death of a sibling that Winnifred knew, and Lawrence would have been one of the infants who was directly under Winnifred's charge.

Edith's favorite, beatific vision of the future was of seeing "all the family grown and settled down and myself, far away from all the noise and confusion, with nothing to do but write a book."[48] With her delicate health, this seemed almost unattainable. Winnifred, by contrast, was strikingly robust and cheerfully described herself as "almost abnormally healthy and strong . . . even if I look thin, I'm the wiry kind."[49] With her bouncing energy and buoyant personality, Winnifred was able to turn out her many books in spite of whatever was going on in her life. She was thus able to give up working at office jobs and to support herself and her family solely by her writing while still in her midtwenties—something Edith never managed.

Years later, Winnifred recalled, in an amusing newspaper piece, the rough-and-tumble of her Hochelaga days. She was playing mud pies when a lady of fashion strolled down the street, with a "radiantly clad" toddler. "Come along, pet. Mamma's 'ittle 'osebud must keep away from the dirty 'ittle girl!" the lady exclaimed. Winnie's feelings were hurt. She had just "emerged from the worst rubbing and scrubbing and drubbing" of her life and was emphatically not a dirty little girl. Also, her father had placed her on a highchair and cut her hair close to the skull, using a sort of "lawn mower" over her "sore and protesting pate." This fashion was in vogue among the French Canadians but was most disfiguring to Winnie. With her freckles, wide mouth, and missing teeth, she looked like a monkey according to her brothers. But she was not dirty. "My mother was an apostle of the God of Cleanliness—if there is such a God—there ought to be anyway," she recalled.[50] So Winnie was clean even when making mud pies. She got her revenge on this occasion by smiling engagingly at the rosebud infant and placing a mud pie in each of her tiny lace pockets.

In another typical reminiscence, from *Marion,* Winnifred related how her mother would send the children to pick maggots off the currant bushes and bugs off the potato plants and would pay them one cent for every pint of bugs or maggots. It was a distasteful chore, but the children would lighten it by pretending that gnomes and fairies were hiding inside the potatoes. Little Winnifred, hearing this fancy, would not eat a potato for weeks, for fear she might eat a fairy. Maggots amidst the fairies, or fairies amidst the maggots—and gardens, always gardens.

A healthy tomboy life, running free with her sisters and brothers; more attention to household chores than to schooling; poverty, shame, and ridicule but also blithe play and the vigorous exercise of fanciful storytelling—that was Winnifred's Hochelaga childhood.

As the Eaton children grew up, they were, as one of the suitors in *Marion* calls them, "like little steps and stairs" (58). The household must have been a lively one, and Winnifred gives a spirited, exuberant portrait of it in this autobiographical novel, which remains the source for almost all that can be conjectured about Winnifred's girlhood. In later life she wrote little about her teenage years, and even her daughter never knew such details as what her formal education consisted of or what work she did. Her statement in *Me* confirms what we may have guessed: "I had not been happy at home" (3).

Yet plenty of outside entertainment—plays, dances, and gadding about—was available to the young Eatons. The girls were mad about Gilbert and Sullivan, and a passion for Japanese styles hit Montreal hard, culminating with an elaborate production of *The Mikado* in 1886. Mounted by the troupe of the Castenet Club, "dans un montage signé par Eugene L'Aricaine," this featured thirty-two performers in Japanese costume. A photograph shows a fancy set, complete with a balcony, and kimono-clad girls waving fans, holding musical instruments, and posing with chopsticks stuck in their hair.[51]

The effect of this stylish production on the young people of Montreal—and in virtually every other city where *The Mikado* disseminated its dazzling pseudo-Japanese brio—can hardly be overstated. A family photograph shows three of the Eaton sisters—Sara, Rose, and May—waving fans and wearing kimonos about this time. The most enthusiastically Japanese of them all, Winnifred, is not among them, but perhaps she took the picture. These young women are obviously a gay, jolly lot, devoted to fun, with a bohemian, raffish air that must have been the despair of their serious eldest sister, Edith.

In Edith's early womanhood at home, she does not much resemble the altruistic Sui Sin Far she later became. Winnifred depicts her as a thoroughly bossy big sister, tart-tongued, sarcastic, and shrewish. This portrait of "Ada" in *Marion,* one of Winnifred's best works, has the unmistakable ring of being true to life. Yet Edith's sharpness was plainly derived from her anxious concern for them all, and her young siblings knew it well.

By the time Winnifred was ten years old, Edith was already working as a journalist. "My 18th birthday saw me in the composing room of the Montreal Star, where for some months I picked and set type. While there I taught myself shorthand," she wrote.[52] Winnifred scarcely needed to point out, "Life was a serious matter to [Edith], who had enormous ambitions."[53]

In 1888, Edith published several stories in the *Dominion Illustrated.*[54] These were love stories, not Chinese themed, and were signed Edith Eaton, but they marked the beginning of the writing careers of these two sisters, and no doubt the teenage Winnifred regarded Edith's achievement with genuine admiration and wanted to emulate her.

It was in the early 1890s, when Edith had established herself as a stenographer with an office of her own and Winnifred was just embarking on her own jobs, that a clergyman asked their mother to call on a young Chinese woman newly arrived as the bride of a local merchant.[55]

Montreal's small Chinese population was increasing rapidly. The U.S. passage of the Chinese Exclusion Act in 1882 and the completion of the Canadian Pacific Railway in 1885 led Chinese immigrants—nearly all men—to seek work in Montreal. Articles in the Montreal newspapers anxiously examined the possibility of a Chinatown developing in their city. "Are the Chinamen desirable as citizens?" asked the *Star*. To find out, the paper consulted an authority, the Reverend D. C. Thompson of the Presbyterian church, missionary to the Chinese in Montreal. Thompson had lived and worked "in the Christian cause" in China, and he now made it his duty to find every Chinese person in Montreal and advise them on spiritual matters.[56] He must have been well known to Grace, who was a regular Presbyterian church-goer.

Thompson tried to play down the "Chinese menace," estimating that Montreal's Chinese population was under six hundred. He admitted that the location of the "Mongolians" in one district, with the introduction of their "Oriental habits and customs," might be a problem, but his opinion of the Chinese was benign; they were no danger to civilization. Though well-intentioned, Thompson was incapable of rising above the prejudices of the day. "A good Chinaman makes an ideal servant," he observed, "they are docile, obedient, and most faithful."[57]

The epochal visit Grace and Edith made to the Chinese woman, at the behest of their minister, was the start of Edith's mixing with the Chinese community. "With the exception of my mother there was but one other Chinese woman in the city besides the bride," she wrote.[58] Grace began to teach at a Chinese mission school, no doubt under the auspices of the Reverend Thompson. There is no evidence that Winnifred, or indeed any of the other sisters, joined their mother and Edith in their visits to the Chinese community.

Some of the siblings were ashamed of their ethnicity. Edith's description of a "half Chinese, half white girl" who plastered her face with a thick, white coat of paint, blackened her eyelids and eyebrows, and moved to California, refers to her sister May. "It is not difficult . . . to pass as one of Spanish or Mexican origin," wrote Edith. "This poor child does, tho she lives in nervous dread of being 'discovered.'"[59] May's concealment of her Chinese blood was complete; the knowledge was not even passed down to her own grandchildren. The oldest brother, Edward Charles, was also ashamed of his background and took pains to hide his Chinese heritage. Like Winnifred, he particularly valued the English side of his background and became so English that he belonged to "whites-only" clubs frequented by the aristocratic English of Montreal, such as the Montreal Gun Club. Edith's pride and May's and Edward Charles's shame over their racial makeup were widely different attitudes. Winnifred's own feelings fell in between the two extremes, as did those of Grace, another busy and pragmatic career woman.

Grace was the equal of Edith and Winnifred in intelligence and capability—Winnifred herself called her "the cleverest one of all the family."[60] Unlike her sisters, Grace had no ambition to write fiction, but she shared their interest in fine literature, as is evidenced by her selfless devotion to the service and goals of her writer husband. The result of her idealistic marriage, however, was to make her, by necessity, even more practical.

Walter Blackburn Harte, an Englishman, was an ambitious, talented, but sadly unlucky young writer. He worked for the Montreal newspapers at the same time Edith did and was instrumental in helping her in her journalistic career. Although little is known about the intellectual influences in Winnifred's youth, it is safe to assume that Harte was one of them, perhaps the first professional writer she ever knew, apart from her own sister. The knowledge she gained through him of the world of journalism was surely significant in her young life, if only as a negative object lesson.

Harte exemplified the fin-de-siècle bohemian literary life, in which Edith and Grace joined, while their younger sister Winnifred, a scribbler and observer from an early age, undoubtedly watched the doings of this older trio with rapt interest. Harte spent his short working life in Montreal, Boston, and New York, but his milieu was something out of the pages of George Gissing's novel *New Grub Street,* a world of pushy hack writers, artistic authors starving in garrets, and cynical jockeying for editorships of small literary magazines. Winnifred likely took Harte at Grace's estimation and his own and held him in awe as a literary genius. But it is evident from her references to him in *Marion* that she sincerely liked him for his gentle character and his loving relationship with her sister.

Harte emigrated from England to Canada in 1868 at age eighteen and worked at the *Montreal Gazette.* His intimacy with the Eaton family was natural. Many exiled young Englishmen made a pilgrimage to Edward Eaton's home in Hochelaga to talk about the England they missed, to enjoy the educated conversation of a gentleman, and to flirt with his lively daughters. Pleasant examples of this sort of intercourse abound in *Marion.* In one scene, a young man sings "In the Gloaming" to the girls, and the narrator explains that many Englishmen were sent to Canada because they were "not much good in England. . . . They liked to hang around papa, whose family most of them knew" (29). He enjoyed showing them his sketches of Macclesfield.

One of Harte's early bylined stories was an article on Japanese art, which included a description of Japanese silk products and lacquered wares—information that more than likely came from Edward Eaton. Edward, who studied art in Paris and traveled in Japan less than a decade after it was opened by Commodore Matthew Perry, was in his own person an exponent of "Japonisme."

Winnifred had the example of the Harte marriage, with its brevity, its joyousness, and its tragedy, before her when she came to make her own marriage to a journalist. But where Harte played genius and Grace was the worker, with dire results, in Winnifred's marriage she was both genius and worker—with results hardly less dire, as we shall see. However, there can be little doubt that the young Hartes helped form her opinions about marriage, independence, and work.

Attitudes about working, specifically the way workers—even intellectual laborers, such as Harte—were regarded are an issue Winnifred addresses in *Marion.* In a passage that reveals Winnifred's own attitudes, the heroine is courted by a snobbish Englishman who argues with her about the status of the working girl: "But there's no disgrace in working. Poor people have to do it. Only snobs and fools are ashamed of it. . . . All of us girls have got to work. Do you think we want poor old papa to kill himself working for us big, healthy young animals just because we happen to be girls instead of boys?" (78).

The Englishman sniffs at this, arguing that a girl can work at home without losing her dignity but that "nice girls" don't go out to work. The heroine retorts with spirit, "Oh, you make me sick. My brother-in-law . . . would call that sort of talk rank snobbery. In the States women think nothing of working," to which the Englishman caustically replies, "As for that brother-in-law of yours, I say, he's hardly a gentleman, is he? Didn't you say the fellow was a—er—journalist or something like that?" The heroine snaps back, "He's a better kind of gentleman than you are! He's a genius, and—and—How dare you say anything about him!" (79).

In addition to glimpses of the young Hartes, Winnifred also paints a picture of the young Eaton girls and their suitors, and their high-spirited way of coping with poverty. Her sketches bubble with life as she shows the family dynamics in youthful days. Clearly they were a set of flibbertigibbets, reminiscent in their high spirits and bad behavior of the bumptious Lydia in Jane Austen's *Pride and Prejudice,* and it is hardly surprising that there are so many sharp pictures of Edith trying to improve her younger sisters' behavior. "Marion," or Sara, is the wildest of the girls. (In the family, Winnifred was said to be the cleverest—though as we have seen, she herself thought Grace was—

Edith the finest character, Rose the best dressed, and Sara the prettiest.)[61] "To [Edith], I was a frivolous, silly young thing, who needed constantly to be squelched, and she undertook to do the squelching, unsparingly, herself," she remarked in *Marion* (41). Of course the heroine's doings—such as posing in the nude as an artist's model—may have been spiced up for purposes of fiction.

There are several alarming episodes in *Marion,* in which the girls go out alone with older gentlemen who have dishonorable intentions. If anything like this actually happened, these unchaperoned girls would have been considered decidedly "fast" for the period. Again, these passages may have been a figment of Winnifred's imagination, but her parents exercised little authority, and they could not be depended on for help in financial straits. Rather, it was the other way around, for there was something feckless about the Eaton parents. Winnifred says in *Me* that "my father and mother were in a way even more helpless than their children. It was almost pathetic the way in which they looked to us, as we grew up, to take care of ourselves and them" (90).

An example of their lax discipline is shown in *Marion,* when the heroine wants to move into a flat paid for by her lover, who assures her that her father will never "bother his head" about it. As for her mother, if told the studio was free, she "would think that was just the usual thing and that you were doing the landlord an honor in using it. . . . Your mother is a joke, there's no mistake about that" (109).

Edith had her mind firmly fixed on these family realities and was determined that all her younger sisters must follow her own example and work. With Grace, her next sister, she clearly had no need to push or persuade; Winnifred, too, was a ball of enthusiastic energy from early youth. Sara and May may have needed some directing. They were the artistic sisters; both painted on china—some of May's pretty pieces survive—and family tradition holds that Sara worked for an artist at the Chateau Ramezay. Winnifred describes her work and gives a charming picture of "le Vieux-Montréal" in *Marion.*

Her portrait of Edith in this novel is almost all she ever wrote about her oldest sister, and there are no surviving letters between them. Edith died in 1914, while Winnifred lived almost exactly forty years longer. Very few of Winnifred's personal papers date back before 1914, the earlier ones being lost in her travels, a loss she lamented. No doubt, in her early working years, Winnifred received many admonitions from her older sister on the perennial theme of "Send money." In *Marion* she gives a fictional example of such a letter containing the revealing advice that "there is no need to get married if you can earn your own living. I think most men are hateful" (173).

This was not advice Winnifred ever took; her weakness for men at times landed her in very hot romantic waters. This is another fundamental difference between the two sisters—perhaps almost as much a result of their physical health as their psychological makeup.

Proximity also seems to have had a good deal to do with the sisters' intimacy with one another. Later, when Winnifred and Sara both lived in New York, they became close and collaborated on writing projects. Winnifred and Edith, however, never actually resided as adults in the same city at the same time. The single act of closeness, or mutual aid, that bears witness to a collaborative sisterly relationship is that Winnifred sent for Edith to take over her reporter job in Jamaica when she gave it up.

The literary "Grub Street" life that Edith and the young Hartes were leading was dauntingly hard. The story of the penurious, desperately struggling Hartes, the dreadful spectacle of the idealistic Harte beating his head against the wall of literary success, was a cautionary tale for Winnifred as a young writer. Small wonder she made up her mind that to be artistic and poor was a path emphatically to be avoided. She had had enough of that all her life.

Evidences of the hardships of this existence, anything but emblematic of the "Gay Nineties," are some of the most eloquent, rueful, heartfelt words to come from poor Harte's pen. He wrote, "The Wit—a woman it is, too—in our little circle . . . says: 'It is better to be a good journalist than a poor inarticulate genius.'"[62] Winnifred would have agreed. With such heartrending examples of suffering for art and being squarely up against the same exigencies herself, she determined to strike out a different path—commercial fiction.

Harte wrote about his circumstances with a mixture of idealism, grinding poverty, attempts to be cheerful, and contented matrimony, tinged with the accepted condescension of the period toward women. In his literary magazine, the *Fly Leaf,* Harte depicts a lively scene in which the young couple sees a crowd of "swell people" pouring into the opera house, and Grace yearns to go "up into the gods" to hear Melba sing or see Irving act. The young Hartes spin dreams about what they will do when his magazine becomes successful. He will collect "Posters and first editions," and they will have their portraits done by Beardsley or Whistler. But Harte refused to do "Jack the Giant Killer stories," even though "refined literary tastes crave *gore,* and plenty of it." He reflected bitterly, "We cure any tendency to thinking by letting blood."[63]

No pleasant success ever came to the young couple. Instead, Harte worked away at his literary endeavors, with Grace helping him as "sub editor." He gave her credit, albeit in his lofty masculine style. Perhaps his shame at owing so much to a mere woman, and not even a literary woman, led him to couch his tribute in sardonic and humorous terms. His lordly depiction of his devoted wife as his sub, his drudge, his slave, sits uncomfortably a century later: "The creature may be a male thing or a female thing: it never has a recognized name in the literary world, but is under the power of an exalted and Superior Personage. . . . I throw encouraging smiles across at her as she swings back from the typewriter, worn out, nervous, actually exhausted, at midnight, but still good-humored."[64]

It may seem odd to us that Winnifred's sister, a woman of intelligence and accomplishment, was satisfied to be in such a subservient position to a husband who described himself whimsically, but with more than a shade of truth, as an autocrat. But it was the convention of the day, and her own background and education were humble enough; she was only a young working girl when they met, though she abundantly proved her mettle both in her marriage and afterward.

It was in Harte's *Fly Leaf* that Edith's first Asian-themed story, "The Gamblers," was printed in 1896. He ran more of her pieces in another journal, the *Lotus,* commenting, "these sketches of Chinese life promise to bring a modest fame to the author in a very little while."[65]

If Edith's fame was to be a long time coming, worse was in store for Harte. His health declined, and Grace took over editorial chores while working full time as a court stenographer, even after the birth of her son, Horace. Harte died half a year later, in 1899, after eight years of marriage.

He died as he had lived, in the most proverbial of artistic garrets, but Grace had to go on. She remained in New York until 1903, then relocated to Chicago, where she raised her son, studied law while working, and was admitted to the Illinois bar in 1912 at the age of forty-five. Her specialty was real-estate law, but her many professional causes over the next forty years included new state laws to empower women to serve on juries and a federal equal rights amendment. One of her articles, in the 1947 *Women Lawyers' Journal,* was the first published history of women lawyers in the United States.[66] She never remarried.

According to James Doyle, her husband's biographer, Grace consistently "maintained her aloofness toward her Chinese heritage." In an interview in the *Women Lawyers' Journal* in 1940, Grace did not refer to her Eurasian background but emphasized her British heritage and the fact that her grandfather was a judge in England. Doyle concludes that she remained publicly silent about her Asian heritage rather than complicate her "already difficult struggle to succeed in a profession beset by rampant sex discrimination." However, her work for women's rights demonstrated her "enthusiastic and sometimes militant character, as well as her commitment to her vocation."[67]

Oddly, there is evidence that Grace, like Winnifred, also at times pretended to be Japanese. In a letter written to a friend, the writer A. S. Cody, after Harte's death, she mentioned that his publisher had published "the book of a sister of mine, whose nom de plume is Onoto Watanna." The book was *Miss Numè of Japan,* and Grace, who was writing from England where she stayed with her late husband's family while trying to find a publisher for his works, lamented that "that kind of writing will sell and get a publisher while Walter's goes a-begging!" She added, "I don't know whether you were already aware of the admixture of Oriental blood in my veins. It was not generally known among Walter's writing friends, as neither of us wanted to see the reviews or notices of his work discussing the uniqueness of the situation, and forgetting the merits of the work in the romance of the personal life of a writer—as in Lafcadio Hearn's case somewhat."[68] Lafcadio Hearn, a writer, was the son of an Anglo-Irish major in the British army and a Greek woman who migrated to Japan in 1890. He married a Japanese woman, became a Japanese citizen, and took a Japanese name.

Many years later, Cody's son wrote that Grace Harte, whom he had known well, was "half Canadian and half Japanese . . . a fascinating woman and very oriental."[69] In claiming Japanese ancestry, Grace was doubtlessly trying to protect her sister's charade. Grace and Winnifred were always allies; Winnifred respected and looked up to her older sister, kept in touch with her throughout her life, and consulted her in the various professional and legal difficulties that beset Winnifred: divorce, lawsuits, and writing contracts.

Winnifred's other siblings, some of whom flash in and out of the pages of *Marion* as dirty-faced urchins and flirtatious girls, did not take up writing careers, but they worked hard and were adventurous spirits, like Winnifred herself. In the struggle against poverty, all the poor and "half-caste" young Eatons improved their lot in life.

After their early years in Montreal, Winnifred's brothers and sisters scattered to San Francisco, New York, Boston, Chicago, and Seattle. The eldest, Edward Charles, we have seen, became a successful businessman and married a snobbish woman. Sara married a German artist, Karl Bosse, and led a happy, bohemian, childless life in New York. Christina Agnes married a French Canadian in Notre Dame Cathedral; she and Edward Charles were the only Eaton children to remain in Montreal. May converted to Catholicism and spent a few months in a convent; then she moved to San Francisco and married.

Rose, born in 1881, six years Winnifred's junior, married an impoverished descendant of French nobility, Harper de Rouville, but when he left her a penniless widow, she proved to be another capable Eaton sister and supported herself by running an oil company office and working for the Red Cross during World War II. George, the second Eaton son, was considered "the genius of the family," for he was an inventor who took out patents on car improvements and worked for Kodak and General Electric. Though delicate in health, he fought in the Spanish American War. Hubert (born, like George, in 1879 in one of their mother's more exhausting feats of fecundity), drowned in 1902 at the age of twenty-three, swimming off the Ile St.-Helene. The youngest Eatons, Florence and Beryl, born in 1885 and 1887, were the babies Winnifred helped care for. They remained close to her, as they both moved to New York and she saw them frequently. Florence married a con man who created a harrowing life for her and their four children; Beryl became a nurse.

And where was Winnifred in those Montreal days? Those years between fifteen and twenty, before she left home, were not ones she wrote about, although she committed almost every other phase of her life to paper. Ironically, that was the age of most of her heroines. But if Winnifred deliberately wanted to keep the events of those years in her own life secret, as if they never happened, she effectually succeeded in doing so by cutting three years off her official age of entry into the world, making herself seventeen when she was nearly twenty-one.

During those years, Winnifred may have left Montreal on occasion, perhaps to visit the Hartes in Boston or New York, as family tradition hints; but probably she lived as her sisters did, working at what jobs she could get. Of one thing we can be certain: during those years she was writing stories as fast as she could think of them and sending them to newspapers, in hopes of becoming a writer more successful than her sister and less tragic than her brother-in-law.

Of all these fourteen children with their peculiar heritage, to Winnifred fell the largest share of the daring spirit of both parents. In her first essay in the world beyond Montreal, she impulsively ventured far afield—abruptly, dramatically, like the picaresque little adventurer she was, she unexpectedly took a ship for the exotic and unknown (to her) land of Jamaica.

2. Jamaican Adventure

> "That kid! What on earth is she going to do?"
> "Oh, Nora's not so young. She's nearly seventeen. . . . She's going out to the West Indies. She's got a position on some paper out there."
> "Whee!" Reggie drew a long whistle. "West Indies! I'll be jiggered if your parents aren't the easiest ever. Your mother is the last woman in the world to bring up a family of daughters, and I'm blessed if I ever came across any father like yours."
> —[Winnifred Eaton,] *Marion*

In March 1896, a poem with the byline of Winnifred Eaton appeared in *Gall's News Letter* in Kingston, Jamaica.[1] How did Winnifred turn up so surprisingly in Jamaica? Her own account is given in *Me,* written nearly twenty years later: "It was a cold, blizzardy day in the month of March when I left Quebec, and my weeping, shivering relatives made an anxious, melancholy group about my departing train. I myself cried a bit, with my face pressed against the window; but I was seventeen, my heart was light, and I had not been happy at home" (3).

If articles and interviews about Winnifred must be approached with caution as to their veracity, such a caveat is doubly necessary in regard to *Me.* Winnifred was not seventeen when she so daringly left her home, but twenty; however, seventeen had more éclat. Her account of the circumstances in *Me* is as follows: "I had overruled my father's weak and absentminded objections and my mother's exclamatory ones, and I had accepted a position in Jamaica, West Indies, to work for a little local newspaper. It all came about through my having written at the age of sixteen a crude, but exciting, story which a kindly friend, the editor of a Quebec weekly paper, actually accepted and published" (4).

By 1896, Edith Eaton was well established in newspaper work, so Winnifred's first contacts in journalism may have come through her or through their brother-in-law Harte. Perhaps her early story "A Poor Devil," published in the *Metropolitan Magazine,* was the one published by the family friend.

Winnifred indicates that this man thought she might replace a young woman in Jamaica who wanted to return to Canada. “With the alacrity of youth I cried out that *of course* I would go,” says the narrator. As for the distance, she “airily dismissed that objection as something too trivial to consider. Was I not the daughter of a man who had been back and forth to China no fewer than eighteen times?” (5). And so it was arranged, in life as in fiction.

There seem to have been no serious objections. For “Nora,” just as for Winnifred, “I was the fifth girl in our family to leave home. I suppose my father and mother had become sadly accustomed to the departing of the older children to try their fortunes in more promising cities than Quebec; but I was the first to leave home for a land as distant as the West Indies, though two of my sisters had gone to the United States” (6). Grace and her husband were living in Boston, and Sara was in New York.

Winnifred’s picture of herself in *Me* as a callow young woman displays her characteristic egotism: “I was not beautiful to look at, but I had a bright, eager face, black and shining eyes, and black and shining hair. My cheeks were as red as a Canadian apple. I was a little thing, and, like my mother, foreign-looking. I think I had the most acute, inquiring, and eager mind of any girl of my age in the world” (6).

Was 1915 a time of such unselfconscious individualism that a woman could so openly and naively express her admiration for her own uniqueness? Other literary heroines—even Canada’s own Anne of Green Gables (“all ‘spirit and fire and dew,’”)—were praised for their singularity, but Winnifred’s brand of self-congratulation was at times almost breathtaking. Part of her boundless enthusiasm for life included an enthusiasm for herself.

Winnifred’s reference to her mother as “foreign-looking” is the closest she comes in *Me* to indicating Grace Eaton’s race. Winnifred had not yet been captured by the romance of the Orient: “I myself was dark and foreign-looking, but the blond type I adored. In all my fanciful imaginings and dreams I had always been golden-haired and blue-eyed” (41).

At the time of Winnifred’s journey to Jamaica, a one-way winter cabin passage from New York to Jamaica cost fifty-five dollars, which was borne by her new employer. Starting in Montreal, the entire journey would have taken six days. In *Me,* the heroine, dressed in rough, woolen Canadian clothing, sets out with only ten dollars in her purse. The journey is exciting; she develops a crush on the ship’s purser, whom the captain has assigned to look after her, and spends the last of her money buying lighter clothing from another girl. Whatever the journey was really like, it is indisputable that Winnifred’s first byline appeared in *Gall’s News Letter* on March 10, 1896, under a poem. This debut piece (which, it must be said, sounds suspiciously unlike anything she ever wrote at any other time in her life), was entitled "Sneer Not":

> Sneer not, ye cynics, who to school once went
> And talked with knowledge at her many marts;
> Who through long days and longer nights have spent
> Your peace of soul to strengthen mental parts. . . .

It seems probable that Winnifred actually arrived in Jamaica in February, not March, for it was on February 29, 1896, that the first piece likely to be hers appears in *Gall's News Letter,* though uncredited. This is a story entitled "A Summer Girl," a light romantic piece about a young man who is attracted to a girl in a watering place because of her lustrous singing voice, yet he takes her for a trivial "summer girl"—until he learns that she really does have deep feelings for him.

Another story that apparently is Winnifred's appears toward the end of her stay in Jamaica, nearly five months later, on July 18. "The Little Dressmaker" displays a sprightly style and an ironic plot structure typical of Winnifred's writing. A "little dressmaker" sews a bridal gown and laments that her lover is going to marry a rich girl. Asked to the bride's house for a final fitting, she finds the bride making love with another man. The dressmaker tells her lover what she saw, and he marries her instead. But it is a case of mistaken identity: his own sister was trying on the dress.

This early story has several Winnifred earmarks. The plot turns on an absurd contrivance yet is genuinely compelling. The girl is of low social status, but a sour final twist keeps this from being a straight Cinderella story: she wins her lover by an error, and it is not at all certain that he will be happier with this uneducated girl than with his chosen bride.

The *News Letter* was run by a Canadian, James Gall, described in *Me* as "a lame old man running a fiery, two-sheet little newspaper in this tropical land far from his native Canada." Gall sent back home for "bright and expert young women reporters to do virtually all the work of running his newspaper" (25).

The paper relied mainly on news items imported from the English press, but it also carried columns of local news, such as exhaustive coverage of the proceedings of the legislature, detailed accounts of horse and dog races, crime stories, and society and fashion news. There were elaborate descriptions and illustrations of the fancy millinery of the late Victorian period, all available for purchase at the Kingston emporiums and looking much like the fashions Winnifred would have read about back home in the *Montreal Star.* Many of the advertisements for items like Pears soap and the myriad cures for eczema and digestive disorders are identical in the two papers. Far apart though they were geographically, colonial Jamaica and provincial Canada were not so widely separated in matters of fashion.

Although *Gall's News Letter* for the period of Edith's stay in Jamaica survives, most of the issues that Winnifred published in are not available. It does appear, however, that writing fiction was an important component of Winnifred's contribution to the *News Letter,* although in *Me* she gives a long and daunting list of much more extensive duties. These included reporting on the debates of the Legislative Council, city council proceedings, and court cases; interviewing government officials and elected members; covering political speeches, races, and sporting events; representing the paper at social functions; writing a weekly advertising column and a woman's column; reviewing books; and answering correspondence, correcting proof, and editing in the editor's absence.

The *News Letter* pieces that Edith wrote indicate this job description is no exaggeration. The job was no sinecure; the young woman assigned to this arduous set of tasks hurried about all day long, often in conditions of extreme heat, and her assignments continued far into the evenings.

Fortunately, Winnifred was housed in some comfort. Advertisements for the Myrtle Bank Hotel where she stayed, one of Kingston's social centers, show a luxurious-looking, rambling structure surrounded by palm trees and benches and canopies attractively arranged in front. The grounds featured tropical gardens, wide lawns, a bandstand, and summer bowers—before the advent of air conditioning, shade was an important attraction in a resort. The hotel advertised its fine table, featuring tropical dishes. Other inducements to stay at the Myrtle Bank Hotel included billiard tables, a swimming bath, "livery" stables, and magnificent views of mountains, Kingston Harbour, and Port Royal.

Despite the comforts of her lodging, Winnifred found herself in an utterly foreign world. In *Me,* she relates how, on disembarking from the ship, her heroine felt "a genuine thrill of excitement and fear" upon seeing for the first time a "vast sea of upturned black and brown faces. Never will I forget that first impression of Jamaica. Everywhere I looked were negroes—men and women and children, some half naked, some with bright handkerchiefs knotted about their heads" (20).

At the time of Winnifred's stay in Jamaica, *Whitaker's Almanac* listed the racial composite as follows: "Whites, 14,692; Blacks, 488,624; Coloured, 121,955," plus "a number of coolies and Chinese."[2] But to read *Gall's News Letter,* one would assume the island's racial makeup was exactly the reverse. It was a white newspaper for white people, with white tourists pictured in advertisements for homeopathic remedies, corsets, and confectionery. Occasionally there is a glancing reference to the nonwhite population: a man is arrested for practicing obeah; or in the police court column, it is noted that a man fined for fighting is darker skinned than his opponent.

Jamaica was just opening up to the tourist trade and conditions for visitors were in a transitional state. An elaborate international exhibition had been held a few years earlier, in 1891, in an elegant, newly constructed Moorish festival hall, ceremonially opened by Prince George of Wales. On display were such items as fruit-drying devices. It was hoped this exhibition would spark a tourist boom, and the building of hotels was encouraged. However, new laws intended as a panacea for depressed economic conditions resulted in saddling the taxpayers with what was called "the hotels loan incubus."[3]

Building was not the only activity the Jamaicans undertook to prepare for the hoped-for increase in tourism. An attempt was made to get the residents themselves into shape, to keep their houses and yards clean and tidy to avoid pestilence.[4] Arriving a few years after this surge of activity, Winnifred and Edith saw a somewhat less primitive Jamaica than had existed only recently. Among the improvement projects undertaken in Kingston, the Myrtle Bank Hotel, owned by Winnifred's employer James Gall, had been rebuilt. With his interest in the hotel, it is not surprising that Gall chose this location to house his young journalist. Most of the hotels lost money, and there were endless complaints of mismanagement: at Myrtle Bank, it was intriguingly reported that the manager was in a state of "maudlin drunkenness" for weeks. The hotel was often closed, and a *Jamaica Post* editorial labeled such places "aristocratic alms houses."[5]

At this troubled time in Jamaica's tourist economy, visitors, such as the young Winnifred, would have found an unsettling atmosphere of racial tension, even in the insulated hotel world. Relations between both European and American tourists and the hotel staffers were uneasy, as the "superciliousness and cultural arrogance" of the whites collided with the often mock-servile attitude of those who waited on them. In his study of the hotel industry in Jamaica, Frank Fonda Taylor describes these conflicts: "The hotel industry served to resuscitate the dying master-servant culture of the Great House era in Jamaica. Little wonder, then, that the hotels became an arena of subtle black-white confrontation. . . . Uppishness, feigned stupidity, clumsiness, and deliberate inefficiency were part of the resistance kit of these early black hotel staffers."[6]

Edith, a fair-minded and unprejudiced observer, commented on the situation, displaying an attitude toward working much like Winnifred's own: "Jamaicans are continually complaining about 'the lazy nigger,' the lazy laboring class . . . [but] they are the most humble and servile lot of humanity that I have ever come in contact with. . . . Free born, educated men regard work as a blessing. Slavish and ignorant people regard it as degrading and something to be shunned."[7]

Both sisters had difficulties adjusting to life in a foreign and racially complex culture with an oppressive colonial history. Black Jamaicans had won full citizenship as far back as 1838, but the ruling class had found ways of restricting the number of people who could vote, and requirements for membership in the assembly were so high that only rich landowners could meet them.[8] The government promoted Jamaica as a holiday spa and urged construction of "elegant lodgings for transient whites," but the housing needs of local blacks were largely ignored.[9]

Despite such realities, Jamaica was promoted as a winter resort, an isle of sunshine, marked by the "smiling faces, joyous laughter, and blithe behavior" of the blacks.[10] Travelers were urged to shed their fears of fever, dangerous reptiles, and the locals. The white woman visitor was assured that she need never fear being raped by the natives, as the island's blacks had "'an almost divine affection' for the white woman because during the reign of a woman they became freedmen."[11]

To see Jamaica through Winnifred's eyes, one must appreciate how radically unlike Montreal her new home was. She may have been like her heroine in *Me* who claimed to have seen only one black person in her life before—in church, when an older sister told her he was the "Bogy man" (19).

As depicted in *Me,* Nora's new employer is appalled to find his new editor and woman-of-all-work is "a green, green girl" who earnestly declares that she taught herself shorthand with a book and "acquired practice and speed by going to church and prayer-meetings and taking down sermons" (24). The heroine is taken to the Government House to learn her new duties. It seems safe to take Nora's narration as a fair description of what Winnifred saw: "At the council table, on one side, were the Parliament members, Englishmen . . . on the other side were the elected members, who were, without an exception, colored men" (36).

Nora is introduced to Mr. Burbank, a wealthy champion of the press, and is so surprised to find that the greatly respected man is "pure black" that when he holds out his hand, she panics and does not take it. She is thereupon warned that if she has the slightest feeling of race prejudice, she had better "kill it at once or clear out of Jamaica" (40).

Our narrator protests that she had "literally never heard the expression 'race prejudice' before":

> I was as far from feeling it as any person in the world. It must be remembered that in Canada we do not encounter the problem of race. . . . One color there is as good as another . . . my own mother was a foreigner. What should I, a girl who had never before been outside Quebec . . . know of race prejudice?
>
> Vaguely I had a feeling that all men were equal as men. I do not believe it was in me to turn from a man merely because of his race, so long as he himself was not personally repugnant to me. (41)

Nora may have been unprejudiced, but her contradictory creator, Winnifred, was either being disingenuous or blocking out her own unpleasant life experiences in claiming that her alter ego could know nothing of race prejudice: her mother, as well as she and her siblings, had suffered its effects directly. If there was anything Winnifred knew well, it was how it felt to be a member of an ethnic minority.

The social rules in Jamaica, as they are laid down to the heroine of *Me*, would, in truth, have been unlike anything Winnifred ever encountered in Canada. Nora's employer spells out the distinction between black and white in Jamaica: "The richest people and planters were of colored blood; though they were invited to all the governor's parties and the various official functions . . . there was a fine line drawn between them and the native white people who counted for anything." She is told to act in such a way as to "never in the slightest to hurt or offend the feelings of the colored element whose good-will was essential," but, equally, she must "stoop to no familiarity" (42).

Winnifred claimed to be "a great favorite" with the governor and his wife, Sir Henry and Lady Blake, who "petted and spoiled" her, as did the Earl of Carlisle, even though she thought he was a shopkeeper the first time she saw him.[12] Winnifred always did like to drop the names of titled people, but it actually was the reporter's job to get close to the rich and famous folk visiting the islands. Edith, for example, interviewed John Jacob Astor, visiting him aboard his yacht, the *Nourmahal.*

No matter how hard she worked or what the conditions, for Winnifred there would always be time for romance. Even early in her career, she depended on the kindness of strange gentlemen in an emergency—and Winnifred's life was full of emergencies. The world of *Me* is populated with helpful and gallant strangers who give the heroine a hand at difficult times. She develops crushes on them, has her heart broken by them, breaks their hearts—but whenever she is in trouble, she straightaway finds a beau to help her over the rough spot. Always resourceful, Winnifred was fundamentally a person who relied on herself and on her own hard work; but at the same time she saw no harm in accepting help from an obliging man. Men were there to be used, and her attractiveness to them was one of her natural resources that she never hesitated to employ.

Winnifred certainly did not sleep her way to the top—or to writing and journalistic success. There is no way of knowing which or how many men she had affairs with or how many she teased. But she would have lost her proud view of herself as an independent career woman had she relied too exclusively on sex to further her aims. In her view of morality, there was nothing wrong with borrowing money from a man or flirting for a free meal. Not only was such behavior often urgently necessary, but also it was natural to her, for she had a decided enthusiasm for men. Flirtation was the spice of life to Winnifred.

In *Me,* she writes of being pursued by an older man, "Dr. Manning," who thought that "a girl like me deserved a better fate than to be shut up in this country" and that she should go to the United States as his secretary to avoid the hot season (51).

But the incident that dictates Nora's departure from Jamaica—if not Winnifred's—is a startling encounter with Mr. Burbank. This occurs one evening when she stays late after the council session and is approached by the black gentleman. "God! how I love you!" he exclaims, seizes her in "a pair of powerful arms," and presses his lips hard on hers. She fights and screams and rushes out into the street, sickened by "that great *animal* who had kissed me" (55). Nora determines to leave Jamaica at once. Her employer scolds her for her foolishness. "Don't you know better than to stay alone in *any* building where there are likely to be black men?" he asks (60). She accepts Dr. Manning's offer to pay for her passage to Boston and promises to go work for him in Richmond.

What should she know of race prejudice? Any woman might have a horrified reaction to being suddenly assaulted by a man. But Winnifred, in protesting that her character never felt race prejudice, did not recognize its traces in her Nora.

More surprising than any prejudice her heroine is shocked into betraying at age twenty is Winnifred's utter unawareness of what she was describing, when writing about the incident as a woman of forty. The young Montreal woman's sickened reaction to being admired, approached, and kissed by an older black man appeared entirely natural to the adult author, and she made the perfectly correct assumption that it would seem so in the eyes of her readership. There were numerous details about her life that she concealed in her memoir, such as her age and racial makeup, yet she did not remotely conceive that it might be wise to cloak her heroine's reactions to put her in a good light. Even years after the supposed event, she did not blame her fictional self for such feelings; but, of course, even in 1915 she did not live in a world that might look askance at them. Always a good, canny judge of what was popular and acceptable in current usage and morality, Winnifred judged her audience correctly. Nearly a century later, it is Winnifred's uninhibited account of the incident that seems more startling than the incident itself; another reminder that the past is, indeed, another country.

Me contains other incidents when the heroine is preyed on by men, such as the terrifying moment when her employer Dr. Manning creeps into her bedroom. As in the Mr. Burbank situation, Nora's horrified response is to clear out of the place as fast as she can. In recounting these two incidents, Winnifred is depicting the susceptibility of an unprotected young female to predatory attacks by older men who take advantage of her lone situation. Both black and white prey upon her: being vulnerable and at risk is another of the trials the heroine endures on her difficult road.[13]

We might expect Winnifred to show some special open-mindedness and sensitivity to racial issues, due to her own half-caste status, but in *Me* she shies away from any mention that her heroine is of mixed race. Part of the perplexity engendered by Winnifred's racial postures is due to her own shifting stance. As Winnie Eaton, working in Jamaica, she saw and presented herself as a white woman, nothing Asian about her at all. She then proceeded to spend many years working out—and exploiting—her conflicts about being Asian, by posing as Japanese. But when that charade ended, she went back to presenting herself basically as a white lady for the rest of her life—one who may have had exotically mixed blood but who functioned as Mrs. Reeve of Hollywood and Calgary, an unremarkable, white North American.

We cannot be certain that the Mr. Burbank contretemps that precipitated Nora's departure from Jamaica incident ever really happened—it may be pure fiction—but Winnifred gave it some prominence in her anonymous memoir. We can only conclude that if it happened, it was deeply upsetting to her.

Whatever the actual circumstances of Winnifred's departure from Jamaica, she did spend about five months there, and when it was necessary for someone to replace her, the replacement was none other than her sister Edith. Edith did not set out immediately but arrived in Jamaica in December 1896, six months after Winnifred's departure. More of her newspaper pieces survive than Winnifred's, and she wrote many lively observations of Kingston life, usually signed with the nom de plume "Fire Fly." In her autobiographical writings, Edith has little to say about her Jamaican experience, though amusingly, she, too, misstates the age she was at the time, saying she was in her "27th year" when she was actually thirty-one.[14]

Edith probably attracted less attention at thirty-one than Winnifred did at twenty, with her coltish "greenness" on flamboyant display. On the evidence of *Me,* Winnifred latched on to men for all sorts of aid—a young admirer to help her write her reports, another man to help get her out of Jamaica. The older Edith depended on no one. Clearly she was more the kind of woman *Gall's News Letter* had been accustomed to hiring. No black Mr. Burbank ogled her, yet she wrote in "Leaves," "When it begins to be whispered about the place that I am not all white, some of the 'sporty' people seek my acquaintance," only to retreat on learning that she is a "very serious and sober-minded spinster."[15]

By contrast, no one ever mistook Winnifred, during her Jamaican period or at any other time in her life, as a serious, sober-minded spinster. No one seems to have identified her in Jamaica as "not all white" either, though Edith was recognized as Chinese (one man suggestively offered to tell her "all about the sweet little Chinese girls I met when we were at Hong Kong").[16] This was a potential problem for both sisters. Annette White-Parks suggests that the "'colored distinction' could apply equally to Eurasians, as Winifred and Sui Sin Far knew. Both also recognized that if they were identified as the daughters of Lotus Blossom,[17] they might not be traveling at all, unless as Chinese traveled, in bond."[18]

The difficulties of traveling for a Chinese person at that period could be enormous and humiliating, involving questions and physical examinations. However, the Eatons were in small danger of being forced to comply with such regulations, which were aimed at Chinese immigrant workmen, not at Western–born and educated individuals. Even if being challenged on such grounds was extremely unlikely, the sisters knew of these laws and may have felt uneasy about them. They took the precaution of calling themselves Miss Edith Eaton and Miss Winnifred Eaton when traveling, not Sui Sin Far and Onoto Watanna.

Edith's stay lasted not much longer than Winnifred's, about six months. She explains, "I got very weary and homesick tramping the hot dusty streets of Kingston; and contracted malarial fever, the only cure for which, in my case, was a trip up north."[19] Even the amenities of the town's refurbished hotels (a typical one boasted "Electric Light, Electric Bells, and complete up-to-date Sanitary arrangements") were not sufficient to keep poor Edith in good health in such a climate and with such stressful work.[20]

Returning to Montreal in the summer of 1897, Edith recovered, continued her peripatetic career mostly on the West Coast, and went more or less out of Winnifred's life. They may have corresponded, but geographically speaking their paths did not cross.

Winnifred sailed back to the United States just before her twenty-first birthday. She was determined to make her way as a writer in surroundings more congenial to her than Jamaica and closer to the important writers' markets. In the big cities of Boston, Richmond, Cincinnati, Chicago, and eventually New York, she would throw herself heart and soul into the struggle for success and recognition that lay ahead.

3. Chicago

"Poverty, in a way, is a state of warfare."
—Winnifred Eaton, "Starving and Writing in New York"

"Who can analyze a coquette?"
—Onoto Watanna, *Miss Numè of Japan*

WINNIFRED LEFT Jamaica in July 1896. Where did she go? It is tempting, in tracing her movements, to follow literally the narratives of *Me* and *Marion.* Some articles about her early writing years corroborate her experiences as she described them in these books, while others contradict them. Although hardly an exact outline of her adventures, these autobiographical fictions are useful as a clue to some of the events of her life.

According to *Me,* after leaving Jamaica, Winnifred traveled to Boston, using the last of her savings from her salary—which could not have gone far, since she earned only ten dollars a week and the ship fare was approximately fifty-five dollars. She may have depended on a loan or gift from her employer or one of her men friends for the balance; in *Me,* Dr. Manning pays Nora's fare.

In both *Me* and *Marion,* Nora has a chance encounter with her sister Marion—in real life, Sara—in a basement dining room patronized by Harvard students. In *Marion,* a young woman comes in with a little white fox terrier, and to her amazement Marion sees it is her "little sister, Nora! I had thought she was in Jamaica" (157). She notices that Nora looks more sophisticated, with her hair done up, and has a new "older-sister" way about her, "which was very funny, for I had always snubbed her at home as being a 'kid' while I was a grown-up young lady" (158).

Nora's dog is described in *Marion* as "not very good, for if she left him a single moment you could hear his cries all over the neighborhood" (159). She evidently insisted on taking the dog everywhere, though her sister tells her she is crazy; no girl can go looking for work with a dog along. Winnifred did have a white fox terrier, at least at the time of writing *Me;* photographs show her enthusiastically cuddling the animal.

Marion advises her sister to take the job with Dr. Manning (who is mentioned in both books, as if repetition makes his existence more likely) and sees her off for the South, commenting, "She looked pathetic and awfully childish" (161).

Little more than the dubious testimony of this fiction suggests that Winnifred went to Richmond to secure employment or that she met on the train the wealthy "Mr. Hamilton," an older, married man Nora falls in love with. It is impossible to know if there really was a Dr. Manning or a Mr. Hamilton or if they are purely imaginary creations, superimposed on a backdrop that realistically reflects Winnifred's own life. But an early publicity piece that appeared at the time of her first novel, *Miss Numè of Japan,* in 1899 mentions that Winnifred was in the South at about this time. In this article, she did not, of course, bring up Dr. Manning or Mr. Hamilton, if they existed; instead, we are told that "for awhile after leaving Jamaica, Miss Watanna lived with her father's relations in the South."[1]

Nora's employment with the doctor, as related in *Me,* does not last very long, for he proves to be a predator who slips into her bedroom at night. Terrified, Nora knows she must get away. Before bolting, she makes a fine departing speech to the villainous doctor: "If I work for a man, I expect to be paid for my actual labor. That's a contract between us. After that, I have my personal rights, and no man can step over these without my consent." She adds, "They were pretty big words for a young girl, and I am proud of them even now" (87).

Winnifred was always a creature of contradictions. She made many noble speeches about supporting herself, being unafraid of hard work, and never wanting to owe anybody anything; and much of the time she was as good as her word. She did work hard, took whatever job was offered, made good through her own efforts. But perhaps because of her feckless streak, her propensity to do the rash, ill-considered, impulsive thing, she often found herself in risky, desperate situations, and when in one of these, her natural instinct was to turn to a man.

It must be recalled that Winnifred had absolutely no support system in her early working life. She could not draw on her parents for any kind of help; her sisters, in far-flung cities, were in such financially precarious straits themselves that they could be of no assistance. Furthermore, it was a time when the vast majority of women did normally depend on being "kept" by men in some way or another; their husbands, fathers, brothers—or their lovers—

were their "keepers," in ways either sanctioned or unsanctioned. For their part, men expected to give women money as a matter of course and did not necessarily hope for an immediate return. This was the gray area into which Winnifred adroitly inserted herself in her dealings with men. She took the money and returned it when she could; or else she got out of the tight spot by bolting away before any reciprocal favors were demanded. At least this is the impression she gives of her own behavior, and it is consistent with what we know from her correspondence and circumstances. Such maneuvers were possible, even commonplace, when the sugar daddy era was in full bloom.

The completely independent working woman just coming into being was ordinarily considered a "common working girl," not in a position of much respect. Wherever the working woman went, she was prey for men. To accept the favors of these eager men was tempting. Men buzzing around her, in some stage of being in love, were so omnipresent that it is not surprising that Winnifred looked upon them as a kind of resource, to be tapped in a real emergency. Furthermore, with her vivid imagination and healthy ego, Winnifred frequently imagined that men were in love with her even when they were not. She saw herself surrounded by an inexhaustible supply of that intoxicating, fascinating, most helpful commodity: men.

Winnifred protested that she would never bestow her sexual favors in exchange for anything and that she paid back gifts just as soon as was humanly possible. Perhaps she did. With all the effort she lavished on her career, she would have felt herself a failure and would have been humiliated had she been categorized in the eyes of the world as being "kept" or "fallen," living on the tender mercies of lovers. Still, she was never shy about asking men for money, loans, or handouts.

It is natural to assume that she had love affairs, even though her day was a century before our own supposedly more liberated times. With her strong attraction to men, her excitement in their company, and her independent single life, it is possible she did. Yet it must be remembered that love affairs generally had consequences in those days, and Winnifred had a strong moral streak; virtue may very well have won out after all. In any event, she wasn't telling. Shocking as her confessional novel of 1915 was then considered, it was not as revelatory as would be the case nowadays. In *Me,* the closest she came to addressing the question is as follows: "Some one once said of me that I owed my success as a writer mainly to the fact that I used my sex as a means to help me climb. That is partly true not only in the case of my writing, but of my work as a stenographer. I have been pushed and helped by men who liked me, but in both cases I *made good* after I was started" (147).

It is illustrative of Winnifred's solution to problems in life and in fiction that when her alter ego Nora feels the urgent desire to leave the wicked doctor's employ, she does not give up the idea of asking men for help. No, she merely goes to the next kind male stranger, Mr. Hamilton. Used to such approaches, he asks lightly, "Well, how many thousands or millions of shekels do you suppose it will take to support a little poetess in Chicago?" Hurt, she replies, "You don't have to support poetesses if they're the right sort. All I want is enough money to carry me to Chicago. I'll get work of some kind then" (95). And she tearfully vows to pay back every penny: "I will die of starvation, I will sleep homeless in the streets, I will walk a thousand miles, if need be, in search of work rather than take money from him again . . . I will prove to him that I indeed am different" (102).

Like her heroine, Winnifred went to Chicago as a young woman with little money. "The colossal city . . . bewildered and amazed me," she wrote in *Me* (104). At the end of the nineteenth century, the "furnished room" districts of big cities were first identified by urban investigators as regions where unconventional, immoral behavior thrived. By the late 1910s, sociologists identified "a new code of sex relationships" in the furnished room districts of Chicago. The transient nature of this culture meant that lodgers were anonymous, unknown to their neighbors. There was less pressure to "conform to conventional familial roles." Young women might have good intentions of seeking work, but, as Joanne Meyerowitz points out, "not securing very lucrative positions, they soon learned how to supplement their wages by allowing young men to stay with them."[2] The "experimenters" in the Chicago's North Side bohemia are seen by historians as "vanguards of modern sexuality, women and men who experimented freely with new sexual possibilities learned from Sigmund Freud, Havelock Ellis and other sexologists."[3]

Winnifred identified her own family as bohemian and unconventional. Mixing with writers, intellectuals, and artists and living in a casual rooming-house atmosphere in Chicago and New York, she remained comfortable in bohemian circles. During these years of her early working life, her economic circumstances may have reflected Meyerowitz's observation: "Because employers paid self-supporting women wages intended for dependent daughters and wives, many women lodgers worked in low-paying jobs that barely covered subsistence. . . . By entering sexual relationships, however, they could supplement their wages."[4] Although there is no evidence that Winnifred engaged in any untoward behavior, she wrote many lively descriptions of how she and her girlfriends, in their common circumstances of poverty, youth, and high spirits, made a game of getting such things as free meals from gentlemen.

Reformers did their best for poor, working young women, and in Chicago as in other cities, they opened subsidized boardinghouses. Winnifred often told of staying at the Chicago YWCA and may have shared the opinion of several residents who wrote a letter to the newspaper at about the time of her stay there, describing themselves as self-respecting, self-supporting, and properly chaperoned by a matron. By her account in *Me,* she was much impressed with this institution, for her heroine says, "I had never been in a building with an elevator before. . . . We did not have one in Quebec when I was there" (110). The "Y" is gratefully described as a useful haven for young working women: "There in the reading room . . . I found not only paper, pencils, pens, but all the newspapers and journals" (115).

Winnifred places Nora's arrival in Chicago in May, although we know Winnifred herself did not leave Jamaica until July 1896. Perhaps she spent the fall and winter of 1896–97 in Boston, the South, Cincinnati, or New York, all places where we hear of her, and she probably did not actually settle in Chicago until May of 1897, when she was nearly twenty-two.

Her amusing, reminiscent piece called "Starving and Writing in New York" was written in 1922. Here she declares that she was "not quite eighteen years" when she made her entrance into New York City, carrying with her an encouraging letter from an editor of *Frank Leslie's Magazine.*[5] Of course she was not really eighteen, but the lie at least tallies with the lie about her age in *Me* and shaves off the same three years. Winnifred remained generically eighteen for a long time.

In the same piece, she describes storming into the editor's office, being turned away, and resorting to tears, until he promised to buy a story. Tears, importunings, displays of talent, and persistence: she never gave up. "Whatever I lacked in talent, I made up in pertinacity. I was determined, by hook or by crook, by fair means or foul, to get my stories and poems read and published" (66).

The "Starving and Writing in New York" story is full of vivid details of Winnifred's struggling youth, a time when she "wrote and wrote and wrote" and was "undaunted by the unflattering return of my manuscripts in every mail." And she notes, "Curiously enough, in spite of privations that, looking back upon them now, seem to be appalling, when considered in connection with an extremely young and ignorant girl, my heart was always light and my head teemed with plots and ideas" (66).

She describes living with two other young women in a dingy room on the top floor of a house on East Sixteenth Street. They were all "penniless and improvident," but they managed to have fun; and they staked each other during "broke" periods. "That plan worked very well, except when we were all 'broke' at the same time. Then we were sore put to make ends meet." The young women used their wits to keep themselves fed. "Some of the ways and means we resorted to, it is true, might not have been considered ethical by our more affluent sisters, but poverty, in a way, is a state of warfare" (67).

One roommate was Jocelyn, an aspiring opera singer, a "practical young person, who always seemed out of place in our rackety-packety room." The other roommate, Anna, a beautiful young Danish woman, "was built on a grand scale, and her feet and hands were of a size to match her great, graceful body." "*I* had discovered Anna," Winnifred states proudly. She was a waitress who, Winnie decided, was destined for greater things. "I knew a man who knew a stage hand who knew the stage director at Weber & Fields Theater. To this man, I piloted my willing Anna" (66). Anna secured chorus work and also proved useful in the cold apartment: "Anna was a human furnace. She was better than any hot water bottle or hot water bag ever invented. Snuggled up against her I slept as snug as the proverbial 'bug in a rug.' That first night I slept between my two friends, a sort of dividing link between them, but the next day, expatiating loudly upon the beautiful warm sleep I had enjoyed, the shivering Jocelyn . . . bitterly suggested that I was a pig to keep a good thing all to myself" (67).

Anna had other uses as well. A prosperous man who lived on the "parlor floor" had "cast a sentimental and appraising eye" on her. The roommates marked him as a possible meal ticket and encouraged Anna to dine with him. Winnifred lent her her only party frock: "It was pink and fluffy, and I was small and dark, and therefore, showed up well in it. At that time I weighed about a hundred pounds. Anna tipped the scales at close to a hundred and eighty." But they somehow got Anna into the dress, and she was taken to dinner, with instructions to bring food home to the others. Then to a dance hall—where the worst happened. "I ban busted!" she whispered to Winnifred, who was also there. "I ban busted on dam corset, and I ban busted on dam dress on dam back." Winnifred good-humoredly urged her to conceal the damage by fainting (67).

As her early fiction was being accepted by magazines, the first articles about Winnifred, in the persona of Onoto Watanna, began to appear. These stories often make it difficult to pin down whether an event occurred in New York or in Chicago, for accounts conflict.

One clipping, a "Chicago Letter," written at the time of the publication of her first novel, relates, "In the scrap-book in which she keeps a copy of her published stories, and in which she makes delightful and original marginal notes, she has written opposite a story entitled 'A Japanese Girl': 'This is the first Japanese story I ever wrote. It appeared in the Commercial Tribune of Cincinnati.'" A Cincinnati editor who liked her work encouraged her to write "something of Japan."[6]

Another clipping, based on an interview with Winnifred in 1922, sets out the sequence of events differently, saying that she "came to Columbia University to complete her education and in 1895 went to the West Indies as a reporter on the *Jamaica News Letter.* Shortly after that her first serial appeared in *Conkey's Magazine,* Chicago. It was entitled 'The Old Jinrikisha.'"[7]

Still another piece, in *Current Literature,* dated October 1897, gives a fanciful mix of facts and fiction and is principally interesting for the breathtaking disregard for the truth with which Winnifred fashioned her new writerly image:

> Kitishima Kata Hasche is the real or family name of the clever Japanese girl who is living in Chicago at present and winning fame by writing for the magazines and newspapers of Chicago and the East under the pen name of Onoto Watanna, while more dollars come from her work as stenographer. Miss Hasche, or, as she prefers to be called, Miss Watanna—the two names meaning the same thing, but belonging to different Japanese dialects—though scarcely past her twenty-first birthday, has seen more of life and experience than the average woman of twice her age.

This article, the first we have in which Winnifred's new identity is deliberately set forth, actually comes close to the truth with regard to her age. As for the Kitishima Kata Hasche sobriquet, the writer of the profile is correct in only one particular: that the two names mean the same thing because, in truth, neither name meant anything. The article's inventions continue: "Born in Yokohama, Japan, she was taken by her parents, and in company with the three brothers and nine sisters who shared with her their care and supervision, to Liverpool, England, and from thence to Manchester, before she was eight years of age. The journey from Japan to England was made by sailing vessels, and occupied an entire year."[8] There is not, of course, a word of truth in this statement. Winnifred was not Japanese and was not born in Yokohama; the number of siblings is inaccurate; she never went to England; and the journey by sailing vessels happened, if at all, in the early youth and stories of her father.

The article also states that after "some months" in New York, Winnifred settled in Chicago, where she was helped by a woman lawyer named Florence King, who corresponds to a character in *Me.* If these hints are true, perhaps this New York stay is when the events of "Starving and Writing in New York" took place, but it is difficult to trust an article so filled with what would now be called "spin." It is not, however, composed entirely of untruths, for it gives an accurate list of magazines that were then publishing her work (*Mumsey's*, the *Ladies' Home Journal*, the *Black Cat*, and *Iroquois Magazine*).

This article turns up in the scrapbook of her early pieces, with a note indicating that in this instance the lies and misstatements did not originate entirely with Winnifred. "This paper also had a picture of—well—supposed to be me anyhow. *I* never knew this article had been written till I received a marked copy of the paper—It therefore made me feel quite funny to note that on top of my supposed picture—were the following words—'Taken specially for the N.Y. World'—I am wondering whether there is such a thing as photography by proxy."[9]

A lavishly illustrated article in *Harper's Weekly* in 1903 chronicles the growing fame of the now-glamorous author. "Two years ago the name of Onoto Watanna was entirely unknown except to a coterie in Chicago; today it is known everywhere." We are told that with the sum she received for the serial use of *A Japanese Nightingale* in a women's paper, "she left Chicago in the spring of 1901, and came to New York to take a course in Columbia, and to try her fortune in the East."[10]

This is another curious juxtaposition of facts and dates. Winnifred's arrival in New York as late as spring 1901 as a published author of twenty-five, shortly before her marriage, does not square very well with the image of a poor girl who is "broke" and using the monumental Danish Anna as a hot water bottle. But perhaps not much credence ought to be given to these articles, other than to observe that canny marketing publicity with a cheerfully blatant unconcern for the truth was a phenomenon already well developed a hundred years ago. Our American know-how for self-promotional publicity did not arise from nowhere; it has a long history.

Another profile appears in *Frank Leslie's Popular Monthly* in September 1899. This places Winnifred still in Chicago and mentions her residence in Cincinnati. The piece continues Winnifred's deliberate deception, calling her "the only Japanese woman writer of fiction in this country" and noting her fame in Japan. "Even her fellow countrymen have so far overcome their prejudice against women writers as to read her contributions in the Kokumin-no-Toni and the Hansei Sasshi, two magazines published in Tokyo. The prominent Japanese in America are proud of their clever and charming young countrywoman. . . . In appearance she is decidedly Japanese."[11]

Her description in *Me* of her search for work is a vivid evocation of what a young single working woman faced in turn-of-the-century business offices. She tells of tramping the streets, going from office to office, "selecting a building, and going through it from the top to the bottom floor. It seemed as if a hundred thousand girls answered every advertisement." She continues:

> I have known what it is to be pitied, chaffed, insulted, "jollied"; I have had coarse or delicate compliments paid me; I have been cursed at and ordered to "clear out—" oh, all the crucifying experiences that only a girl who looks hard for work knows!
>
> I've had a man make me a cold business proposition of ten dollars a week for my services as stenographer and type-writer, and ten dollars a week for my services as something else. (124)

The narrator notes that her YWCA roommate, a typical young working woman in Chicago, earned fifteen dollars a week as a "stenographer and type-writer" and contributed three dollars a week to her family. Winnifred's resourceful Nora thinks she could do better, with her "superior education—Heavens and earth! compared with Estelle, I called myself 'educated,' I whose mind was a dismal abyss of appalling ignorance!" And she wryly observes, "Confidence carries youth far" (122).

Winnifred often told the story of how she secured a position as a secretary without knowing how to type. Puzzled about how to make capital letters, she typed without them and told the manager that "the capital was broken." A repairman was sent for, and Winnifred paid him from her "slender purse" for a lesson.[12]

In *Me,* the naive Nora is befriended by a young woman called Lolly Hope, the daughter of a prominent politician, with ambitions to be a reporter. Lolly probably really existed. Her characterization is carefully drawn, and *Me* is dedicated "To Lolly, the friend that was, and to Jean, the friend who is." Jean was Jean Webster, who wrote the introduction to *Me.*

Lolly, older and more sophisticated, advises Nora of the difficulty of securing a position as a reporter. She tells her that there are "five thousand and ninety-nine positions for stenographers to one for women reporters, and . . . if I got a good place, I would find time to write a bit, anyway" (131). This is just what Winnifred did. She did not give up her stenography until she was earning a decent income from her novels. In *Me,* Lolly introduces Nora to a man in the stockyards. Winnifred did work in the Chicago stockyards, and her fictional descriptions of them are lively. As Nora rides through the stockyards on a sunny June day, she thinks of her "father's vivid stories of old Shanghai, the city of smells" (138).

At the stockyards, Nora finds herself in an enormous office with what seem like thousands of clerks. She immediately attracts the attention of men, which is hardly surprising considering the male-female ratio in the stockyards. She describes, with rueful humor, the mash notes and compliments she receives:

> We girls were all appraised when we entered, and soon afterwards were assigned certain places in the estimation of the men of the yards. That is to say, a girl was "good," "bad," a "worker," a "frost," or a "peach." . . . There was a wavering disposition at first to put me in the "peach" class, but I rather think I degenerated within a few weeks to the "worker" class. . . . Twenty-four men asked me to "go out" with them the first week I was there. . . . In the yards there was probably one girl to every three or four hundred men. (154–55)

In another passage that reveals some of the working girl's usage of men friends, as well as the bohemian status of such girls, the cynical Lolly shrewdly advises Nora to get herself a sweetheart. "You talk," says Nora, "as if sweethearts were to be picked up any day on the street." "So they are, as far as that goes," retorts Lolly. Nora is shocked and calls such behavior common. "Pooh! Lord knows I was brought up by book rule," says Lolly, "but now I'm just a working-girl" (133).

With an honest attempt at self-knowledge, Winnifred addresses an issue that obviously disturbed her:

> People who have called me clever, talented, etc.—oh, all women writers get accused of such things!—have not really reckoned with a certain weak and silly part of my character. If as I proceed with this chronicle I shock you with the ease and facility with which I encouraged and accepted and became constantly engaged to men, please set it down to the fact that I always felt an inability to *hurt* by refusing any one who liked me enough to propose to me. I got into lots of trouble for this,—call it moral lack in me. (149)

In *Me,* Winnifred's Nora is introduced into a new social sphere when she does some typing for a dramatic school. The school's head is an "imposing and majestic woman of about fifty," who has a "little salon" frequented by celebrities and authors (323). Nora herself is not one of this set: "I was, in fact, simply on the outskirts, a rather wistful, perhaps envious, and sometimes amused observer of those great people" (324).

This ties in with accounts of Winnifred's own doings in Chicago literary circles, where she attended lectures, made friends among other aspiring writers and poets, and ventured to read her poetry in public, giving readings at the Cipher Club and before the Chicago Women's Press League in 1897.[13]

But there were still plenty of grindingly bad employment experiences to come. One of Nora's worst moments, typical of the trials of poor young working women, occurs when the drama school owner asks Nora to type eight copies of "a closely written manuscript, a play in six acts, for a well known Chicago author." After performing this heavy piece of labor, Nora submits her bill, only to be arrogantly told by the author that he expected her to do the work "for nothing" (327).

Some of the characters Nora meets are intriguing, for they are evidently based on people Winnifred really knew in her early writing days. There is the young reporter "Dick Lawrence," whom she describes as ambitious, impractical, and visionary. "He wrote astonishingly clever things, but never stuck at anything long enough to succeed finally. He was a born wanderer, just like my father, and although still in his early twenties, had been well over the world" (213). Dick is sent to Cuba by a newspaper syndicate, and before he goes he proposes to Nora, who is "sorry to think of his going out to hot and fever-wracked Cuba." But he is "a big, wholesome, splendid-looking boy," so she answers "All right" (214).

Dick Lawrence may have been Frank Putnam, a Chicago journalist who went to Cuba. In 1898, Putnam wrote a slender book of poems entitled *Love Lyrics* and dedicated it to his friend Onoto Watanna, who wrote the introduction and praised the poetry.[14] This was an early tryout of Winnifred's new pen name and persona; at this time she had not yet published her first novel.

When Winnifred wrote in *Me,* "A poet wrote lovely verses to me, and the Chicago papers actually published it" (300), she may have meant Putnam—though it is true she was quite capable of having more than one poet in love with her at once. By this time she was already beginning to be a literary "name" in Chicago, and she wrote the flattering introduction with some suavity: "Only a lover could have written 'Love Lyrics.' All poets are lovers, but few of them write love's language in the expressive way in which Mr. Putnam does. . . . In these days of poseurs and affected poets it is refreshing to pick up a little volume that vibrates with its genuineness."[15]

In Putnam's collection of verses, there is one in which the poet expresses romantic feeling for Winnifred herself:

ONOTO-SAN

Love is the spirit's dream of beauty;
Love is the flower of dear desire;
Love's call is man's supremest duty,
Hope glows in Love's immortal fire. . . .

"Onoto-san" is implored to "receive Love kindly," because "Fame's meed is dust on Age's tongue," and "Love only lives forever young."[16]

Yuko Matsukawa has considered the collaboration between Winnifred and Putnam, an arrangement that she calls an intriguing and gleeful "inside joke," hilariously disingenuous. Winnifred was qualified to authenticate Putnam's aspirations in poetry, says Matsukawa, "because she seemed authentically Japanese or exotic enough to pass as 'Other.'" And Winnifred's "tongue-in-cheek" assertion about the "genuineness" of Putnam's poetry "acquires a comical double edge because Eaton as Onoto Watanna could not help but be cognizant of herself as a poseur and Putnam as an affected poet. Putnam's poetry drips with maudlin affectations and shmaltzy sentimentality."[17]

No doubt Winnifred did enjoy some sly, conspiratorial fun with her masquerade, but both she and Putnam took themselves and their work quite seriously, certainly at this period of their lives. Furthermore, although Winnifred was skilled at narrative fiction from a very young age, she lacked ability as a poet and quite likely sincerely meant what she said about her adorer's verses. Putnam's later letters reveal him as a highly sentimental person who loved to sigh over his lost youth, and Winnifred's letters are filled with romantic nostalgia. They corresponded as late as twenty-five years after *Love Lyrics* was written, and he lent her money and advised her about her affairs like an old friend and lover.

It was through Frank Putnam that she met the Japanese poet Yone Noguchi, who had come to the United States at the age of eighteen. Noguchi's first reaction on hearing about her from Putnam in early 1899 was, "You say Onoto Watanna? Such is not Japanese name. Is she real Japanese lady?"[18]

By June of 1900, Noguchi and Winnifred were good friends. He wrote to his friend Charles W. Stoddard that he was visiting Putnam, who was "himself not fine poet, but has such a nice and graceful soul that pleases me very much, he does everything to entertain me." Noguchi wanted Stoddard to write to him at Winnifred's address: "But you will write to me at 3105 Groveland Avenue where my dearest friend lives and I visit nearly every evening. She is a half caste woman with the name Onoto Watanna; her mother was Japanese, father being an English; she herself being very bright writes now and then very clever short stories for magazines. . . . She published one book from Rand McNally & Co., last year, I believe. She is awfully clever; but she has no sound mind and sweet philosophy. She is woman after all!"[19]

Noguchi did not find his way into *Me* as a character, though Winnifred must have found the Japanese writer a useful and charming friend. As for Putnam, if he is not the prototype for Nora's first fiancé, Dick Lawrence, that honor may belong to Thomas W. Steep, another on the roster of men in Winnifred's life. It may seem remarkable that she should have had not one but *two* serious suitors who were journalists who went to Cuba, but it is natural that many of her men friends were journalists, and the war in Cuba coincided with Winnifred's most marriageable stage. Steep was reportedly an "able correspondent" for the Associated Press of New York. Born in Ohio in 1878 and educated at Lebanon University, Steep began his newspaper career with the *Cincinnati Commercial,* which also published Winnifred in 1897. As a war correspondent, he went to Santiago with American troops and, acting as special correspondent for the *London Daily Mail,* reported uprisings in Russia and Mexico.[20] Winnifred's correspondence indicates that she considered marrying Tom Steep as late as 1916, when she was divorcing her first husband.[21] Steep was as old a friend as Putnam was, and the men knew each other.

Most of Winnifred's legion of lovers, male friends, flirts, and meal tickets are harder to identify than the poetical Frank Putnam and the dashing Tom Steep. However, her romance with "Dick Lawrence" helps fix the date in which *Me* supposedly takes place. Their engagement occurs just prior to the Spanish American War, when Dick goes off as a war correspondent. It was on February 2, 1898, that the U.S. battleship *Maine* was destroyed in Havana Harbor. If this first of Nora's engagements took place in late 1897, Winnifred would have been twenty-two years old—which tallies with her taking three years off her age for the book.

But in *Me,* Mr. Hamilton is Nora's chief lover. He may have been a fictional construct, superimposed to give the book a romantic plot; or perhaps she was pouring out the story of a genuine early passion. Mr. Hamilton raises a fraught issue by giving young Nora clothes and furs. Winnifred had few reservations about accepting gifts from men, in real life or in fiction; and she allows her heroine to acquire sables that she naively believes are "astonishingly cheap" (229). The narrator's protestations about her ignorance due to her youth and her status as a greenhorn are disingenuous. A young woman from Quebec, where furs come from, could hardly have been unaware of their value. "I had been less than a year in America. I was just eighteen. I came from a large, poor family. I did not know the value of clothes or jewels any more than poor, green Irish or Polish immigrant girls would know it in that time. What could I know of sables?" (320). This protest echoes Nora's earlier, equally disingenuous, "What could I know of race prejudice?"

Despite her vaunted ignorance, Nora is sharp enough to know that her only hope of impressing her lover is by retaining her virtue. "I wouldn't be exceptional or wonderful," she protests, "if I took your money. I'd be common" (237). And her most impassioned statement of her moral values is quite impressive, though couched with melodramatic emphasis: "What I had, I honestly earned. I was no doll or parasite who needed to be carried by others. No! To retain my belief in my own powers, I must prove that they actually existed. Only women without resources in themselves, without gifts or brains, were 'kept' by men, either as mistresses or wives or from charity, as Hamilton wished to 'keep' me. I had the youthful conviction that *I* was one of the exceptional souls of the world, and could carry myself" (244).

It is hard to doubt Winnifred's sincerity here, as either author or heroine. She undoubtedly considered herself superior to women who could be nothing more than kept mistresses, and she was proud of her ability to work and be independent. Despite her susceptibility to men, her propensity to fall in love, and her fondness for flirting, she was determined not to compromise herself but to succeed according to her own lights.

Two of the most interesting characters Nora meets are very different from the other men in her life or in Winnifred's. George Butler is a Socialist and a charity worker from Cincinnati who has a "thick baggy-looking mouth, and he dressed like a poet." Then there is Robert Bennet, a news editor, whose face has "an almost shining quality of *honesty*" (257). Both young men are graduates of Cornell and room near Jane Addams's Hull-House, where they teach night classes for free. The narrator respects them both deeply and remarks, "No man like Bennet can come into a woman's life and not make a deep impression" (261). She describes a poetry class Bennet teaches to "chiefly foreigners—Russian Jewesses, Polish and German girls,—and for the most part they worked in factories and stores; but they were all intelligent and eager to learn. They made me ashamed of my own indolence. . . . Those were clean, inspiring days" (262).

Bennet and Butler plan a reading course for Nora, hoping she can enter Cornell. The narrator wryly notes that everyone who became interested in her at this point in her life "seemed to think himself called upon to contribute to my education. I must have been truly a pathetic and crude little object; else why did I inspire my friends with this desire to help me?" (295).

It is, of course, Nora's natural instinct to accept the proposal of any new man who dazzles her, and she hasn't the "strength" to refuse a proposal from Bennet—even though she is already engaged and does not love either of the young men. There are numerous other entertainingly detailed proposals, which Winnifred told her family were taken from her real life. The suitors include one of her bosses and his son, an insurance agent, an engineer, an Irish politician, two clerks, and a plumber. That was not all: "I had a proposal from a Japanese tea merchant who years before had been my father's courier in Japan. Now he was a Japanese magnate, and papa had told me to look him up. He made a list of every person he had ever heard me say I did not like, and he told me if I would marry him, he would do something to every one of them" (300).

Then there was a western magazine editor, who became another fiancé.

"You see, he had accepted my stories, and how could I reject him? I was now, as you perceive, actually engaged to three men," she explains, adding, "I lived a life of not unjoyous deceit" (300).

Since joyous deceit was a condition in life that Nora relished as much as her creator did, any attempts by such an earnest character as Bennet to teach her the decent conventions were ultimately doomed. Youth, sex appeal, ego, and sense of fun were just too strong. Nora reveled in being engaged to three men at once—just like Winnifred herself, who often spoke with amusement of this youthful predicament.

For all her brashness and seeming confidence, Winnifred had spasms of being uncertain that she knew the right way to behave. Nora is uncertain, too, despite her success with men, and she falteringly asks Mr. Hamilton, the one man she cannot win, what would happen if she went to college, became more cultured, dressed better, and improved her manners. "Wouldn't I be good enough to be your wife?" (309). Evidently not.

Finally disgusted with her own behavior, Nora breaks off the engagement with Bennet. Butler bluntly reproaches her for playing with the feelings of a serious man who deeply cared for her. In a scathing speech, he lets her have it, saying that he suspected her from the first and never knew what Bennet saw in her. "He's head and shoulders above you in every way. You're not in his class at all. I don't mean that in the cheap social sense—simply morally. . . . It's damned hard luck, I can tell you, for me to see him come up against a proposition like you" (317).

Winnifred's portrayal of Nora's reaction rings so true that it is hard to believe something like this was not once said to Winnifred herself:

> And that was the opinion of me of one of the brightest men in the United States, a man who subsequently became internationally famous. Nothing could have equaled the contempt of his looks or his cutting words. He had stripped me bare. For one startling moment the scales dropped from my eyes. I *saw* myself! And I shrank before what I saw—shrank as only a weak coward can. . . . I was capable of staring wide-eyed at my own shortcomings only for a little while, and then, like every one else, I charitably and hastily and in fear drew the curtains before me. (318)

Winnifred adds tantalizing hints about Bennet that make us long all the more to know who he was, if he existed. "Bennet achieved all that I tried to do. Such fame (if fame I may call it) as came to me later was not of a solid or enduring kind. My work showed always the effect of my life—my lack of training, my poor preparation for the business of writing, my dense ignorance. I can truly say of my novels that they are strangely like myself, unfulfilled promises. But Bennet! He climbed to the top despite me, and there he will always be" (319).

In *Me*'s denouement, Nora discovers that Mr. Hamilton is a married man who leaves his wife for another woman of his own social class. She is devastated, but her pain centers not on his wife but on his mistress, who is "all the things that I was not, a statuesque beauty, with a form like Juno and a face like that of a great sleepy ox." Still, she declares, "No, no, she was not better than I. Strip her of her glittering clothes, put her in rags over a wash-tub, and she would have been transformed into a common thing. But I? If you put *me* over a wash-tub, I tell you *I* would have woven a romance, aye, from the very suds. God had planted in *me* the fairy germs; that I knew" (349).

Nora melodramatically considers suicide, but her friend Lolly Hope urges her to start over again in New York, because, Lolly tells her flatteringly, she can *write.* It is Lolly who finally commits suicide. As Linda Trinh Moser wittily observes, when the hope of marrying her man disappears, so does Lolly Hope.[22]

Winnifred, at her most clear and convincing in portraying her own character, was not so successful with Mr. Hamilton. Perhaps he was not based on reality after all but was a fictional "fairy godfather" partly inspired by Jean Webster's book *Daddy-Long-Legs,* which Winnifred deeply admired. So many of the peripheral facts in *Me* are true, however, that it is tempting to give credence to the main romantic story as well. Mr. Hamilton remains a mystery figure; but if he did exist, he certainly was important in Winnifred's life.

At the end of *Me,* Winnifred depicts her Nora as heading for New York still poor, hopeful, and clutching her suitcase of writings. In real life, when she departed for New York in 1901, it was as a published novelist who was already beginning to make a name for herself. She was still comparatively poor, but she was on the move and ready for the big city.

4. Becoming Japanese

> Sometimes, if I came in early enough, and if I were not too desperately tired, I would write things. Odds and ends. . . . I wrote a little story of my mother's land. I had never been there, and yet I wrote easily of that quaint far country, and of that wandering troupe of jugglers and tight-rope dancers of which my own mother had been one.
>
> —[Winnifred Eaton,] *Me*

IT WAS WHILE she was living in Chicago that Winnifred began to have success selling her Japanese-themed stories. In *Me,* her heroine Nora tells her admirer Mr. Hamilton that she has "an instinctive feeling about that country. A blind man can find his way over paths that he intuitively feels. And so with me. I feel as if I knew everything about that land" (176).

Drawn to the idea of writing Asian-themed stories because of her feelings and conflicts about her ancestry, she may have chosen Japan over China partly because she wanted to distance herself from Sui Sin Far's "Chinese" territory. It was also true that prejudice against Japanese people was not so strong as against the Chinese, who were perceived as heathenish coolies. At least Winnifred might have obtained such an impression from reading her local newspaper while growing up in Montreal. Typical of material she might have read in the *Montreal Star* is a letter of January 4, 1895, which argued against the establishment of Chinatowns: "Chinese never change; they have not changed for 4,000 years; they came a few hundred of them to San Francisco 40 years ago; there are 30,000 of them there now, and that city would ask nothing better than to be rid of them at any price!" Another *Star* article describes the practices of examining Chinese who crossed the border from Montreal into the United States, which was illegal after the passage of the Geary Act in 1882. Chinese methods of slipping into the United States are described as "ways that are dark and tricks that are mean."[1]

Reading such stories, knowing about such laws, Winnifred could understandably have gotten the idea that Chinese blood was nothing to flaunt in a writing career. Edith, at any rate, was not having marked success in doing so.

At the same time, as a romantic young woman, Winnifred was swept up in the tide of interest in things Japanese that peaked at the turn of the century. This craze for "Japonica" began after Commodore Matthew Perry "opened" Japan in the 1850s and was reflected in art, such as the paintings of Whistler in the 1860s, in literature, in fashion, and in all kinds of merchandising. Even the *Lotus,* a small literary magazine edited by Winnifred's own brother-in-law, Walter Blackburn Harte, had Japanesque cover drawings and carried advertisements for ultrafashionable Japanese posters. Examples of the entrancements of Japanese culture were everywhere.

Japan had the prestige of being seen as a powerful modern nation, and its people were admired for being a strong, warlike race. An account in the *Montreal Star* of the massacre at Port Arthur is typical in its bellicose descriptions of "the savagery of the Japanese": "Chinese prisoners were tied together in groups, riddled with bullets and then hacked to pieces. . . . Mutilations were carried on in every form that Oriental cruelty has ever invented. The Japanese soldiers were apparently unchecked in their deeds of blood by their commanders."[2]

Amy Ling, writing about the attitudes toward minorities at the turn of the century, quotes a remark recorded by Edith: "'A Chinaman is, in my eyes, more repulsive than a nigger,' [says] a town clerk. 'Now the Japanese are different altogether. There is something bright and likeable about those men.'" Ling observes, "The Japanese were at the top of the ladder, respected in part because this island nation had won wars against China in 1895 and Russia in 1905, and in part because few Japanese had then immigrated to the United States. . . . The Chinese, however, were not only regarded as an incomprehensible subhuman species, but with the completion of the transcontinental railroad in 1869, the thousands of Chinese laborers imported for its construction had become a threat to white workers."[3]

As a young writer, Winnifred would have had access to an abundance of literary material, travel diaries, and histories of Japan that were readily available in the Chicago and New York libraries and bookstores; she would have had little trouble doing enough research to form a background for her Japanese novels.[4] Her father's reminiscences about his long-ago travels to Japan may have partly inspired her in the first place, but she could hardly have relied on them as research for books written years later.

Some popular works available for Winnifred's perusal in her early writing years might have included Alice Mabel Bacon's *Japanese Girls and Women* and *A Japanese Interior;* Isabella Bird Bishop's *Unbeaten Tracks in Japan;* and *Letters from Japan* and *Custom of the Country* by Mrs. Hugh (Mary Crawford) Fraser, the sister of the author Marion Crawford and the wife of the

British minister to Tokyo until 1894.[5] These books were published by major houses, and a study of them would have given Winnifred sufficient grounding in Japanese culture to spin her romances.

Among Winnifred's early published works are a number of nonfiction articles, which reflect her research on Japanese subjects. These factual pieces, with such titles as "Every-Day Life in Japan," "The Japanese Drama and the Actor," "The Marvelous Miniature Trees of Japan," and "The Life of a Japanese Girl,"[6] bear more than a touch of the lamp and are not written in Winnifred's usual lively imaginative style. Strictly research pieces, they were a way to make some money while not letting her background work go to waste. It is possible that her husband, Bertrand Babcock, helped her in some of this work; he had more academic training, and the pieces show more of his fact-bound style than Winnifred's touch.

Winnifred's daughter, Doris, remembered that her mother often spoke of taking courses at Columbia University during her New York days, and she may have studied about Japan there.[7] She wrote just one short story that was set at Columbia, a frothy piece about young male undergraduates seeking a girl's dancing slipper.

The novel that most directly influenced the creation of Winnifred's Japanese stories was *Miss Cherry-Blossom of Tokyo,* published in 1895 by John Luther Long, who later wrote the novel *Madame Butterfly.*[8] But Long owed much of his inspiration to the earlier work of Pierre Loti, whose novel *Madame Chrysanthemum* (1888) dealt with the story of his "marriage," a temporary contract with a doll-like *mousme* (the book was, incidentally, a favorite book of Vincent van Gogh). The strange and sensual French writer's groundbreaking tale of a meeting between East and West must have held a glamorous, powerfully evocative appeal for a Victorian audience used to Western views about the sacredness of marriage vows.

Loti, a more evolved and layered author than Winnifred, wrote in a lush style, almost like a hallucinatory opium dream, with exquisite romantic images of the soulless beauty of Japanese life and culture. At the same time, he had a cold contempt for all things Japanese: the people were ugly; the customs were absurd; a woman was a slave, without a soul. "Does she think she has one? Her religion is an obscure chaos of theogonies as old as the world, treasured up out of respect for ancient customs. . . . what a muddle, therefore, must not all this become, when jumbled together in the childish brain of a sleepy mousme?"[9]

Winnifred, too, would occasionally make fun of her Japanese heroines' beliefs, but in a warmer, gentler way, portraying them as charmingly superstitious. She always emphasizes that the Japanese woman has as powerful emotions as any Westerner does. Her heroines may be as quaint and doll-like as Loti's, but they have a soul and are often more honest and down-to-earth than their white lovers are.

John Luther Long was no Frenchman and traveler like Loti. He was an American businessman who claimed authenticity for his story based on travelers' tales. Long's style was closer to Winnifred's than Loti's and more sentimental; his melodramatic sympathy for the plight of his Butterfly may be a reaction against Loti's coldheartedness. There is little doubt that Winnifred was inspired by his work.

The idea of trying her skill in a new and popular genre was a shrewd move on Winnifred's part. After reading Long and others, she must have felt confident that she could do as well. Some of Long's stories are so like Winnifred's and hers like his that they could have been written by either. She seems to have taken particularly close notice of his style of rendering Japanese pidgin talk, which now seems one of the most dated and awkward elements of these books. Winnifred's characters use the same pidgin words as Long's do (e.g., "aexcuse"), which can hardly be coincidence.

Beyond the initial inspiration of *Miss Cherry-Blossom,* the tales Winnifred went on to tell were her own, and she had her own motives, even if she never fully defined them to herself. Loti and Long may have adored the exotic East, but Winnifred, the first Asian American novelist to write on such themes, had a personal investment in her cultural and racial explorations.

Winnifred may initially have needed a model to work out how to proceed in such a stylized, artificial genre; but she had a fertile and inventive brain, and she related her tales with an urgency abetted by her own underlying agenda and a vigor that made whatever she wrote interesting and compelling. It was a recipe for success, and it is no surprise that her Japanese stories prepared the way for her early fame. Winnifred's stories did not have the cold elegance of Loti's, nor were they as sunk in treacly sentiment as Long's; they conformed to certain standards of formula romances, yet they displayed unexpected deviations of their own that gave them a feeling of originality.

A look at *Miss Cherry-Blossom of Tokyo,* the novel that most influenced Winnifred in her early Japanese-writing days, reveals that the volume is beautifully illustrated with color scenes of Japan, and the appearance is very much like that of one of Winnifred's books. Long's style is labored and prosy, as he describes the tangled love affairs of a set of foreign legation officers. The American grande dame of this community, Mrs. Haines, coyly introduces her protégée, Miss Cherry Blossom, into this social world, assuring the officers that they will be fascinated "by her baby-wise ways" (23)—for a day.

Winnifred's Japanese young women have a coyness similar to what Mrs.

Haines calls Cherry Blossom's "baby-brightness and wisdom" (67) or what Dominika Ferens calls her infantilism.[10] The coupling of a big blond barbarian and a charming little Japanese maiden is the hallmark of both Long's stories and some of Winnifred's, and a powerful, sexually potent coupling it was for their turn-of-the-last-century audience. The cross-match between Japanese men and white women is less acceptable, however, and when Winnifred depicts such a couple in *Miss Numè of Japan,* the romance ends tragically.

It is significant that neither Long nor Winnifred ever went to Japan. Not surprisingly, their Japan is not as realistically drawn as Loti's but more dreamlike, a rosy Japan that never was. At least one reviewer had his suspicions about the authenticity of Winnifred's Japanese tales and her ancestry and felt that her stories were fundamentally American in style and sensibility. Winnifred carefully saved this particular review of *Miss Numè* from the *Chicago Tribune* in her scrapbook: "She is said by those who ought to know—namely the publishers of the story—to be herself a Japanese . . . but the reader cannot escape the conviction that some bright American girl who has traveled in Japan is coquetting with him under the guise of Onoto Watanna." Beside this shrewd evaluation, Winnifred scribbled a comment: "This man read the book and has voiced his frank opinion."[11]

Of course Winnifred was not an "authentic" avatar of Japan. Some scholars have even called her a trickster. Yuko Matsukawa makes a fascinating attempt to "decode" Winnifred's activities. Proceeding under the assumption that Onoto Watanna's name may be a kind of cipher-code, Matsukawa points out that the facsimile of her autograph, printed in the frontispiece of her novel *The Wooing of Wistaria* (1902),

> is written not only in Japanese but also in the order in which Japanese names are written: surname first and then the first name. Out of the five characters that comprise the signature, the first two represent the last name "Watanna" written in *kanji* or Chinese ideograms and the remaining three spell "Onoto" in *hiragana,* one of the Japanese phonetic alphabets, though this part of the signature is more illegible than the first. The legible half, the top two characters, represents that last name "Watanna," composed of the Chinese ideograms (Japanese pronunciation) for "to cross": *wata[ru],* and "name": *na.*[12]

Matsukawa believes that "the name Onoto takes on great significance when one realizes that this was the name of a celebrated fountain pen manufactured by Britain's De La Rue company from about 1905 to the late 1950s." By the time the first Onoto pens were introduced in 1905, Onoto Watanna was already a best-selling writer, but Matsukawa comments that "given Eaton's predilection for playfulness and crossing, it is curiously appropriate that Winnifred Eaton's pen name turned out to be, for most of her life, also the name of a pen."[13] Winnifred's daughter remembered that her mother often told her that manufacturers of the Onoto pen asked permission to use her name. This she gave, though disclaiming royalties.[14]

Matsukawa speculates that the cross-naming "foreshadows Winnifred Eaton's career as a tricksterlike figure who assumes multiple identities in order to straddle different spheres and disrupt the sense of reality and complacency of those worlds."[15] It is not hard to imagine Winnifred enjoying her clever stratagem, but her motive was probably not so much a desire to disrupt people's complacency as simply to make a glamorous, successful, exotic name for herself.

In discussing *The Wooing of Wistaria,* Matsukawa contends, "The orientalized bindings of the book, the illustrations, and of course the contents of the novel contribute to the overall packaging of Onoto Watanna as an 'authentic Japanese.'" Matsukawa observes that Winnifred's trickstering apparently was not obvious to her readers, who uncritically accepted her as Japanese: "She gave them what they wanted to see."[16]

Throughout 1898, living in Chicago and dividing her time between stenographic work and writing, Winnifred wrote and wrote. Not all her early stories survive, and in her very scrappy scrapbook is a note: "Owing to my foolishness and idiocy I lost nearly all my former stories and articles—and the ones I have saved, are incomplete—so that I was obliged to typewrite part of most of the stories in order to make a clear record."

Her scrapbook contains a fragment entitled "Japanese Women," in which she shows less knowledge about Japan than she later displays. In a patronizing tone, posing as one who has spent time in Japan, she notes the "deferential, almost slave-like, courtesy of Japanese women." She opines that they lack "the brilliancy and cleverness of their European sisters, but they possess one trait which has made it possible for them to exercise a marked influence upon the destiny of their nation—obedience. If they wield any power, it is the power of trustful silence."

One partial story in her scrapbook contains elements of Winnifred's first novel, *Miss Numè of Japan.* A young Japanese man named Karo is sent to the United States to study at "a great college called 'Harvard.'" He sends his sweetheart, Yedo, a picture, in which he appears changed; his college friend Howard has slipped his own photo into the envelope. When Karo and Howard go to Japan, Yedo assumes Howard is Karo, and they fall in love. Karo insists on fulfilling his duty by marrying Yedo, and when Howard and Yedo meet at night, Karo stabs the lovers to death and kills himself.

Already several ingredients of an Onoto Watanna story are here: whites and Japanese mixing, misunderstandings, broken hearts. It is a strange mixture of almost farcically lame plot devices and a surprisingly assured authorial voice. But Winnifred was not pleased with it. At the end of this tragedy, she appends, "This story was written but not published until '98—I used to be quite fond of it, but it passed through unscrupulous hands of editors—who chopped . . . leaving in merely the sensational and anecdotal."

Another interesting fragment in her scrapbook has a theme of war between China and Japan—unusual for her fiction, in which wars usually occur offstage and the only battle is between the sexes. A prince's soldiers kill his beloved's old mandarin father and brother, and in a fury the prince slaughters several of his own sleeping men. In one battle scene, the Chinese "fall like grass beneath the scythe," unable to "hide from the sharp eye and alert ear of the Japanese." Winnifred's notes identify it as one of her earliest published Japanese stories, first appearing in 1897 in the *Iroquois Magazine,* a Sunday supplement, and later copied by other magazines. "I don't particularly care for it," she noted. "It is too warlike . . . and immature."

The early "A Japanese Love Story" was also, as James Doyle points out, published by "the obscure *Iroquois Magazine* . . . signed with her new pseudonym, 'Onoto Watanna,' in 1897, less than a year after Edith first appeared in the *Fly Leaf* as Sui Sin Far."[17]

"A Noble's Daughter," another of her early stories, tells about a boy, Omi, with a mother of gentle birth and laborer father, whose sweetheart, Yuri, is betrothed to a rich man. They consider suicide, but on the wedding day they plead their case to the rich bridegroom, and he shows himself a great man by adopting Omi and giving Yuri to him. This reads as if it was written in haste, and indeed Winnifred's note tells us, "I wrote this story inside of an hour—one morning, took it to the Editor of the *American Home Journal,* waited while he read it, and it was accepted on the spot—cheque being handed me at once—quick work—and profitable! However the story is trite—poor—."

A few clippings about the rising young author survive in her scrapbook. A biographical piece in the *New Orleans Picayune* says, "She cannot be classed as a painstaking writer, since she produces her stories much too rapidly to bestow much care upon them." Quoted about "'Boo-Boo,' the pathetic story of a half-Japanese who finds life too hard," Winnifred says, "This story is in my mind, the best thing I have written. It is human, and after all that is more than being extraordinary." The article also notes that Miss Watanna, who is "Japanesque" in appearance, is also a clever business woman, and during the last presidential campaign was "the chief stenographer in Cincinnati."

Another of Winnifred's research pieces, "New Year's Day in Japan," which appeared in *Frank Leslie's Popular Monthly* in January 1900, is accompanied by a small drawing of Onoto Watanna looking excessively Japanese. This is chock-full of book-learned details ("Outside a typical Japanese house will be found the shimekazari, which represent the three Chinese ideographs."). New Year's customs are described, with the comment that there is "always some one who has broken down from overwork. Perhaps she is an older sister who has had to make not only her own but her sisters' gowns." (Shades of Edith.)

Winnifred's revealing essay on "The Half Caste," published by *Conkey's Home Journal* in November 1898, is also featured in her scrapbook. It contains her own observations about the Japanese-Caucasian "half breed," who held a "pitiful and undesirable position in society." According to Winnifred, the half-breeds are brave and generous, with unusual qualities. They are "wonderfully precocious, their sharpness and brightness being almost abnormal, though as a rule they are so versatile that their cleverness is too general for them to accomplish much in any one direction. Furthermore, they are extremely erratic and moody." Her analysis of the half-caste seems to some extent based on her intimate knowledge of the one she knew best: herself. "To a supersensitive nature such as is that of the half breed, the smallest cut or slight is felt. This is how cynics are made. Half breeds are either cynics, or they are philosophers or geniuses. They are seldom ordinary—seldom normal."

Winnifred felt that the half-caste suffered the most in childhood and that those who have "in their early youth been ridiculed and tortured by companions . . . usually make the very best or the very worst of men or women." However, she ignores certain realities of her own "half-caste" family when she writes, "The Japanese half breeds seldom make good sons or daughters, nor do they have that great reverence and love for the parents which is common among children of ordinary parentage." The half-caste Eaton family members as a whole were loyal and supportive to their parents, but it is true that they may not have respected them overmuch.

She is probably summing up her own nature in her revealing description of the Eurasian, for Winnifred did possess numerous of the contradictory qualities she listed here:

> They generally enjoy fine physical constitutions, though they are nervous, highly strung, jealous, conceited, yet humble and self-deprecating and overly modest at times, sarcastic, skeptical, generous and impulsive. It is hard to analyze their natures, because they are so changeable. They are born artists . . . extremely ambitious, but generally meet with so many disappointments and hamperments that it is not a common thing for any of them to be more than ordinarily successful in life. Often the greatest impediment to their success is their own erratic, proud natures.

A year after "The Half Caste" was written, Winnifred wrote a fiction piece, similarly entitled "A Half Caste," which appeared in *Frank Leslie's Popular Monthly* in September 1899. It has a John Luther Long–like theme about an American man making a "Japanese marriage" with tragic results. The American, Hilton, sails to Japan with a friend who, like him, has a weakness for Japanese girls. He admits that he married a girl in the Japanese fashion and left her in the American fashion. He knows she is dead, but he wants to find her child. Hilton is charmed by a dancing girl, Okikusan, who scornfully tells him, in the exact patois of Miss Cherry Blossom, "Tha's way all big mans come from the West. They thing my! we so *nize*!" Hilton wants to marry her, but she reveals that he is the "fadder" who abandoned her. She pulls down her long brown curls and shows him the "white purity of her arms." "Thad lig Japanese girl?—thad? thad?—thad? Thad?"[18]

This disturbing tale, with its incestuous theme, is a harsh mockery of the charmingly romantic cross-cultural tale, and it shows Winnifred writing in anything but a formulaic, stereotyped manner. It is an example of the unsettling themes she raises, while simultaneously spreading the emollient of all the "Japanese" charm she could muster.

Dominika Ferens points out the novelty of Winnifred's miscegenated plots, each of which is "a skeleton straight out of the American closet. . . . The drapery around the skeletons is conventional, as is the creaky machinery of 'mistaken identity' and 'changing places' she used so often."[19] But these devices allowed her to explore racial themes in a way that was acceptable to her public.

Winnifred had published many stories and was earning good money for them. Then, in 1899, came her first, great realized goal: her first novel, *Miss Numè of Japan,* was accepted for publication, by Rand McNally in Chicago. She wrote *Miss Numè* in Chicago, and in *Me* she describes the intensity that she must have felt during the process: "I lived now with only one avid thought in my mind—the story I was writing. It infatuated me as nothing I had ever done before had infatuated me" (321). Nora's future is tied up in her writing, and Yuko Matsukawa perceptively comments that "the act of writing will not only make her feel at home but will become home as well."[20] This was as true of the nomadic, restless Winnifred as of her heroine; writing became, and would remain, a constant, a necessity in her life.

When interviewed a few years later, the now-famous Onoto Watanna let it be known "with pardonable pride" that she was "anxious to forget" her first novel.[21] It is difficult to see why she should have felt this about *Miss Numè,* for it is a compelling tale, fresh and vigorous, and it works out daring themes.

Perhaps it was the reworking and borrowing from *Miss Cherry-Blossom* that she was anxious to forget. *Miss Numè* distinctly shows its cousinship to John Luther Long's work. Even the first edition's title, *Miss Numè of Japan,* echoes *Miss Cherry-Blossom of Tokyo; Numè* means plum blossom. Dominika Ferens writes that "Winnifred maintains Long's cast of major and minor characters, including a Japanese girl and an American diplomat, a scheming married woman and an abandoned fiancée, but inserts several figures that alter the balance of power in the story."[22] Her intention, Ferens contends, was to conduct "a double experiment in sexual selection . . . to construct an Asian male as a romantic hero to whom several white women were attracted." This was "an unprecedented step in American fiction."[23]

The novel, illustrated with studio photographs of Japanese women, is "affectionately dedicated to my friend, Helen M. Bowen, because I love her so." It is interesting that Winnifred dedicated her first novel not to a family member—parents, the older sister who may have inspired her—or one of the men in her life but to a writer friend, the author of *A Daughter of Cuba.*

The story of *Miss Numè of Japan* concerns young Orito and Numè, the son and daughter of two merchants who want them to marry after Orito returns from being educated at "the great college called Harvard." On the ship home, Orito meets a beautiful American girl, Cleo, who is traveling with her cousin Tom, Orito's classmate. Cleo, a great flirt, breaks hearts, but "as long as she did not see the pain she did not feel it. Who can analyze a coquette?" (16).

Cleo is engaged to the American vice-consul Sinclair, and she knows that the Japanese man can never really be anything to her. Yet Orito decides that he loves her, and he proposes. Cleo stalls him, and Tom warns her, "You are the greatest moral coward I know. . . . It's a wonder you are not engaged to a dozen at once" (53).

Numè is visiting an American woman, Mrs. Davis, who is at the center of the English and American colony. Their friendship is reminiscent of that of Miss Cherry Blossom and Mrs. Haines. When Mrs. Davis asks if she loves Orito, she replies, "Luf? Thad is so funny word—Ess—I luf," echoing Cherry Blossom's, "Oh! loave-loave-loave! What *is* that loave?" (69).

Cleo finally tells Orito that she cannot marry him because of Sinclair. That night there is the sound of drums, and the terrible news comes that Orito, his father, and Numè's father have all killed themselves. Learning that the tragedy was the result of the way Cleo led Orito on, Sinclair marries Numè. Sadly, when Cleo hears about Orito's suicide, she realizes that she really did love him. In the end, she marries her cousin Tom.

Winnifred profitably worked a mine of story variations on Eurasian relationships that may have been initially touched off by the success of Long's stories. In her first novel, however, it is not the romance between a white man and a Japanese woman that assumes center stage, as in Long's work. Instead, the most vibrant and truthful characterization is that of the young American woman, Cleo.

Winnifred obviously put a good deal of herself into Cleo: she understood very well how incapable Cleo was of refusing Orito and how she egotistically relished being adored. Winnifred gives an unsparing view of Cleo's selfish, heartless characteristics—which she shared—but she knew that despite Cleo's despicable behavior, her heart was in the right place. And Winnifred is remorseless in her punishment of Cleo: she makes her pay the price, in shame, in regret, in self-loathing. Yet, bowing to the convention of popular fiction, she provides a happy ending—after Cleo has suffered.

Winnifred's depiction of Cleo's behavior must have been written directly in the aftermath of Winnifred's own humiliation by a man like Butler—if we believe, from the evidence of *Me,* that something like this actually happened. It seems likely that it did, since it is a theme she returned to again and again. Winnifred was by her own admission an incorrigible flirt, who led men on because of her craving for admiration and security. Perhaps she handled her shame and remorse by putting a similar circumstance into a book and punishing the heroine.

It is Cleo's volatile behavior that gives the book its edge, its immediacy, as well as its strong sense of the unexpected. Winnifred often employed formulaic methods, contrivances, and coincidences, but along side creaky plot devices are strands of sophistication, such as the examination of Cleo's complex vanity and her destructive attraction to a Japanese man. Also in evidence is Winnifred's streak of dark unpredictability: her proclivity for bringing in some startling jolt—like the suicide of Orito and his elders. Winnifred is at her most spellbinding when she spins this kind of plot.

It is tempting to think that the character of Orito may have been based on Winnifred's friend Yone Noguchi, but they did not meet until after the book was published.[24] Winnifred's Sinclair is the standard American male who is charmed by a Japanese maiden, and as such he is recognizable as a descendant of Loti's and Long's male characters. Miss Numè is Winnifred's first charming Japanese heroine to appear in her novels, the kind of young woman she had been writing about in her stories for some time. Miss Numè is also a genre figure, and though Winnifred was charmed enough by her to put variants of her in several other books, she is not Winnifred herself. In *Miss Numè of Japan,* the more Winnifred-like figure is the young white woman who enters the Japanese world.

Amy Ling characterizes Onoto Watanna's heroines as "a far cry from the demure, deferential, totally self-negating, stereotypical Asian woman. They are, like their creator herself, sturdy survivors who use whatever means is nearest to hand—their ingenuity, beauty, resourcefulness—to achieve their own ends."[25] Yet for Ling, too, the portrait of Cleo is more convincing and deeper than that of Miss Numè. Numè is seen from the outside, "a dainty piece of Dresden china—a rose and lily and cherry blossom in one. . . . But Cleo and the emotions of a flirt are analyzed in depth." She notes that "Winnifred Eaton's special talent as a writer is exactly that of this coquette; she knows how to 'pull the heart-strings till they ache with pain and pleasure commingled.'"[26]

Miss Numè of Japan is constructed around a Japanese couple and a Caucasian couple, with the Japanese man falling for the white woman and the white man falling for the Japanese woman. In her future books, Winnifred created various permutations of the cross-racial love affair. Amy Ling points out that her "interracial romances seemed acceptable as long as they took place in Japan and as long as the couple were white male/Japanese female." (True enough, in *Miss Numè,* the romance between a white female and a Japanese male is tragically aborted; it cannot happen.) She observes that seven of Onoto Watanna's novels couple American men or Englishmen with Japanese or Japanese European women, but that "despite the 'between-world' relationships . . . 'the Caucasian perspective is nearly always maintained.'"[27]

Miss Numè received warm reviews. In the *New York Times Book Review,* the reviewer "thanks Miss Watanna for the delightful evening given to him by her charmingly written little story," full of "much of the pleasantest kind of love-making between Occident and Orient."[28] Not all were charmed. The *Brooklyn Eagle* reviewer seemed to see the character of Miss Numè as a Japanese version of a dumb blonde, "that dainty and pretty, undeveloped doll of a creature, the Japanese girl. . . . It is ridiculous to think of them as women, for mentally and morally they are as ignorant as six-year-old children."[29]

A century ago, reviewers did not seem to find the "Cherry Blossom" pidgin of *Miss Numè of Japan* objectionable, though modern writers do. Amy Ling comments that *Miss Numè* is "entertaining, engrossing, and effective and at the same time somewhat offensive, ignorant, and contrived." The English speeches of the Japanese characters are "embarrassing in their inaccurate strangeness. . . . this version of English does not show the traits characteristic of the Japanese: the substitution of r's for l's, and the addition of a vowel to end consonants. Instead, it sounds as if the young lady has a stuffy-nose."[30]

It may occur to us to wonder how Winnifred's older sister Edith felt about her success with her startling device of a "Japanese" identity. Success of this commercial kind eluded Edith. We have only the evidence of her veiled but scornful comment in "Leaves": "I also meet some funny people who advise me to 'trade' upon my nationality. They tell me that if I wish to succeed in literature in America I should dress in Chinese costume, carry a fan in my hand, wear a pair of scarlet beaded slippers, live in New York, and come of high birth."[31] Edith could not have escaped a complete knowledge of Winnifred's doings, her publishing, her fame. By the time she wrote this comment in 1909, Winnifred had published most of her "Japanese" novels. Edith vented her feelings by sardonically imagining how she might take a similar line in her own "Chinese" sphere. She could talk about Confucius: "They forget, or perhaps they are not aware that the old Chinese sage taught 'The way of sincerity is the way of heaven.'"[32]

Winnifred herself had some doubts about her own tactics, particularly years after the fact, and it cannot be said that she was fully satisfied with the results of her deception. There are several allusions to this in her letters, and in *Marion* her heroine's musings about honesty in art sound heartfelt. "I recalled my brother-in-law's remarks on literature, and I knew it must be the same with all art," she wrote. "I thought of my father, and I wanted to cry. I realized that there were times when we literally had to do the very things we hated. Ideals were luxuries that few of us could afford to have" (257). In *Me*, she reflected, "It seemed a great pity that I was not, after all, to be the savior of the family, and that my dreams of the fame and fortune that not alone should lift me up, but all my people, were built upon a substance as shifting as sand and as shadowy as mist" (194). Even though troubled that she was not practicing the highest or truest art, she must have been thrilled her Japanese stories were selling. That was something real.

Winnifred had positively reveled in her experiences as a poor working girl, even as she suffered them. Despite much misery and anxiety, she had succeeded in rising above her circumstances through her own efforts. She undoubtedly felt all the enormous satisfaction of the self-made person. She had set out to conquer the world with nothing but her energy and her pen, and she was going to New York as a published novelist. There could be no question, now, that the game was worth the candle. Another passage in *Marion* surely reflects her feelings on the subject:

> It seems to me one does not regret passing through scorching fires. It's the only way one can get the big vision of life. I used to feel bitter, when I contemplated the easy life of other girls, and compared it with my own hard battle. Now I know that, had I to go through it all again, I would not exchange my hard experiences for the luxury that is the lot of others. I can even understand what it is to pity and not envy the rich. *They miss so much.* Money cannot buy that

> knowledge of humanity that comes only to him who has lived among the real people in the world—the poor! (269)

Winnifred was perfectly safe in saying that, because real poverty was finished for her. At the age of twenty-four, she had already achieved several of her dearest goals, and she had only begun her journey.

5. The Lady of the Lavender Books

> Dreams, too, came of the days when I would be famous and rich, and all my dear people would be lifted up from want. My poems would be on every one's tongue, my books in every home. And I saw myself facing a great audience, and bowing in acknowledgement of their praise of my successful play.
>
> —[Winnifred Eaton,] *Me*

It was early in 1901 that Winnifred arrived in New York City, where she was to find her husband, begin her married life, and make her home for the next fifteen years. She was not a poor, green girl with a suitcase full of unsold stories. She was twenty-five and a successful writer, in the triumphant morning of a career that promised much. She had sold dozens of stories and articles, had made a name for herself in Chicago as the exotic, fascinating Onoto Watanna, and her first novel, *Miss Numè of Japan,* had already been published.

A *Harper's Weekly* article gives the sequence of events: "Then she wrote *A Japanese Nightingale,* and with the sum she received for its serial use in a woman's paper, she left Chicago in the spring of 1901, and came to New York to take a course in Columbia, and to try her fortune in the East. After several rebuffs she found a publisher at last for the manuscript she had brought with her."[1] *A Japanese Nightingale* was published by Harper and Brothers and received its first reviews in November of 1901. This was the book that would be a mammoth success and sweep her to fame.

Yone Noguchi wrote to Frank Putnam, "Miss Onoto—the young butterfly lady wrote to me, telling me she found a place in Frank Mansey's [*sic*] and she enjoys much of New York. Such a happy, perhaps bright—in some small way—woman! At once every body falls in love with her, I suppose."[2] But Winnifred's days as a butterfly were ending.

Soon after her arrival in New York, she met the man who became her husband when they were both working on the *Brooklyn Eagle.* They were married on July 16, 1901. There is little to indicate why she chose Bertrand

Whitcomb Babcock over a myriad of other suitors—literary men, rich men, ardent men—who sought her. She clearly had a range of choice. Even if men were not quite as wildly bowled over by her as she implies in *Me* or if she sometimes imagined admiration where none existed, she was involved with any number of men. And she was surely attractive: if not beautiful, she was vivacious, bright, lively, different.

The man she married was not rich, but his family, the Babcocks, were of old colonial stock, which must have impressed Winnifred. If she couldn't catch a genuine English lord, American nobility was the next-best thing. After her own weary history as a "mongrel," she must have been delighted to know that there had been eleven generations of Babcocks in Rhode Island and New York; the family even had an coat of arms, an unnerving cock's head and three pale cocks on a red band, which even a book of Babcock genealogy calls "belligerent": "'Tis true the cocks are pale, but paleness in a fighter sometimes denotes great determination."[3] If symbols have their meaning, Winnifred might have taken warning, for her husband developed during their marriage into a wife-abusing alcoholic.

Babcock's father was an exemplary, solid citizen. Charles Almanzo Babcock graduated from Hamilton College in 1874 and was a science teacher and school principal of the Fredonia, New York, Normal School who studied law during his vacations, receiving his degree in 1883. That year he went to Oil City, Pennsylvania, as superintendent of schools, a position he held for twenty-five years. Babcock traveled to Europe to study school systems and was once Democratic candidate for the state legislature. The pinnacle of his life was undoubtedly when he became the originator, in 1894, of National Bird Day.

This bird-loving gentleman's wife, Emma Whitcomb, was said to have family connections to the popular poet James Whitcomb Riley and to Commodore Perry, whom Edward Eaton so much admired. That must have meant something to Winnifred.

The Babcocks had two sons, Bertrand and Paul. Paul was an assistant trainmaster with the Pennsylvania Railroad Company and, like his brother, turned out to be an alcoholic, no doubt to the distress of the respectable senior Babcocks.

Hamilton College's "Alumniana" lists Bertrand, class of '98, as "a prosperous reporter on the staff of *The New York Sun*" in March 1899, shortly before he met Winnifred. Five years later, another alumni note mentions that he "is receiving much congratulation on the success of Mrs. Babcock's career as a literary woman who is receiving much attention at the present time with hope for a very bright future." The emphasis had already shifted to his wife.[4]

A class statistics column tells us that Babcock's nickname was "Babs," he was 5'10" and weighed 150 pounds, and his religion was "Catholic, if any." He liked to play whist, drink beer, smoke a pipe, and dance. The class verdict on him was that he was the class poet, which may have significance, since his son grew up to be a poet and his wife claimed to have the true poetic soul. More alumni notes reveal that Babcock at various times wrote for the *New York Times, New York Tribune, New York World,* and *New York Journal.* Later he worked for the Schubert Theaters. A classmate complimented his extensive vocabulary, "easy flow of language in debate," and "complete confidence in his own ability." He was compiling a dictionary, for fun.[5]

The young Babs may well have been hopeful, ambitious, amiable, and talented. Later, however, he evolved into the man who claimed, when drunk, that his youngest son, Charley, was not his child but a "red-headed bastard"—this, although his own brother Paul had red hair. This son, as a result, loathed him all his days and in adulthood changed his name and refused ever to see him. Doris had a more civil relationship with her father and kept in touch with him until his death from diabetes and alcoholism in 1947.

In happier times, Winnifred and Bertrand may have done some of their courting at the Ramble in Central Park, for Babcock, in his serialized novel *A Syndicated Prince,*[6] gives a pleasant image of young people waltzing in the park to the music of the merry-go-round. Once, this might have been Winnie and him.

Their wedding was performed by the oddly titled curate of the transfiguration at "The Little Church Around the Corner" on East Twenty-ninth Street in Manhattan. This pretty church, more formally known as the Church of the Transfiguration, was the fashionable place to get married for members of Winnifred's and Babcock's theatrical and literary bohemian set. In some of her stories as well, the characters seal their happy endings at "The Little Church Around the Corner."

The bride's address was given as 146 West Forty-sixth Street, the groom's as 700 West Fifty-seventh Street, the latest in a series of ever-shifting New York temporary addresses for both of them. The witnesses were G. E. Kennedy and Winnifred's older sister Grace Harte, who had been widowed only two years earlier and was still living in New York, prior to her move to Chicago. Winnifred, instituting a practice of matching her fictions to documents, gave her age on the marriage license as twenty-two.

Babcock must have had some charms to attract the budding literary star. He was not the "blond type [she] adored" but was dark, saturnine, with a narrow face and somewhat receding chin. But he was a handsome, intelligent-looking man; in photographs he wears his hat and dangles his cigar at a jaunty angle. Clever and well-spoken, Babcock was promising and had literary ambitions like Winnifred's own. He was her professional equal, though not on a higher career rung, since she was already a published novelist. But with the benefit of hindsight, we know that he possessed neither her talent nor her will to succeed.

Several of Babcock's published stories survive. They are uniformly written with a clunky, heavy hand, utterly lacking Winnifred's charm and gift for gripping narrative. They do, however, shed some light on his personality. "The Psychological Investigator," written for the *Eclectic* in April 1907, is a curious example. The hero of this story walks in the fields surrounding his Bronx home (at this time Bertrand and Winnifred lived in the Bronx, then a bucolic setting) and ascertains the "color sensations of his wife as she stood wide-eyed, with her face uplifted to the sun, while he sheltered under her red silk parasol."[7] A bull attacks the man, and he climbs a tree while his wife dexterously gets rid of the bull. To further test his color theories, he walks down Broadway carrying a white flag, but the black residents attack him. He tries an orange flag in an Irish neighborhood and gets beaten. In an Irish pub, he concludes that green is the color of peace.

In the light of our knowledge of the Babcocks, it is tempting to contemplate the symbolism of this story. Does the parasol stand for primacy in the relationship? For talent? Then there are the story's sociopolitical stereotypes, the drunken Irish, raucous blacks, and so on. However interpreted, this peculiar story, with its contrived plot, graceless language, and ominous ending in a bar, is not the product of a natural writer.

Babcock's style is no more inspiring in his workmanlike research piece entitled "Horses in the Big War." Here he is at his happiest (if most boring) wielding statistics and observing, "If the horses used in the Allied Armies were placed in a single file, as closely as animals can walk, the procession would stretch across the American continent several times."[8]

Babcock's most ambitious work, *A Syndicated Prince*, is a novel-length serial that appeared in the *Eclectic* in eight monthly installments during 1906. This story does possess a colorful theatrical and newspaper background, and it also gives the clue to what may have been Babcock's own assessment of himself, when a journalist character says, "I really believe I'm a writer; not a novelist or a fiction man, but a good square sort of fellow that the newspapers'd take up."[9] In this story, a European prince, down on his luck, considers working as a newspaper reporter but is repelled at being asked to write such pieces as "How a mother feels when she murders her child, by a mother now in Sing Sing."[10] A theatrical producer helps him form a syndicate of rich men, who pay for his presence at parties and make him the king of society.

This story sporadically shows some of the color and interest of Winnifred's writing, but the theme of marketing a social position is unlike Winnifred's. Though she grew more cynical in her Hollywood days, she was not given to this sort of cold satire.

Perhaps Babcock's most interesting surviving article describes the nefarious practices of theater ticket scalpers, a subject he really did know something about because of his work in the theatrical world. Titled "The 'Deadhead' and What He Costs the Theatre," it capably details the abuses in the turn-of-the century New York theater world.[11] Ironically, a "deadhead" is how Babcock himself might be described as far as his marriage went. As soon as Winnifred began to be successful, early in the marriage, he gave up reporting and took to calling himself her manager. During most of their marriage, Babcock was supported largely by Winnifred's writing efforts. Winnifred periodically earned large sums, but she was not a saver. Perhaps this is the reason for some of their frequent moves from one house to another. These were Winnifred's most productive writing years, but her writing was the only income, and since it flowed in unevenly, there were undoubtedly flush periods and alarming "broke" periods.

After the children were born, the young Babcocks sometimes lived in Manhattan apartments, sometimes in country houses with a staff of servants. The children might be with them; or they would go to stay with the senior Babcocks in Oil City or with her sister Sara Bosse on Staten Island; or the boys might go to a farm for the summer.

To give an idea of the peripatetic nature of this family, in May 1902, Mr. and Mrs. Babcock had an apartment at 25 West Thirtieth Street in Manhattan. By February 1903, while awaiting the birth of their first child, Perry, they were living unfashionably far uptown, at 311 West 111th Street. By November 1903, they were at 2445 Grand Avenue in Fordham Heights, a rural locale at that time. When baby Bertie was born the next September, they were at another Fordham Heights address, on 183d Street. At the time of Doris's birth, in January 1906, they were at 70 West 128th Street in Manhattan; when Charley was born in 1907, they were at 196th and Bainbridge Avenue in the Bronx.

The Babcocks bought their Mamaroneck house, at fashionable Orienta Point, from the actress Adele Ritchie—or, by another account, from Mrs. Guy Bates Post,[12] though Ritchie's name is on the deed[13]—for $6,000. They owned it from April 1905 to 1907. Halfway through their residence there, in March 1906, Winnifred bought Bertrand's half of the house for $2,500. In the end, they could not pay the mortgage and lost the house.[14]

During this hectic period, Winnifred still wrote stories nonstop. Two months before the publication of *A Japanese Nightingale*, her story "Two Converts" appeared in *Harper's Monthly.* Close in theme to *The Love of Azalea,* published several years later, it has a slyly humorous tone. John Redpath, a missionary, meets Otoyo, a typical Onoto Watanna bright-as-a-button little Japanese miss with childlike pidgin language that masks a sharp brain. She wants to teach him Japanese, and he consents, in exchange for teaching her about Christianity. One day she drops a bombshell: she has been forced into an arranged marriage with a brutal man. He objects to Redpath's teaching his wife and divorces her. The missionary baptizes and marries Otoyo, and thus there are "two converts . . . one a convert to Christianity, the other a convert to divorce."[15]

Another Japanese story, "Kirishima-san," was published in the *Idler* in November 1901. This is a generic tale of Jack, an American young man in Japan, who learns Japanese from the usual charming young Japanese woman, Kirishima. Jack thinks he can learn quickly, because he has friends in the United States who are "authorities" on Japan after living there briefly. This is a self-tweak at Winnifred herself, the newly Japanese authority. Jack falls in love with Kirishima, but she overhears him tell a friend he is just "having fun" with her, so she announces she is going to be married. The misunderstanding is quickly sorted out: she did not lie when she said she was going to be married—because she will marry *him.* This slight piece, like "Two Converts," is representative of many stories Winnifred conceived during this period that played out permutations of Asian-Caucasian romances.

Another story, "Margot," published in *Frank Leslie's Popular Monthly* in December 1901, is unusual at this point in Winnifred's writing because it is a non-Japanese story. A young country girl brings milk to a group of artists who are camping out. They call her "Maude Muller" after the Tennyson poem and paint her dark hair and eyes. When she does not show up for a few days, they go to her humble home and find her caring for her mother's new baby. Margot is a talented, self-taught violinist, and the artists pay to have her educated. At her boardinghouse, all the stylish young people snub her except a kind young man named Manning. Receiving a love note from him, she writes back, and he is forced to tell her he did not write it—it is a practical joke. Margot is mortified. Soon after, she hurts her hand, and her violin career ends. Manning ends up loving her after all.

Although Margot is not an Asian heroine, a true racial "other," she is one of Winnifred's gypsy girls, a rustic naïf of wondrous talents. And she goes through the same boardinghouse hardships as several of Winnifred's poor, romantic heroines who hark back to how she saw herself when young.

But it was Winnifred's Japanese genre tales that were building to a crescendo of popularity and consequently becoming ripe for satire. Her poet friend Yone Noguchi wrote a story that seems like a parody of her work: "The American Diary of a Japanese Girl," which ran in *Frank Leslie's Magazine* in November and December of 1901. The Japanese heroine, Miss Morning Glory, simultaneously naive and wily, pokes fun at the sort of stories Winnifred was writing: "Authorship is nothing at all nowadays, since authors are thick as Chinese laundries."[16]

Winnifred's sister Edith wrote a similar story three years later. "Wing Sing of Los Angeles on His Travels," published in the *Los Angeles Express,* also has piquant viewpoints on American culture, as seen through the eyes of a newly arrived Asian, writing in pidgin.[17] Although she was now based in the West, Edith occasionally returned to Montreal, "whenever I had a little money put by, some inward impulse would compel me to use it for a passage home." (Winnifred does not seem to have felt a similar urgency.) In about 1901, Edith used her savings to "pay for a passage out West for one of my younger sisters." We can guess at the date, because Edith writes of "a shock of sudden grief" that occurred a year later.[18] This would have been the death of her brother Hubert, who drowned while swimming off the island of St. Helene in Montreal in August 1902, at the age of only twenty-three. Two Eaton babies were already buried in the Montreal cemetery, but Hubert was the first adult in the Eaton plot. Born in 1879, four years younger than Winnifred and fourteen years younger than Edith, Hubert would have been one of the sisters' rambunctious charges.

Winnifred's life was at its most frenetically busy and distracted in 1902. Newly married, pregnant with her first child, she wrote the novel *The Wooing of Wistaria* and many stories. She was also involved in troubled negotiations concerning her Broadway play. Living in New York, frantically involved with all this new raw material of life, she would have had little time or energy left to think about the people back in Montreal and their grief.

It was at about this time that Edith's editor at the *Express,* Samuel T. Clover, wrote the *Century* editor that he thought "she really has more talent than her sister who writes over the name of Onoto Watanna . . . [and] has claimed to be half Japanese and half English, but of course she is not."[19] Those in the know were obviously well aware of Winnifred's deception. Edith might have felt some envy tinctured with scorn at the "Japanese" books piling up on the East Coast, but in her personal life she clearly relished her freedom and was unlikely to envy Winnifred's marriage to the difficult Bertrand W. Babcock.

Winnifred now had the entrée to New York literary society. In *Between Worlds,* Amy Ling writes that Winnifred "moved in a distinguished circle including such luminaries as Edith Wharton, Anita Loos, Jean Webster, David Belasco, Mark Twain, and Lew Wallace. She was propelled into this elite society by her first big best-seller, *A Japanese Nightingale.*"[20] Published in 1901, the novel was more flowery than the comparatively simple and straightforward *Miss Numè of Japan,* and it had a more conventional "Japanese plot"—that is, more like that of *Madam Butterfly. A Japanese Nightingale* sold in the vicinity of 200,000 copies (or at least so Winnifred claimed). Not only did *A Japanese Nightingale* become a Broadway play (her only one), but years later, in 1918, it was filmed by Pathé as a silent movie. Neither the play nor the film was successful, something Winnifred never understood because she considered it the *Gone with the Wind* of its day.

The book was exquisitely produced, with a pink petal–strewn cover, color plates, and delicate monochromatic page illustrations by Genjiro Yeto, a young Japanese artist living in New York who also illustrated Yone Noguchi's "American Diary of a Japanese Girl." As Susan G. Larkin pointed out in her recent article on Genjiro Yeto, "Yeto's exotic name lent authenticity to novels such as *A Japanese Nightingale.*"[21]

The novel opens in a teahouse, with visitors to Japan watching a dancer in the moonlight. A rich young American, Jack Bigelow, is charmed by the half-caste with genetically improbable blue eyes and red hair. His Japanese college chum, Taro Burton, has warned him not to make a temporary marriage, for "the Eurasian is born to a sorrowful lot" (19). But the dancing girl, Yuki, pleads with him, "Oh, jus' for liddle bit while marry with me" (30). He gives in, and they are blissfully happy together, though he suspects her of being an adventuress because she begs for money, blatantly lying, "I god seventeen brudders and sisters!" (76). She often seems sad, and asked why, she says, "You also los' liddle bird? . . . Jus lige unto my same liddle nightingale?" (124).

Taro arrives from the United States, delayed because his people had had difficulty sending money for his passage. Jack introduces him to Yuki, and everyone is appalled because Yuki is Taro's sister. Their mother brokenly admits that the family had lost their money and could not afford to keep Taro at the university. So Yuki had became a geisha and had married the rich foreigner. Taro is sickened. "It was for me, me, my little sister sold herself," he exclaims (161). Yuki runs away, and Taro becomes ill and dies. Jack swears that he will never cease searching for Yuki. At last she returns to the home she shared with Jack, and they are wedded "for ever an' ever" (226).

The narrative of *A Japanese Nightingale* is often lush and lyrical, with flowery, descriptive "poetical" passages: "The moon . . . clothed in glorious raiment, and sitting on a sky-throne of luminous silver, was attending the banquet in person, surrounded by myriad twinkling stars, who played at being her courtiers" (3). This labored fancifulness may seem excruciating to us today, a tortuous attempt at lyricism, but Winnifred's contemporaries considered it exquisitely dainty and refined.

No less a respected litterateur than William Dean Howells admired *A Japanese Nightingale.* In an essay entitled "A Psychological Counter-Current in Recent Fiction," he positively gushed about the book: "If I have ever read any record of young married love that was so frank, so sweet, so pure, I do not remember it. . . . There is a quite indescribable freshness in the art of this pretty novelette—it is hardly of the dimensions of a novel—which is like no other art except in the simplicity which is native to the best art everywhere. Yuki herself is of a surpassing loveableness."[22]

It may seem surprising that such a clever arbiter elegantiarum should be so charmed by the "novelettish" *Japanese Nightingale* and could think it fresh, as if he had not been exposed to any fictional Chrysanthemum or Butterfly. But *A Japanese Nightingale* had its fans, and although it contains less incident than some of Winnifred's other books, the hero's honorable feeling and Yuki's martyred sacrifice have strong sentimental appeal. It is therefore not surprising that it was singled out for a Broadway dramatization.

There are autobiographical glimpses of Winnifred in the character of Yuki. Yuki is a half-caste; she claims to have a large family of brothers and sisters; and she is a newlywed, as Winnifred was. The story of Yuki's parents strongly resembles that of Winnifred's own parents. Their marriage, like the Eatons', is performed by an English missionary, and Yuki's father is "the son of a rich silk merchant [who] had come to Japan in order to extend his knowledge of the silk trade and expand his father's business. But Stephen Burton had become infatuated with the country, had married a Japanese wife. . . . Old Sir Stephen Burton had never forgiven what he considered the *mesalliance* of his son" (189).

A Japanese Nightingale was warmly reviewed. The *New York Times Book Review* commented that it was written "by a young Anglo-Japanese girl whose opportunities for observing her countrywomen have been exceptional and whose mind has been trained to the European point of view." The reviewer admired the heroine, a type like Chrysanthemum and Butterfly: "the same delicate, melancholy charm, the same emotional force, they alike illustrate the element of childishness allied to the elaboration of their complex civilization."[23] Winnifred's heroine does share the truthfulness of Chrysanthemum and Butterfly and their ilk, who are artificial from their tiny Japanese toes to their butterfly hairdos.

The myth of Onoto Watanna showed up in numerous publicity squibs. *Harper's Weekly* had a fetching photo of the charming young Eurasian in kimono, head atilt, with an elaborate Edwardian coiffure, and a note congratulating her on her "sudden conquest of the Occident."[24] The *New York Her-*

ald Tribune stated that "the young Americo-Japanese woman . . . was born at Nagasaki, and was at work on a new novel, to be published by Harper's in the fall."[25]

This new novel was *The Wooing of Wistaria,* a considerable departure for Winnifred, though still a "Japanese" novel.[26] Perhaps irked by reviewers who noted the shortness of her previous novels, she turned out what was unarguably a full-length work, of 388 pages. Quite different from *Miss Numè of Japan* and *A Japanese Nightingale,* it was a historical novel set in 1853, when Commodore Perry opened Japan to the West, and it contained material unfamiliar in Winnifred's works: a background full of political events and a masculine array of battle scenes.

The story concerns the Lady Wistaria, who is brought up by her uncle, Lord Catzu, and seldom sees her cold, withdrawn father. An admirer visits the household in disguise and manages to penetrate her cloistered existence. The family is unaware that he is really Prince Mori, the young ruler of another province. Lord Catzu is adviser to the Shogun, while the rival Mori clan wishes to see the Mikado as the real, instead of the nominal, ruler of Japan once more. When Mori's identity is discovered, Wistaria's father orders her to betray her lover by persuading him to tell his battle plans—or else he will be killed. Her father explains that he hates the Mori because he himself married an Eta woman, of an "untouchable" class, and she was killed by Mori samurai. Wistaria warns Mori to leave the palace, but he is captured. To save his life, Wistaria proposes to her father that Mori be disgraced by being married to an Eta girl: herself. After the marriage, Mori learns of her betrayal and leaves her. War and intrigue follow. Wistaria plays a brave role disguised as a boy and eventually reveals herself to Mori; they are reconciled.

The historical background is broader and more extensively researched than anything Winnifred had done previously. Particularly intriguing is the description of the Eta and the appearance of Perry and his ships, as seen from an apparently Japanese point of view. The love story is uncharacteristically subordinate to the war intrigue. The book's narrative style is also quite different from that of *Miss Numè of Japan* and *A Japanese Nightingale;* it is somewhat dry and pedantic and, as a result, decidedly slower paced. The piquant charm of a "fish out of water" story, in which the reader sees Japan through a Westerner's eyes, as in Winnifred's previous books, is not found here. Even though the pidgin English of some of Winnifred's other tales is somewhat ludicrous, it is livelier than the sedate pontificating of the characters here, who speak formally, use the stately "thou," and have no other quaintness to their speech. This does, however, have the effect of making them seem more intelligent. Winnifred was clearly making an attempt to be serious, and her story has a wider scope than anything she ever attempted before—or than she ever really tried again.

The Wooing of Wistaria was a strange flower. Was it really all Winnifred's own story? Amy Ling makes a persuasive argument that her newly wedded husband may have made substantial contributions to the book, as indicated by its "different style, more formal, somewhat more stilted than is usual with her works. . . . Though the love scenes have the usual Winnifred Eaton stamp, the book is filled with numerous battle scenes and detailed descriptions of artillery and troop maneuvers that have a different writer's voice." The story "Eyes That Saw Not," published in the June 1902 issue of *Harper's,* was written by Winnifred and Babcock jointly, and Ling reasons, "Since *The Wooing of Wistaria* also appeared in 1902, it must have been written during the first year of the Eaton-Babcock marriage. Nothing would be more natural than for two newlywed writers to work on a book together."[27] She suspects that Bertrand Babcock wrote the military scenes of *The Wooing of Wistaria* and perhaps helped with the complex plot as well.

In the light of this possible collaboration, "Eyes That Saw Not" is worth examining, for it eerily reflects the young Babcocks' own lives and abilities. The man and woman in this story collaborate—yet he is literally blind to what is going on. John—like Babcock himself—becomes a newspaper reporter in New York City, but he is struck blind and returns to his small-town home, where his mother and his fiancée, Elizabeth, make him as comfortable as possible. John tries to write, with Elizabeth as his amanuensis, but his work shows all the faults that both Winnifred and Bertrand tried to avoid professionally. Without John's knowledge, Elizabeth improves his writing, and the stories sell. Then a specialist restores his sight. Elizabeth fears John's anger when he learns what she has done, "despising dishonesty as he does, and so greedy and proud of his attainments."[28] Still, she places the printed stories in his hands. He explodes with rage but later admits the truth: the stories were better.

It is hardly likely that Babcock actually saw himself as poor a writer as John is in the story, yet it is remarkable how accurately the assessment of the couple's relative talents is presented. It was Winnifred who was having a thrilling success as a novelist, while Babcock was strictly a reporter, with no talent for fiction. Was he really blind to Winnifred's talent? Was her greater success, at a time when women normally did not outshine or outearn their husbands, a sore point? Did he instigate the story, or did she? There must have been competitive feelings, and perhaps this is why Babcock stopped trying to do any serious work of his own and instead took to the bottle.

The Wooing of Wistaria was an experiment that Winnifred does not seem to have felt succeeded, for she went back to her usual style in her succeeding works. The reviews were positive enough, however. A *Harper's Magazine* reviewer gushed, "The pathos of passion in the love scenes between the Shining Prince and Wistaria in the first half of the book and at the happy close is felt with a fierce joy and poignancy that have led critics to speak of them as a Japanese Romeo and Juliet."[29] The "Book-Buyer's Guide" in the *Critic* called the book a novelty that "must insure the standing of Onoto Watanna." As for the plot, "All improbabilities are sheltered behind Japanese witchery, for—what may not happen in Japan?"[30]

In addition to her novels, Winnifred kept writing stories. Books, stories—and then, the Broadway play. Winnifred's literary agent, Elizabeth Marbury, sold the rights of *A Japanese Nightingale* to the theatrical producers Mark Klaw and Abraham Erlanger. Winnifred did not do the play adaptation herself (which may have been a mistake); William Young, who had adapted the novel *Ben Hur* into a hit play, was hired, and plans were made for a lavish production at Daly's Theater.

This was an important, anticipated event in Winnifred's life, so it was a shock and a disappointment when the famous theatrical impresario David Belasco, who had read *A Japanese Nightingale* and had turned down the proposal to make it into a play, proceeded with his own plans for a "Japanese" play—one that would surely be a major success and would entirely eclipse Winnifred's own efforts. What was more, it seemed to Winnifred and to her producers that Belasco's play, *The Darling of the Gods,* was suspiciously close to Winnifred's own writings. Winnifred therefore filed an injunction against Belasco. The result was that on the eve of the opening night of *The Darling of the Gods,* on December 3, 1902, a startling headline appeared in the *New York Herald Tribune:* "Onoto Watanna Arrested." This was an almost unbelievable development in the life of a young woman novelist just emerging from obscurity into the limelight, but it was no joke. An order for arrest had been issued by Justice Fitzgerald of the New York Supreme Court.

We may well wonder, what on earth had Winnifred done? The powerful Belasco was charging her with libel and seeking to recover $20,000 in damages. "The order for the author's arrest was placed in the hands of two deputy sheriffs, bail being fixed at $500. Last night the author had not been found," the story states. We are told that Winnifred's reasons for filing against Belasco's play were that "it contained an outlaw prince and a giant and three similar characters which appear in one of her stories, *A Japanese Nightingale.*"[31]

A little background is needed to explain how Winnifred found herself in such dangerous, deep theatrical waters, with such a major adversary as Belasco demanding her arrest. When it comes to being a flamboyant figure, Winnifred was dwarfed by Belasco, an intensely dramatic personality who claimed to have been taught by priests in a monastery and to have traveled with a circus and been the first equestrian to jump through a flaming hoop as a boy. It was said that "what he felt he lacked in personal experience he *borrowed,* and when the facts failed to conform to his conception he altered or amended them accordingly until in some instances he came to believe in the amelioration."[32] Of course, it must be admitted, that this might be said about Winnifred too, as well as any number of other theatrical and literary types of a day, when deception was easier to practice and there were no computer files to disprove anyone's claims.

Belasco was found guilty of plagiarizing on at least one occasion in his career,[33] and he was surrounded by equally remarkable characters. One such, his son-in-law, a Russian immigrant theater scalper, earned his first money in the United States by painting sparrows yellow and selling them as canaries.

By 1902, Belasco had enjoyed considerable success as a theatrical producer, but he was threatened by the powerful Theater Trust. Klaw and Erlanger, booking agents of the Syndicate, as it was called, had demanded of Belasco a heavy share in the profits of his plays, in exchange for a first-class touring route for his stars. Belasco was actually engaged in a full-scale war with Klaw and Erlanger rather than with Winnifred herself, who was really just a pawn.

With his play about to open in New York, it was galling to be publicly accused of plagiarism. This threat could easily hurt the production and had to be put down immediately. Belasco therefore went on the offensive with a statement to the papers that his purpose in causing Winnifred's arrest was "to stop, once and for all, the groundless persecution to which I am subjected whenever I dare present a new play." Through her, he hoped to reach "the real instigators of this attack against my integrity as a manager and a man. I have never met Mrs. Babcock in my life, nor have I read either of her books." And he noted that *The Wooing of Wistaria* was not published until the previous September, while his play was finished early in June.[34]

Immediately after opening night came another sensational headline: "Onoto Watanna Surrenders."[35] Winnifred had been arrested, but she was promptly released on bail. The matter was finally settled two months later, with the order of arrest vacated in court.[36] Still another headline trumpeted, "Mrs. Babcock Wins the Belasco Suit." This article related Belasco's contention that "Mrs. Babcock caused to be printed" in a newspaper a statement that he had stolen his play from her manuscript. The judge held that this statement was libelous, but that "there was no proof that Mrs. Babcock was either the author or the instigator of it."[37]

How did Winnifred get pulled into such a public mess? It was probably not difficult for her managers, Klaw and Erlanger, to persuade her to sue Belasco for plagiarism, for she was undoubtedly convinced that she had a valid case. Throughout her life, Winnifred was always suspicious of people "stealing" her ideas; she would question her agents about such claims and often warned her writer son not to show his work to anyone. Her early participation as a charter member of the Authors' League of America was surely inspired by such concerns.

Later recalling the lawsuit, she wrote, "I placed in the hands of David Belasco the book *A Japanese Nightingale* and a synopsis of *Wooing of Wistaria.*" After he rejected them, Elizabeth Marbury sold the rights to *A Japanese Nightingale* to Klaw and Erlanger in the United States and to Marie Tempest in England. A few months later Belasco came out with his play, and Winnifred felt "it closely resembled Wistaria . . . we saw it in Baltimore."[38]

Winnifred's ill-judged action against Belasco did no harm to *The Darling of the Gods,* which was a huge success, but to her undoubted embarrassment and disappointment, her own Broadway play, which opened the following year, on November 19, 1903, was a disaster. The notices were uniformly bad. Erlanger attributed this to critics who were, as he said, "subsidized by David Belasco, who dictated the reviews."[39]

On the opening night, William Young, the adapter, took a bow "for the author," who stayed away, pleading pregnancy though she was actually between pregnancies at the time. Perhaps the truth was she smelled a failure. *A Japanese Nightingale* ran only forty-four performances. This may be contrasted with *The Darling of the Gods,* which ran 186 performances in its first season alone and played through May 1903.

Nightingale's horrendous reviews make curious reading but are interesting for the picture they give of the play. Alan Dale in the *New York American* remarked that "the wise man has long ago fled from the purgatory of books that may be dramatized to the paradise of those that can't be." He also saw nothing Japanese about the Nightingale, apart from "a nice satin kimona and two streaks of makeup in her eyes. In the first act she appears on a balcony in a flood of Loie Fuller light, and after dancing sees a man in the audience and faints. I was asked by certain inquirers in the lobby what this meant, and referred them to the book. . . . I never read Miss Onoto Whatdoyoucalla's book and I never shall."[40]

Another review had a headline as scathing as it was long: "A Japanese Nightingale Suffers from Locomotor Ataxea and Influenza: Its Native Atmosphere Debilitates the Latest Little Stranger from Japan and Has Given It a Cold beyond the Power of Cough Drops, While Its Vaulting Ambition Has

Severely Barked Its Shins—The Actors Worked Gallantly, but without Japanese Ozone Their Efforts, While Gallant, Were Fruitless." The review goes on to say that *Nightingale,* "which was going to wipe out all recollection of any other Japanese drama ever produced the moment that it saw the limelight," was like a poor little bird that had twisted its larynx, and in short, "the play fell down with such a thud that you might have thought it was another explosion on the subway." This reviewer further noted that the first night audience, after waiting for an hour and a half to find out "what it was all about," had the whole action "explained to them in a lump, only to find that it was scarcely worth the explanation." They reacted with grim smiles, sarcastic grins, and finally "audible titters." The reviewer felt sorry for the actors, for whom "it was a night of agony. Poor souls!"[41]

The *New York Times* review was pained and negative in tone, if not as scathing as the locomotor ataxia attack. Such a familiar bag of tricks "will no longer do on Broadway . . . they belong to a period of the theater that is past." The reviewer allowed that the star, Margaret Illington, was sweet, sympathetic, and attractive, "but she is never Japanese, or anything like it."[42] *Theater Magazine* agreed: "A picturesque environment, sumptuously presented, in which is set a group of Orientals and Occidentals, does not necessarily constitute a play. . . . [William Young's] experiments are old, his touch heavy."[43] The *New York Post* chimed in with "We have had our eyes blistered lately by mistaken gorgeousness."[44]

The *New York News* entitled its review "Mediocrity Once More" and noted, "Belasco was not out-Belascoed! That was the trouble. It was very sad, and a howl of managerial rage rent the atmosphere—of which, by the by, there was very little in 'A Japanese Nightingale.' The squirm of the infuriated producer took the usual hackneyed form. The critics were dishonest! The critics were venal! The critics were subsidized!"[45]

Yone Noguchi saw the play and wrote to Frank Putnam, "Onoto's play . . . was a flat failure. It is a pitty [*sic*] but no one can help it. I was sent by some newspaper to criticize it from Japanese eyes. I thought to say nothing was the only way to be kind to the play. Such a poor production! I am afraid the play will be stopped. Onoto expected much out of it, you know."[46]

In the light of the fate of her Broadway play, it is not surprising that Winnifred's later interpretation of the event, in *Me,* was rendered with a mixture of rueful humility, realism, and perhaps more self-knowledge than she had displayed earlier:

> A few years later, when the name of a play of mine flashed in electric letters on Broadway, and the city was papered with great posters of the play, I went up

> and down before that electric sign, just to see if I could call up even one of the fine thrills I had felt in anticipation. Alas! I was aware only of a sad excitement, a sense of disappointment and despair. I realized that what as an ignorant little girl I had thought was fame was something very different. What then I ardently believed to be the divine sparks of genius, I now perceived to be nothing but a mediocre talent that could never carry me far. My success was founded upon a cheap and popular device, and that jumble of sentimental moonshine that they called my play seemed to me the pathetic stamp of my inefficiency. Oh, I had sold my birthright for a mess of potage! (153)

The spectacularly public setback, even humiliation, doubtless shook Winnifred. By the time of the play's failure, her first thrill of success, of being "somebody," was tempered by a more sober assessment of who and what she really was. But if she was no longer the excitable, dream-struck girl, the vicissitudes of being in the public eye and her own hard work had honed her into a seasoned professional writer.

It was in a businesslike tone, very different in style and sentiment from her musing in *Me,* that she wrote a letter in 1915 to her former publishers, Harper and Brothers, summarizing the play's history and expressing her disappointment. The play had suffered bad luck every step of the way. On the road tour, it played to "splendid business" and was about to open at the Iroquois Theatre in Chicago, but the playhouse was destroyed by fire. In short, the play "never got a fighting chance." With hindsight, she thought the Klaw and Erlanger version was "very bad. They turned what was a delicate little romance into a colossal musical melodrama." At one time, she had hoped that Sousa would compose a light opera from the story, but her new agents, the Wilkennings, informed her that "Mr. Sousa had expressed an aversion to the Japanese."[47]

In the wake of the fiasco, Winnifred gave a revealing interview to the *Sunday Telegram,*[48] in which she gamely did all she could to put a good face on the situation. But the grapes were very sour. Winnifred is shown a review in which William Young is blasted, and she asks, "Could any one call such studied maliciousness criticism, or treat it seriously?" Obviously, the criticisms were written by people who had not seen the play. One man, boasting that he would "reduce the production to atoms," criticized material that was cut out at the last rehearsal. "My friends and I have spent several hours in the enjoyment of that joke," she says with a smile. "Surely it is great to entertain."

The interviewer tells us that Mrs. Babcock's manner "is a cunning blend of Japanese graciousness, English repose, and just a dash of American humor." But the interviewer also points out that Winnifred's house is "a typical American suburban home, all eaves and Queen Anne balconies." Nothing indicates "that the mistress of the house is not a New England housewife. There is not a Japanese screen, not a department store idol in evidence." Moreover, Winnifred expounds on "unwise" interracial marriages and "half-castes": "Oh, they are quaint, dainty little things, when the blood is not crossed, but the second generation is not pretty—and is apt to be clever, but often most wicked." When the interviewer remarks that Winnifred's own pictures do not look very "oriental," Winnifred says, "with a merry twinkle that sits oddly in her handsome, almond-shaped eyes, 'No, the photographer is polite enough to retouch the negative, and take out dark spots.'"

The article does say that when Winnifred is asked about the Belasco controversy, she exhibits "a suggestion of the cuddlesome dignity of the little figures that might have come off a fan." She replies that she has promised her family not to speak of that, but the facts speak for themselves. "That annoying affair happened at the time my attention was turned to the nursery, which interesting event has interfered with my literary work," she excuses herself.

Winnifred then proceeds to a highly disingenuous statement about her rival, John Luther Long, who claimed her work was copied from his: "When I decided to enter the literary world, I wanted to adopt a style of work that might be considered characteristic, and to labor in a field that was not overcrowded. Where else could I turn for more interesting copy than my native country?" As for Long, Winnifred notes that he "is forty-five years old, and has written a volume of short stories. I am in the early twenties and have published six novels. At this rate Mr. Long would not last me any length of time for inspirations."

Of course, Long did publish many novels and was hardly unjustified in his protest that Winnifred was partly inspired by his books. Winnifred boldly countered this accusation by blandly citing her own supposed Japanese ethnicity. She hardly needed to exaggerate the number of her published novels, for her genuine achievements thus far were notable. If she was not in her early twenties, she was still only twenty-eight, and during 1903 alone she had written and published her fourth novel and numerous stories, she had seen her play in production, and she had given birth to her first child. Winnifred's desperate strategy was to tell whatever stories were needed to defend her hard-won position in the literary world against powerful adversaries. She did not have as much at stake as Belasco financially, but she had to fight to keep what she did have.

A *Harper's Weekly* article, published a year after her arrest, is illustrated with a lavish spread of photographs of Winnifred in idyllic, prosperous-looking surroundings.[49] In a high-necked lace Edwardian shirtwaist, she looks serious and rather pretty, with dark eyes and piled-up hair. Another photograph shows "Onoto Watanna in her Library," pensively reading; she is also seen "starting from her Home at Fordham Heights, New York, for a Spin in her Automobile." Onoto Watanna sits holding the levers of a very old-fashioned vehicle, wearing an enormous feathered hat, and looking, it must be said, faintly apprehensive. When one considers that in 1902 there was one car for every 1.2 million people in the United States and that two years later that number was increased to one car per 65,000 people,[50] if Winnifred could chauffeur her own little open-topped machine in 1903, she was quite a successful woman. (It should be noted that her grandson, Paul G. Rooney, recollects that she did not actually drive a car until the 1930s.) But the purpose of the article, as Dominika Ferens points out, was to establish Winnifred's appearance amidst elaborate Western tokens of prosperity and to signal that she had arrived.[51]

She kept on writing, as she always did. One of her oddest stories, probably written while she was pregnant, "The Loves of Sakura Jiro and the Three Headed Maid," appeared in the *Century Magazine* in March 1903. It is a tale of a new immigrant in New York, Jiro, who sees a circus poster showing "Ostero, the Spanish Juggler," an Irish-faced man rolling flame out of his mouth. "Any babby in all Nippon do that," declares Jiro, and he presents himself at the circus freak show, where he is hired to do knife tricks. He falls in love with the circus's three-headed lady, Marva, and is jealous that she is courted by Ostero. The snake charmer advises him to do something spectacular, so he sucks gas from a tube and sets it alight. Flame comes out of his chest, and he bakes pancakes with it. He flings flame into the face of Ostero, and Marva tosses off her two fake heads and rushes to Jiro's side. He awakens in the hospital and is happy to find that Marva is his—even if she really has only one head. "Dear leddy, I so happy I shall love you enough for three," he says.[52] This fablelike story interweaves magic and tricksterism in a playful manner—it is not difficult to see the monkeyish child Winnie spinning this peculiar but very accomplished tale.

In another vein entirely is a story published in the *Ladies' Home Journal* in August 1903. "Miss Lily and Miss Chrysanthemum" is subtitled "The Love Story of Two Japanese Girls in Chicago." For once, instead of bringing Americans to Japan, Winnifred brings Japanese to Chicago; the result is unusually convincing.

Yuri, which translates as Lily—Winnifred's own birth name—is the daughter of an English father and Japanese mother. Taken by her father, now long dead, to be educated in the United States, she has struggled to put herself through college and to support herself as a schoolteacher. Her younger sister, Kiku (Chrysanthemum), stayed with "the little mother in Japan" but on her recent death has joined her sister in the United States. The serious, "American" older sister takes motherly care of the playful little Japanese sister. A young lawyer in their boardinghouse loves Yuri, though he has little chance to talk to the busy, studious young woman. He spends time with the unoccupied Kiku, who asks him embarrassing questions about "lofe" (11). But his true love for Yuri wins out.

Yuri sounds remarkably like Edith Eaton. She is described as "supersensitive" on account of "the strange antipathy the English had shown to her in her childhood, because of her nationality"; schoolmates called her "nigger" and "Chinee." "That she was inferior to them she never for one moment thought, but that she was different from them, and one whom it would be impossible for them to understand, she firmly believed . . . hence her strange love for the home she had never known. Holding herself aloof from all whom she met, she . . . lived a lonely, isolated life." So many phrases here echo Edith's own assessments of herself, as suffering prejudice, not believing herself inferior, and so on. The passage also reveals that Winnifred considered such a life—like her sister's—to be lonely and isolated, and her love for the home she never knew as "strange" (11). The way the heroine scrapes and sacrifices to pay for a trip for her younger sibling also evokes Edith.

As Winnifred's stories were becoming more accomplished in both theme and execution, so was her full-length fiction. Her next novel, *The Heart of Hyacinth*, was published in October 1903.[53] Here, she went back to tried and true methods; *The Heart of Hyacinth* is much closer in style and theme to *Miss Numè of Japan* and *A Japanese Nightingale* than to the historical *Wooing of Wistaria*. It is a romantic, bittersweet story with one of her peculiar, strongly felt, half-caste themes. There is less of the pidgin talk that disfigures some of her other books, and much of the overblown, purple prose is toned down; mastering her plot with complete assurance, she has come into her stride.

Widowed Madame Aoi tries to bring up her little boy, Koma, an English sailor's son, to know English ways. A dying American woman leaves her child, Hyacinth, with Madame Aoi, and the two children grow up together. The Reverend Blount arranges to have Koma educated in his father's land, and Hyacinth misses him keenly. Her own school humiliations recall those of the young Eaton children: "Did not the sensei (teacher), on the very first day, perch his spectacles upon his nose, and, drawing her by the sleeve to one side, examine her with the curiosity he would have bestowed on some small animal" (64).

Koma returns home, and Hyacinth welcomes him passionately: "she ran blindly towards him, and he caught her in his arms with a great hug, which was as familiar to her as life itself" (71). Later, Hyacinth's father tries to find her: she was born while her parents were traveling in Japan, and the mother became "morbid" and ran away. Now, he wants to take his daughter to the United States. Hyacinth hides in the mountains, but Koma finds her. They pledge their love and are married by the Reverend Blount.

The Heart of Hyacinth was reviewed in the *New York Times Book Review* by a reviewer who was taken in by Winnifred's Japanese identity. In his opinion, books about Japan written by Westerners "insist on treating the country as one big tea garden." To the Western writer, the Japanese "are charming playthings, puppets which now perform a comedy, now a tragedy, but always puppets." Even Lafcadio Hearn could not be excepted; but this writer is "one who has Japanese blood in her veins and who consequently is able to sympathize with the peculiar 'genius' . . . of the Japanese race."[54] Winnifred must have been pleased by being favorably compared with Lafcadio Hearn, a writer who had lived long in Japan and was unquestionably a finer stylist than she was. Perhaps *Hyacinth*'s successful debut helped make up for the stinging events of the *Nightingale* play.

It would seem excitement enough, but that winter of 1903–4, after *Hyacinth* came out and while she was pregnant with her second child and writing her next book, *Daughters of Nijo,* Winnifred was involved in still another bizarre incident, that of the stolen sonnet. This was the only time in her life that she was outright accused of plagiarism.

This sensational episode was detailed in a story in the *New York Times Book Review* on February 20, 1904, entitled "Tale of a Sonnet: Dispute about the Origin of a Certain Descriptive Passage in Onoto Watanna's Book, 'A Japanese Nightingale.'"[55] The article stated that a month earlier the *New York Times Book Review* had published a letter from Genevieve Farnell about the following passage in the fifth chapter of *A Japanese Nightingale* by Onoto Watanna: "Pink, white, and blushy-red twigs of cherry and plum blossoms, idly swaying, flung out their suave fragrance on the flattered breeze, the volatile handmaid of young May, who had freed all the imprisoned perfumes, unhindered by the cynic snarl of the jealous Winter, and with silent, persuasive wooing, had taught the dewy-tinctured air to please all living nostrils." After quoting this passage Farnell stated that she recognized these lines as "a prose adaptation from a cyclus of sonnets written several years ago by a professional musician and litterateur well known in Cincinnati." In the spring of 1898, the author had sent her the series of nine sonnets, which were entitled "Guinevere, Lancelot, and Arthur—A Heart Tragedy of Three Typical Characters Recounted and Defined in a Cyclus of Nine Sonnets," by John S. Van Cleve.[56]

Here is the opening of the sonnet, "Guinevere's Apology," from which Winnifred evidently gleaned a large part of her material for the quoted paragraph:

> White, innocent twigs of apple, idly swaying,
> Shed a suave fragrance on the flattered breeze,
> Volatile handmaid of young May; she frees
> All perfumes from their prisons, nor delaying
> For stone-ribbed Winter's cynic snarl, inveighing
> 'Gainst gentle joys, by silent soft degrees,
> Teaches the dewy-tinctured air to please
> All living nostrils, with caressive straying.[57]

Farnell related that she was visiting in Cincinnati when she read *A Japanese Nightingale,* and Professor Van Cleve was visiting that city from his home in Troy, Ohio. She read him the lines. He "gasped, then emitted a short, hysterical laugh."

> "Why, it's my sonnet, almost bodily!" he exclaimed. For a moment it seemed impossible for him to understand exactly how the thing could have happened.
>
> "I met Onoto Watanna," he said at last, "while I was living in Chicago during the Summer of 1898. And I now do recall that I recited to her my sonnets. She was immensely enthusiastic—praised me liberally, and finally asked if I should object to her using some part of the work in her book, which she was writing at the time. Naturally, a writer supposes that this would mean to quote his work, and to give him credit for it."

Farnell described her friend's character, saying he "has been blind since his eighth year, and yet he is one of the best educated and most brilliant of men. Besides being a finished musician and musical instructor, he is thoroughly versed in English literature [and] has mastered several languages." In fact, "the Japanese lady" actually honored his work by appropriating it, and Farnell wondered "why this woman, with all her cleverness and capacity for real literary beauty, should have wished to steal a poet's thunder."[58]

That was not the end of this intriguing episode. On February 1, the editor of the *New York Times* received a communication from Messrs. Baldwin and Blackmar, lawyers, on behalf of Onoto Watanna, giving their opinion that the charge in Farnell's communication was serious and injurious to the literary reputation and financial interests of their client. They declared that Winnifred Babcock herself was the author of the sonnet paraphrased in the descriptive passage from *A Japanese Nightingale.* In an interview with the *New York Times,* the attorneys named James McArthur, of Harper and Brothers, Winnifred's publisher, as an authority who could testify as to Winnifred's Babcock's authorship of the sonnet.[59]

The *New York Times* rather bafflingly stated that the editor had received a communication from Winnifred, "which it would be a pleasure to print in full," but that the paper would not be printing it because "Mrs. Babcock refuses to take part in any controversy on this subject, and expressly states that her letter is not for publication." Yet the substance of the letter is then actually given in full. Winnifred claims that she wrote the sonnets in 1896 and read them before the Cipher Club and the Chicago Women's Press League in 1897. She says she was "in the habit then of reading her work to any one who would listen; that Mr. Van Cleve was possibly one of those who listened; that he was merely an acquaintance whom, she thinks, she met twice; that he was, however, a close personal friend of a mutual friend, and that it is possible that he might have secured copies of the sonnets from this person who had them." Winnifred and her lawyers also claimed that about a year before the publication of *A Japanese Nightingale*, she showed the sonnet to Mr. McArthur of Harpers, who "suggested that she embody some of the expressions in the text of the book."[60]

Van Cleve's statements were given on February 8. He confirmed that he had granted Onoto Watanna permission to "use" the poem. "That it was to be mutilated and used without quotation marks I had it not in me to imagine," he said. He also described his acquaintance with the novelist during 1898, when they both lived in Chicago: "I met Onoto on a number of occasions, having first heard her name mentioned by a certain Dr. Dowd. These meetings took place at the Cipher Club, at various dinner engagements, and one Sunday afternoon at my studio. It was then she took a pencil copy of 'Guinevere's Apology.'"[61]

Two weeks later, L. C. Willcox came to Winnifred's defense in the *New York Times Book Review*, commenting that Winnifred had permission to use the sonnet and that "literary 'borrowings' are common among English writers . . . So let the lady of the lavender books take comfort. All conversation is quotation."[62]

What to make of this episode? On the evidence, it seems that Winnifred did incorporate phrases of Van Cleve's sonnet to make her descriptive prose in her second novel even fancier and more romantic. We know that she loved romantic poetry, and her effusive compliments on first hearing Van Cleve's sonnet ring true. Yet what she did cannot really be called plagiarism, and this may be why Van Cleve did not seek further damages. Winnifred had covered herself by asking his permission. That he did not comprehend she meant to use the phrases herself points to a misunderstanding rather than a deliberate crime. It is easy to imagine that Winnifred, with her slapdash methods and impatience for details, assumed that her use of the piece was justified because she got permission.

What is less savory is her attempt in her statement, through her lawyers, to claim entire authorship of the sonnet. This is more unscrupulous than merely borrowing the phrases, when, after all, she had permission to do so. But of course, she was by then acting entirely on the advice of her lawyers and her publisher. The lawyers knew that Winnifred and Harper and Brothers had a great deal to lose, namely a literary reputation that by 1904 was approaching its apogee and was extremely lucrative. There could be no mealymouthed defense; the only course was to go on the offense and make Winnifred appear completely innocent, or she would be tarred with the stain of plagiarism.

John Van Cleve did not really have a legal leg to stand on, since Winnifred did not use the sonnet outright but by his permission. Moreover, it is doubtful that she ever intended to out-and-out steal from a blind man.

This accusation of plagiarism must have been exceedingly uncomfortable for Winnifred, coming as it did only three months after the humiliating failure of her play, and while she was mother of an eight-month-old baby and two months pregnant with her second child. After this public exposure in the *New York Times,* no shade of such scandal ever darkened her name again. She was not seriously derailed by the incident. Instead, she kept barreling ahead, turning out her novels for profit. No one ever accused her of borrowing a story—she had more ideas than she could write down, even writing at top speed. However, apart from occasional doggerel, she never seriously attempted to write poetry. She left the poetry for the next generation, her son Paul Eaton Reeve, who became, to both her pride and chagrin, what his mother often longed to be but could never afford the luxury of being—a poet.

The young Winnifred Eaton in Chicago about the time her first novel, *Miss Numè of Japan* (1899), was written.

Winnifred's father, Edward Eaton.

Winnifred's mother, Grace Trefusius Eaton.

Winnifred's oldest sister, Edith Eaton (Sui Sin Far).

Winnifred's two youngest sisters, Florence and Beryl.

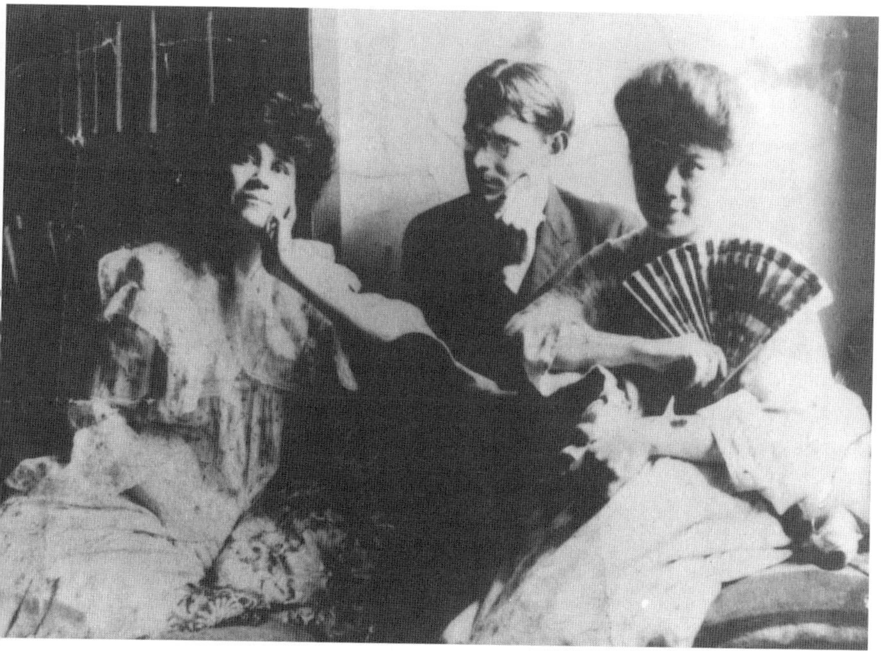

Winnifred's sisters Rose and Sara, showing a Japanese influence in the 1890s, with Sara's husband, Karl Bosse.

ONOTO WATANNA

[*Fac-simile of author's autograph in Japanese.*]

Publicity photos of Onoto Watanna, taken about the time Winnifred's third novel, *The Wooing of Wistaria,* was published in 1902.

Facing page: Frontispiece from *The Wooing of Wistaria,* with the facsimile of Winnifred's autograph in Japanese.

Winnifred in Western clothing at the height of her fame as Onoto Watanna, New York City, 1903.

Winnifred in her library at her Fordham Heights home, photographed for an illustrated article in *Harper's Weekly,* December 5, 1903.

Winnifred posed behind the wheel on an early automobile for the article in *Harper's Weekly,* December 5, 1903.

Winnifred's first husband, Bertrand Babcock, with their oldest son, Perry.

Winnifred and Doris in New York City, about the time she wrote *Me* (1915).

Winnifred's three oldest children, Perry, Bertie, and Doris, about 1907.

Winnifred while she was in Reno divorcing Bertrand Babcock in 1917.

Winnifred in Calgary.

Winnifred's children, Perry, Doris, Charley.

Winnifred in Hollywood as story editor of Universal Pictures in 1924.

Winnifred back home in Calgary.

Winnifred visiting her institutionalized son, Perry, at Camarillo in 1938.

Winnifred's son Charley, by then known as Paul Eaton Reeve, and his bride, Helen Finkelstein, in Miami Beach in 1945.

The biographer, Diana Reeve Birchall, and her father, Paul Eaton Reeve, in a rare happy moment together, 1946.

Frank and Winnifred Reeve, a contented elderly pair, about 1950.

Four generations: Doris Rooney, the daughter of Winnifred and Bertrand Babcock; Winnifred; Frank Rooney, Winnifred's great-grandson; and Paul G. ("Tim") Rooney, Winnifred's grandson, 1952.

Winnifred's grandchildren, Diana Birchall and Paul G. ("Tim") Rooney, Toronto, 2000.

Paul Birchall, Winnifred's great-grandson, and Diana Birchall visiting the graves of Edward and Grace Eaton and their children, where the "Chinese" monument to Sui Sin Far is prominent.

6. A Book and a Baby a Year

> Men don't want wit for a wife. They want sweet, interested intelligence, ready sympathy, but genius, never. And genius goes with dinner never on time.
>
> —Bertrand Babcock, *A Syndicated Prince*

To the Babcock household at 311 West 111th Street came a letter from the Macmillan Company, dated February 25, 1904. Addressed to Mr. Babcock, who handled his wife's business affairs, it announced, "I have had *Daughters of Nijo* very carefully read, and we should be most glad to publish it for Mrs. Babcock, bringing it out here and in London." A $2,500 advance royalty would be made, and the company proposed "some very charming illustrations for the volume."[1] Perhaps because of the affair of the stolen sonnets, Winnifred was changing publishers. It could not have been for lack of sales; *The Wooing of Wistaria* and *The Heart of Hyacinth* had not been the enormous best-sellers that *A Japanese Nightingale* was, but they had done very respectably, and a new novel by Onoto Watanna was still a desirable commodity.

Daughters of Nijo is set at the time of the Restoration. A farmer marries a giddy young woman, who by her bold ways attracts the Prince of Nijo. He abducts her, and she gives birth to his daughter. Born on the same day is the prince's legitimate daughter, Princess Sado-ko. The princess grows up sweet-natured; the other girl, Masago, is discontented and sour. She is betrothed to an artist, Junzo, but he falls in love with Sado-ko. Sado-ko suggests that she and Masago change places, since they look exactly alike, and snobbish Masago is thrilled to be a princess. The Emperor engages her to his son, the crown prince, but she is sad, for she loves another prince. She steals away to her old home, but Sado-ko, about to marry Junzo, insists that Masago is an impostor. The princess is considered mad, and the crown prince breaks the betrothal. Masago marries the man she really cares for and is so happy she becomes nicer.

Daughters of Nijo is not one of Winnifred's most successful books. Her work is at its most charming when Americans are in the picture to form a piquant contrast with Japanese ways; here the contrast is simply between the "good" princess and the "bad" peasant girl. The story is no more than acrobatic contortions to get them into and out of each other's positions, and perhaps because it is set among courtiers, the language is stilted and formal.

The book's quality may have suffered because 1904 was another feverishly busy year for Winnifred, who had two babies under the age of two at home. Yet *Daughters of Nijo* does not suffer from sloppiness; although some details proved erroneous, the book is replete with descriptions of the court and the elaborate historical setting, and the plot is laboriously worked out. This may be another book that bears the blighting hand of Bertrand Babcock. In any event, the *New York Times Book Review* was the least unkind: "The decorations and the pictures which accompany the text are really truly Japanese and have a Japanese name signed to them. The persons of the book are really truly Japanese too, perhaps. Certainly they are the Japanese after the most charming pattern of Western day dreams."[2]

Winnifred's "Japanese" deception was wearing thin. Reviews were growing increasingly cynical, and the New York literary establishment seemed aware that Winnifred was not Japanese. Far from New York, at least one reviewer was skeptical: "*Daughters of Nijo*, by Onoto Watanna, is a sufficiently ingenious and readable story; but its name, its illustrations, and all its elaborate stage-setting no more make it a Japanese story than the author's name makes her a Japanese woman."[3] The editor of *Out West Magazine*, Charles F. Lummis, Edith's patron, knew the truth.

Reading the reviews, Winnifred may have suspected that she could not continue her imposture indefinitely and that exposure could be embarrassing. At the moment, there was nothing to do but keep playing the Japanese author. Her pose was still taken seriously in some quarters; the *Evening Telegraph* conducted a major interview eliciting her opinions on the Russo-Japanese War. For this occasion Winnifred put on her very best act, and the resulting article was headlined "Natural Fighters, She Says of Japs: Woman Who Writes Books on Eastern Nation Talks of the War with Russia."[4]

Here Winnifred reaches her pinnacle as an ardently patriotic Japanese woman. "If I were not married and did not have a baby nothing could keep me away from Japan," she declares. Her mother was Japanese, and her father was an English army officer (a warlike version of Edward Eaton, surely), "but she is all Japanese at heart and has lost none of her passionate love for the land of the Mikado, where she spent her childhood."

The article gives us a glimpse of Winnifred in her setting and on her soapbox:

> She did not have time even to talk about *A Japanese Nightingale* and *The Wooing of Wistaria*, two of her most popular stories, so interested was she in the latest war news when seen at her home, No. 2445 Grand Avenue, Fordham Heights. Her husband, who is a playwright and an American, is hardly less interested, and Mrs. Babcock declares her seven-months-old son, a cunning little Japanese American, has been heard to cheer in his baby language for Japan.
>
> "I probably know less about the war than you do," [she told the reporter disingenuously] "but I know Japan and the Japanese, of course, and in their time of trial all my sympathy goes out to them. I certainly hope the Japanese—No, I mean I know the Japanese will win. If you knew them as I do, knew their courage and skill in arms, you would not have any doubt either.
>
> "Isn't it splendid the way my people have been giving it to the Russians? I guess people here will not have so much to say about Asiatics being an inferior people now. No country in this world has ever jumped into war the way Japan has."

In the midst of all this fevered patriotism for Japan, she manages a favorable mention of her real Asian connection. In a rhetorical move that must surely have confused her readers, she ventures to speak of the Chinese as her relatives: "The Mikado has no desire to seize China. Japan had to whip China, as a father whips his bad son, but it was only to make her better. The Chinese, you know, are really our brothers, for we all came from China in the beginning. I myself have great love for the Chinese. I ought to have, for some of them are my relatives."

Winnifred's second book to be published in 1904, and her sixth novel, was *The Love of Azalea*. Dodd, Mead and Company brought it out in October, a month after the birth of her second son. Again, it was a romance about a Western man and a Japanese woman. In a little Japanese village, people come to hear a young minister, the Reverend Verley, solely because he is a white man and a curiosity. A young woman, Azalea, seeks his help, for she wants to leave the home of her unkind stepmother, Madame Yamada. Her father is dead, and she has two half-sisters; Azalea is a Cinderella. She promises to be the minister's convert.

The rich merchant Matsuda asks Madame Yamada for Azalea's hand. She is furious that he wants her despised stepdaughter, but Matsuda is determined: Azalea's samurai father once insulted him, and he will take her in revenge. Azalea and the Reverend Verley have come to care for each other. She painfully informs him that she has only been pretending to be a convert, but now she is sincere, and they marry in a Christian ceremony. Matsuda is furious, but he is sure that "foreign devils" do not make lasting marriages with Japanese. Verley is recalled home, promising to return soon; but after her baby boy is born, Azalea is reduced to begging in the street, and Matsuda takes her in. When Verley returns, he is shocked to find his house torn down, his bride gone, and his church nailed up. After many trials, Azalea escapes Matsuda and is reunited with her husband.

The Love of Azalea is a melodramatic tale, but its depiction of the missionary's situation is interesting. He is seen through the eyes of the heathen "natives" as someone to prey upon. Winnifred had rather a soft spot for heathens, and Azalea is essentially one herself. Her conversion never seems truly profound; in her desperation, she goes so far as to destroy her Bible.

The exaggerated stage villain who systematically tries to manipulate and win the heroine is balanced by the saintly, bloodless stick of a minister husband. Winnifred's focus tended to be more on her female characters, and here both males are stereotypes. Azalea herself, however, is not a typical maiden who marries at the end of the story. Instead, she becomes a wife fairly early on, and her trials and tribulations are those of a wife. It is true that the heroines of *A Japanese Nightingale* and *The Wooing of Wistaria* are married too—and the Nightingale, like Azalea, is married to a white man and endures separation from him—but Azalea is more of a woman: she is a mother. It is as if as Winnifred matured, so did her generic Japanese heroine. There is genuine feeling in her depiction of the baby—"The baby grew in strength and beauty, a solemn-faced, large-eyed morsel of humanity, with skin like a peach bloom in color, soft and fat and delightful to the touch of the caressing mother" (143). This is written not by the Winnifred who used to be a big sister tormented by a passel of children but by the happy young mother she was at the time Azalea was written.

The *New York Times Book Review* treated the book casually, merely retelling the "Cinderella" plot and adding dismissively, "But why tell the story. One can read it easily in an hour, printed in a lovely violet-colored book, with wide margins and decorated pages on which appear cherry blossoms and bamboo stalks and little Japanese maidens and grasses and other graceful things."[5]

A more serious review, in the *Independent,* is also harsher, being written by one of those pesky reviewers who saw through Winnifred's disguise and thought she was continuing a "mistaken career as a Japanese novelist." She was taken to task ("Her local color is as erratic, her characters as impossible and their manners as reprehensible as in her previous stories"), but it conceded that she had "made a distinct gain by deserting the dangerous path of the historical novel, so full of pitfalls for the unwary, and cutting herself conveniently loose from all hampering conditions of time and space."[6]

Despite the vicissitudes of reviews, Winnifred was by now well established among the New York literati. Always sociable and vivacious, with an enthusiasm for collecting friends (the more famous the better), she must have delighted in a prestigious invitation to celebrate the seventieth birthday of Mark Twain, on December 5, 1904, at Delmonico's. Winnifred had become friendly with Twain's great-niece, Jean Webster, soon after her arrival in New York. They may have met through Babcock, who grew up in the same small town as Jean, but he was not among the guests. Nor was he present on a similar occasion, a tribute for William Dean Howells's seventy-fifth birthday on March 9, 1912 at the Sherry. This was attended by a large, elegantly dressed crowd; President Taft was present, and a spread in *Harper's Weekly* lists Mrs. B. W. Babcock among the guests. A literary figure in her own right, she went about socially on her own, without her husband.

Yet she did not have infinite time for gadding about. During the first decade of the century, she not only worked hard but also had all four of her babies. It was a stock joke of hers that when her work was in vogue, she turned out "a book and a baby a year."[7]

Winnifred's first book in 1906 was *A Japanese Blossom* published by Harper and Brothers (a return to the publisher of *A Japanese Nightingale, The Heart of Hyacinth,* and *The Wooing of Wistaria*) and dedicated "To my children." It is easy to see why this, of all her books, is the one so dedicated, for the book is all about children. It has less of a formal plot than any other of her books, and little attention is given to adult characters. It is no wonder that Winnifred was so bound up in children; in this year, Perry was three years old, little Bertie two, and she had a newborn daughter. With children very much on her mind, she conceived *A Japanese Blossom.* It is the story of the Kurukawa children, whose mother is dead and whose father is in the United States. Their elderly grandmother breaks the news that their father's new American wife has had a son. The children are upset, especially the oldest son, Gozo, seventeen, who is so angry that his father has put "a barbarian" in his mother's place that he joins the army.

Their father brings home his American wife, who is so gentle, kind, and determined to adopt Japanese ways that the younger children, Plum Blossom, Iris, Taro, and the fat baby Juji, accept her. Everyone adores the new yellow-haired baby, and it is passed around from family to family. The Irish maid "loses" it briefly, but the baby is found, and everyone is happy—until Mr. Kurukawa decides that he must go fight the Russians. He is reported missing, and his wife tries to be proud to give up her husband for his country. Finally, Gozo brings him home, to much rejoicing; they have both been prisoners.

One of Winnifred's most charming works, with its attractive portrait of a family, the book features several stories-within-stories, such as one the father tells about a woman who married seven times to be able to give up her husbands to be soldiers (the last husband dies of "melancholia while in Manchuria" [102]). The character of the Irish maid is an anomaly, who stumbles around the Japanese streets attracting attention with her thick brogue; but Winnifred must have relished depicting her, as a change from her usual gallery of Japanese portraits.

A Japanese Blossom was a particularly prettily designed book, in pale blue with a graceful white orchid pattern and the title and author's name stamped vertically in gold. Imprints of children and flowers cover the pages, adorning the small blocks of deeply inset text. This book was cordially reviewed in the *New York Times Book Review:* "Not so much a story as a child's first book of Japanese life. . . . The author's design, evidently, is to show American children and American mothers what Japanese children are like. . . . While the children of the East and of the West are making each other's acquaintance, you may sit by and look on." As for the war with Russia, the reviewer comments, "To be sure, American wives have devoted their husbands to a country before, but it was not Japan."[8]

The book did not find favor with Winnifred's old friend Yone Noguchi, who, back in Japan, wrote an article entitled "Onoto Watanna and Her Japanese Work." Once enchanted by his butterfly friend, he now deplored her "Japanese" writings, saying that acquaintance with them always made him sad. He noted her ability to "make any new Japanese custom and habit right on the spot when she needs them," and added, "The saddest part about Miss Watanna is that she is still posing as a Japanese, a half caste at the least."[9]

Winnifred probably would have agreed, as she was making clear attempts in her writing to break away from Japanese themes. In the same year she published *A Japanese Blossom,* she had a major two-part Japanese story in *Harper's Weekly* entitled "The Wrench of Chance."[10] Having ventured to introduce an Irish character in her previous Japanese novel, Winnifred leaned further in that direction. Since she was still formally confined to her Japanese subject matter, the combination of Japanese and Irish characters makes a peculiar hybrid. Perhaps for that very reason, this is one of Winnifred's more potent stories.

A foul-mouthed, brawling, red-headed Irishman, Michael Lenahan, jumps ship in Nagasaki, erroneously believing he has killed a man in a brawl. He lives in Japan for the next twenty years, teaching in a small village and evading British visitors. He takes his young pupil, Yugiri, as his wife, and she is his docile slave, though he is a drunken and abusive husband. One day he sees the man he thought he killed and realizes that he is free to leave Japan. Mischievously he tells his wife he is joining the soldiers to fight Russia, and she pictures him as a glorious hero. He drunkenly boasts of his lies in a bar, and two indignant Japanese officers "shanghai" him so he becomes a soldier in earnest. When a doctor, in love with Yugiri, tells her that Lenahan returned to his homeland, she divorces him. But Lenahan does fight bravely and is brought to the hospital wounded. There Yugiri witnesses his death—and she looks at the doctor with eyes full of a terrible reproach.

The brutality and coarseness of the Irishman who turns out to have some noble qualities are drawn with energy and spirit, and the attitudes of his Japanese wife, in response to his alternating nobility and bestiality, are sensitively portrayed by Winnifred in this story of contrasting cultures.

Winnifred's next book was a major departure for her. Weary of being limited almost exclusively to Japanese themes, she decided to try an experiment: she would write a wholly humorous "Irish" novel. *The Diary of Delia,* with the subtitle *Being a Veracious Chronicle of the Kitchen, with Some Side-Lights on the Parlour,* was published by Doubleday, Page and Company, with comic illustrations by May Wilson Preston.[11] Winnifred wanted to publish it under a new pen name, Winnifred Mooney, but her publisher insisted that she use her popular Onoto Watanna name. The resultant spectacle was of an Irish vernacular novel apparently written by a Japanese. Despite this anomalous situation, Winnifred showed herself as shrewd as ever about popular taste.

The heroine of this breezy comedy is a farcical figure, an unglamorous Irish maid. Winnifred wrote the novel in the first person, something she did in only two other novels (*Me* and *Marion*). She used a broadly rendered, comically misspelt Irish brogue, so that although the book is mercifully free of quaint Japanese pidgin, it has another type of mangled dialogue. *Delia* is very much a product of its moment in American fiction, specifically in American humor, when the Irish were seen as a legitimate source of endless, harmless, good-natured comedy. Feather-light, the book is now interesting principally for its picture of manners and class attitudes of bygone days before World War I. *The Diary of Delia* must have seemed very funny in an era when servants were plentiful in middle-class households and when Irish dialect was automatically hilarious in a broad, vaudeville sense. As the taste for Irish comedy passed, the work has come to seem dated. Yet for all this, *The Diary of Delia* is written with verve, spirit, and genuine good humor.

Delia the maid describes a typical day in the Wolley household, which consists of Mr. Wolley, Mrs. Wolley, the *jeune fille* Miss Claire, little Billy, and two grown sons, Mr. John and Mr. James, an "eediotor" and "orthor" respectively. The scene is far from Winnifred's Japanese settings. The family's house is on the "Poynt" in Long Island, just where Winnifred was living in 1906, so she was writing, for once, about a setting she knew and perhaps about her neighbors.

Everyone in the family requests a different breakfast, and Delia, exasperated, scolds them for "Gitting up at these unnairthly ours and bullying the life out of a poor loan hard working girl" (6). Her friend and evil genius Minnie Carnavan calls her a fool ("The Idear of you doing all the wark in a family of 6") and thinks she can do better (9).

Racially themed jokes are blithely sprinkled throughout the book. These were the normal comic parlance of the era, but their offensiveness to modern ears is more evidence of the datedness of Winnifred's comic writing. For example, when Delia goes to visit a "widdy," a "spoonky little culloured maid opened the front door." The widdy calls her Lilly, and Delia exclaims robustly, "My God! The Nigger's name was Lilly and she black as hell" (195).

The reviews were enthusiastic, and one reviewer warmly calls the book "one laugh throughout."[12] Needless to say, there was some explaining to do, to sort out Winnifred's antecedents, and the legend continued to mutate, getting ever stranger: "Onoto Watanna is claimed by several nations. Her father is an Englishman . . . who married a woman of pure Japanese and Chinese descent." All her books, we are told, deal "with life in Japan, where she was born. It is known that even Scotland and Ireland claim the versatile writer."[13] Winnifred managed in one fell swoop to claim English, Japanese, Chinese, Scottish, and Irish blood, covering all possible and impossible bases and giving herself carte blanche to write in the vernacular of almost any nationality she should choose.

Winnifred gave her own verdict on *The Diary of Delia* in a letter to her agent Colonel William Selig years later: "I sold that story anonymously to *The Saturday Evening Post* as I was tired of writing Japanese stories. . . . It ran as they put it for seven uproarious weeks, and I used to see people on the subway reading it and roaring with laughter. I never could understand why it was not sold for pictures. Guess I was a poor business woman."[14]

Winnifred returned to the popular Delia two years later in a *Saturday Evening Post* story entitled "Delia Dissents."[15] The employees of the Poynt form a "yunion," and as "pressydint," Delia makes a fine speech about servants' rights: "We have been crooly composed upon for sinchuries." Rife with cultural stereotypes as the story is, Winnifred's Delia shows a spirit of equality, defending a black character against the prejudice of a southerner who protests that she does not want to join "a yunion where cullered peeple" are admitted. Delia stands up for Lilly. Yet another stereotype is introduced, an anarchist "Rooshun Jew" who hands Delia an "unfirnal masheen," a bomb for workers to use on their bosses (22). There is also a "Jap" character—if the Irish Michael Lenahan can appear in a Japanese story, why not a Japanese in an Irish-American setting—who makes a speech declaring woman an inferior sex (except the maids, of course) (23).

Also in 1908, one of Winnifred's most charming stories, "A Neighbor's Garden, My Own, and a Dream One," appeared in *Good Housekeeping* in April and May, and in it she gives an idealized picture of her Mamaroneck home. The theme is gardens, and Winnifred rhapsodizes about flowers, sighing about her own deprivation: "I have never owned any, hardly."[16]

"About four years ago I bade the city a sincere and cordial farewell," she reminisces in part 1. That places the move to 1904, when Perry and Bertie were babies and when Winnifred's florally named *Hyacinth* and *Azalea* books earned enough to enable the Babcocks to buy their own home. Yet none of the children's birth certificates name a Mamaroneck residence, and in 1904 the Babcocks were living in Fordham Heights, the attractive home described in several interviews. The Babcocks had many different addresses, and how to square them with the home in Mamaroneck is par for the course for their shifting fortunes and changeable locations. Certainly the Mamaroneck idyll was a short one, over by the time the garden piece was published. But Winnifred reminisces about this happy moment in her life in part 1: "For a time we lived in the suburbs, where, on a tiny lawn, I cherished a few pansies and geraniums, but I could not have a garden, for with my work as a writer I found that the most I could do in life was to produce a book and a baby a year. Besides, I wanted the real country for my garden. By and by fortune made this possible" (348). No doubt it did, for family tradition has it that Winnie received as much as $20,000 for some of her books, a very large sum in the first decade of the century.

She continues to detail her home in part 1:

> I dwell now in the heart of Westchester, near the metropolis. I have a little acre of land all my own. Around me are sumptuous homes, mansions set amid grounds kept as perfect and smooth as a well-swept parlor. My little frowsy acre, with its unshorn lawns and overgrown carriage drives, seems a reproach to an otherwise immaculate community. I'm sure my neighbors regard me with suspicion, convinced I am an eccentric individual who prefers my place unclipped. But I keep no man, and have neither the strength nor ambition to push a lawnmower over an acre of lawn.

Here Winnifred harks back to her youth, seeing her house as unkempt and small next to the neighbors' grander ones. We notice, too, that thus far, her husband has not put in an appearance, not even to push the lawn mower. The house is "all my own," and, later, "I purchased the place." Yet in the next sentence is a reference to what a husband might be used for: "When the babies have ceased to come, and when the ones that are here have ceased to need me all the time, then I expect to have flowers of my own" (348).

The Irish girl, Norah, who cares for her "fat babies," summons her mistress to see "three grand ladies in yer parlor!" The author "sprang down as airily as a mother of three may. . . . I forgot my progeny of three and flew houseward as though I was not married at all" (351). The visitors are a mother and her daughters, who have come to welcome her to the neighborhood. The lady, Mrs. C., loves flowers; she created the garden next door and has since moved to a big place with seventeen acres of rolling lands. Her garden is a mass of bloom. "I know no lovelier sight save the blowing cherry and plum blossoms of far Japan," Winnifred sighs, as if she actually did know them (353).

In the second part, she begins to create her garden. "Katy could mind the babies for a time entirely, and the brown-faced girl who did my housework was only too anxious to take full charge of the rest of the work. Fanny was a born housekeeper, and I know she always saw through my various brave devices to make her think I was one also. For I'm not" (484). Perhaps she was no housekeeper, but if we include Norah from the first part, Winnifred was the mistress of at least four servants, which indicates that the lavender books were selling rather well.

Her neighbor patronizingly assures her, "I just know that you are a natural gardener, anyhow. All of your countrywomen are. I'm ever so anxious to see your little garden. I know very well it will reflect the color and taste of your far native land." "Alas for Japan!" Winnifred sighs, rueful about her gardening abilities or having to keep up the Japanese pretense (488). After digging up flowers and planting weeds, she decides that she should have a gardener, as Mrs. C. does: "Next year . . . I, too, will have a man. I can do without a spring hat—or rather, babies thrive just as well in rompers as in expensive, starched frocks. The little dears shall contribute to my garden" (489).

By the time this was published in the spring of 1908, there were not "three fat babies" but four. But the story is set in the previous spring, shortly before the birth of Charley, hence the reference to a time when "the babies will have ceased to come": they were still coming. Winnifred's firstborn, Paul Perry Charles Bertrand Whitcomb—given as many names as a crown prince by his proud young parents at his birth on June 23, 1903, but always known as Perry—would have been nearly four at the time of the story; the second child, Bertrand Whitcomb Jr., born September 29, 1904, was two and a half; Doris, born January 13, 1906, would have been still under a year old. Charles Edward was born on July 27, 1907, so even if Winnifred described herself as running as lightly as an unmarried girl, it is no wonder her mind was on seedbeds and growing things.

Photographs show Perry as a wiry little boy with a clever expression; Bertie is a dark, solemn-eyed, round-faced child, very "Chinese" looking, and already quite as large as the thinner-faced, lighter Perry. Winnifred holds on her lap baby Doris, a dark, serious-looking little girl, and keeps a hand on Bertie, while Perry stands alertly apart. A photograph of Charley shows him as an Asian-eyed baby in the arms of a young, possibly Irish nurse; one wonders if she might be the model for Delia and what she thought about it if she was.

These family photographs are poignant in the light of the story that Winnifred seldom told, that of her boy who died. A garbled version appears in an interview in a Calgary paper in the 1920s by Elizabeth Bailey Price, a journalist who wrote several flattering articles about Winnifred: "Her youngest son's tragic death—he was dropped by a nurse and after several months died from the effects of a trepanning operation—cast a shadow upon her life, and for seven years she ceased to write at all. To get away from the scene of her trouble, and as she was in great need of mental rest, the Reeves came out to Alberta and engaged in the cattle ranching 'game.'"[17]

The first misstatement in the interview is that Bertie was her youngest son; he was her second. Photographs show him as a remarkably stout, healthy-looking little boy, despite his illness. Another piece of misinformation is that Winnifred stopped writing for seven years. This never happened during her children's infancy. There is a six-year gap between *Marion* (1916) and *Sunny-San* (1922), but this had nothing to do with the death of Bertie. It occurred years after Bertie's death, during the period when she divorced Babcock and moved to Calgary as a cattle rancher's wife. Getting "away from the scene of her trouble" meant the divorce, a less presentable reason than the death of her son but the true one. The interview also implies that Frank Reeve, her second husband, was the father of her children, which he was not.

Winnifred's bereavement was, nonetheless, clearly reflected in her writing. The flower piece of 1908 is lighthearted and happy, not written by a bereaved mother but one busy with fat babies. *A Japanese Blossom*, published in 1906, and *The Diary of Delia*, published the following year, are the cheeriest of all Winnifred's books, written in the blithe mood of the flower story. *Tama*, which came out in 1910,[18] is a far different work, strange, rather melancholy, and elegiac. *Tama* does read as if it were written by someone in mourning.

The fact is that little Bertie died on September 11, 1908, just before his fourth birthday. The death certificate says he had suffered from chronic encephalitis for two years and died from convulsions and heart failure, the duration of which was only one day. Most likely the trepanning operation was an emergency measure to relieve pressure from the brain swelling. There is no mention of a nurse, but perhaps one did worsen his condition by dropping him while he was ill.

Winnifred never had any scruples about falsifying such documents as her children's birth certificates. Yet, on little Bertie's death certificate her birthplace is simply given as "Canada." "The poor soul must have been too distraught to lie," in the opinion of her great-granddaughter Elizabeth Rooney, who found the document. Encephalitis was a not infrequent affliction a century ago, when child mortality was much higher than it is today. The fat babies were not always as healthy as they looked. Winnifred had considerable illness to deal with in her children, for Perry also suffered ill health as a boy. In a letter written many years later, his sister, Doris, remembered: "As a very little boy Perry had spinal meningitis, followed by a long series of illnesses. For a time his eyesight and hearing were affected and for quite a long time he was in leg braces."[19]

The death of Bertie and Perry's delicate health may have made Winnifred overly attached to her youngest son, the robust, bumptious Charley, who was only a year old when his brother died. Sturdy and handsome, full of mischief, sticking out his tongue in pictures, loving to ride, proudly termed "wild" by his mother, Charley was all boy. Bertrand, however, was emphatically not fond of this child, to the point of bitterly denying that he was his own son. The family photographs look idyllic—there is a happy set of the children at a country celebration with the elder Babcocks. Perry and Charley, perhaps ten and six years old, and their sister, are seen with their father, who jauntily chews a cigar. The family misery does not show. But Bertrand, who was abusive to his wife, was rough with Charley as well, and Charley never forgot or forgave the mistreatment.

Winnifred wrote a rare account of Bertie's death in the manuscript introduction to a story entitled "Other People's Troubles." In this story, a doctor visits a widow who is contemplating suicide. She feels that she has lost everything, but the doctor tells her "the world has a sovereign remedy for all griefs. It's the contemplation of other troubles greater than our own."[20] And he relates tales of other patients and their sorrows. In her unpublished introduction, Winnifred relates:

> "Other People's Troubles" was suggested to the author through a personal experience of her own. Her little boy of eighteen months was dropped down stairs by a nurse. After several months, he was operated upon—a terrible operation—Trepanning. The mother was told that the operation meant either Death or possible cure, but without the operation the child would never be normal, and she took the chance, from which later her baby died.
>
> During the operation, when she was walking about nearly distraught, one of the doctors came to her and said, "I want you to come with me and look at some of the children in the public ward."
>
> He took her from one cot to the other, and as she saw these tragic little broken castaways of life, there came to her a realization that her own pain was but a drop in the great bucket of the world, and that she was at least able to give her child expert care and the comfort of the private ward. And this and the pity she felt took her out of herself sufficiently to give her the strength and courage to bear her own burden.[21]

In this version, the child is eighteen months old when he suffers the accident or first becomes ill. Since little Bertie actually had chronic encephalitis for two years before he died, his illness may very well have dated from 1906, between the births of Doris and Charley, one of Winnifred's busiest writing years. Even though he recovered enough to look healthy in family photographs taken in 1908, his chronic and critical condition would explain why Winnifred wrote no novel in 1907 or 1908 or in 1909, following his death.

The true specifics of this tragedy Winnifred kept to herself. Even with her habit of pouring herself out in later letters and diaries, it was nothing she cared to write or to talk about. It was one of her secrets. Her daughter said that Winnifred held herself responsible for the boy's death, having consented to the terrible trepanning operation, after which the child "stopped progressing and he soon died."[22] Doris was only two years old when her brother died, but her account tallies with the one Winnifred gave in "Other People's Troubles."

One of the stories Winnifred wrote in 1907—"The Manoeuvres of O-Yasu-san," a long story that appeared in the *Saturday Evening Post* on January 25, 1908, before her son's death—was her first to treat a theme that was to become a favorite: marital infidelity. Her attitude was disapproving, as it would have to be by the conventions of popular fiction, and her adulterous characters were villains; but she was obviously fascinated by this theme. By this time, her wider experience of life and her increasingly unhappy marriage must have shown her many examples of affairs and infidelities. Given her flirtatious nature, there might have been some justification for Bertrand Babcock's continual suspicions about her infidelity. "Manoeuvres" is a sophisticated and cynical tale and portrays its Japanese heroine as anything but a pretty little fool. It is another "half-caste" story, and the heroine has the characteristics that Winnifred deemed innate.

O-Yasu-san, the daughter of a Japanese diplomat and an English mother who dies, is raised in Japan. Her aunt, Mrs. Bailey, a scheming middle-aged woman carrying on an affair with an Englishman, Mr. Middleton, takes O-Yasu-san to the trysts so people will think Middleton is courting the younger woman. Aunt and niece are mutually hostile: "I *have* seen Japanese women appear half-way decent in a Paris frock; but you, my dear, are half-and-half. You look just ridiculous," Mrs. Bailey nastily says (10). O-Yasu-san makes Mrs. Bailey look foolish in Middleton's eyes, showing him her aunt's false hair and devices to make her look younger. After many schemes and counterschemes, O-Yasu-san and Middleton marry, and the stunned Mrs. Bailey sails back home to her husband.

Here, an older, adulterous woman gets her comeuppance—the younger woman is wise and virtuous, the older woman scheming and venial. There is no reason to see any autobiographical undertones in the tale, but Winnifred's disapproving yet titillated fascination with the adultery theme is apparent.

She was starting to deal with older characters. Next, she wrote a story with a "grandmother" theme that appeared in *Lippincott's Monthly Magazine* in December 1909. "An Unexpected Grandchild" is about love and loss. A young woman named Gertrude is engaged to an architect, who is away on business while she and his mother are in Tokyo. In a discussion about mixed marriages, Mrs. Howland declares that if her son victimized a young Japanese woman, she would protect the young woman and her baby. This is overheard by the Howlands' maid and her friend, and the friend soon turns up with a red-haired baby, which she claims is her child by Mrs. Howland's son. Mrs. Howland dotes on the baby, exulting, "He's mine—my very own little grandchild" (690). Poor Gertrude is sickened—"A hideous little heathen imp!" (691). It turns out that a young white woman's baby was stolen from the hotel, and the baby is not Mrs. Howland's grandchild at all. Mrs. Howland is upset. "Two great tears rolled down her furrowed cheeks. 'I—I loved that baby,' she said." Then she adds, painfully, "And I gave her five hundred dollars. I could not conceive of a Japanese adventuress" (696). But she apologizes to her son, and he and Gertrude are reconciled.

One of Winifred's most striking and strongly felt stories, this carries the "half-caste" theme into another generation. The "half-caste" child is seen from two contrasting viewpoints, with the more "rational" view—that the existence of such a child is a shame and a tragedy—being Gertrude's, while

Mrs. Howland is blinded by folly and fondness. Yet her open loving is, ironically, a more truly "moral" response than Gertrude's racism.

Winnifred's next full-length novel, *Tama,* appeared in 1910, two years after her son's death. Another Japanese story, it is perhaps her most somber book. Foreign professor O-Tojin-san (Honourable Mr. Foreigner) is popular with his pupils, though he is an ugly man, with smallpox-pitted skin. The young American woman he wanted to marry had cringed at his proposal, and he now lives the life of an ascetic.

Tojin's household is upset because food is stolen by the Fox Woman, a mischievous mountain sprite whose ghostly cry is heard at night. Her mother was a nun who broke her vows and married a foreign sailor. Parishioners believed she was cursed by having a child with the soul of a fox, and they killed her and her husband at the altar, when the girl was ten years old. She lives in a forsaken temple, an outcast, and is blamed for all ill fortune.

Tojin's students capture the "witch" by digging a trench and covering it with sod and petals, and he finally sees her—a young white woman, with long golden hair and a delicate face, a trembling, hunted creature. And she is blind. Slowly, he gets to know the girl, Tama (Jewel), and feels protective of her.

Owing to political change, the samurai are thrown out of service, and Tojin's involvement with the fox-woman is held to be the cause of the disaster. They hide together, until the prince returns from a journey, and Tojin convinces him that the treatment of Tama was a superstitious wrong. Tojin arranges for Tama to have an operation to restore her sight, though he fears her seeing his ugly face. But she knows him in her heart.

The reviews were admiring, and sales were good. A *New York Times* book reviewer wrote enthusiastically, "Charmingly Japanese in form as well as in atmosphere is *Tama.* . . . It holds the very spirit of Japan, a spirit fragrant, dainty, elusive; capable withal of devotion and loyalty, which, put to the test, esteems death as a little thing. The book has four illustrations in color by Genjiro Kataoka. Each page bears shadowy blossoms, butterflies, birds and scenes of Japan. In its box, repeating the beauty of the cover, it makes an ideal gift."[23]

Winnifred's next book, the last Japanese novel she wrote for ten years—and she only wrote one more—was *The Honorable Miss Moonlight,* published in 1912.[24] It is a story about the young Lord Saito Gonji, who is engaged to marry plump, wealthy Ohano. Before the wedding, he is taken to a geisha house and sees lovely Moonlight, known as "The Spider" for the wondrous dance she weaves. Gonji and Moonlight fall in love, and he informs his family that he will not marry Ohano. When they insist, he prepares to commit seppuku. If Gonji dies, his whole line will die out, so his father reluctantly agrees to let him marry the geisha. When Moonlight fails to produce a child after a year of marriage, her mother-in-law, Lady Saito, insists that she sacrifice herself for the family and be divorced, so Gonji can marry Ohano. Yet Ohano bears no child either, and Gonji goes away to fight the Russians. The family is in despair. In the meanwhile, Moonlight has had a son, and her former master steals the baby and brings it to Lady Saito and Ohano.

Ohano cannot fully love "the Spider's child," and when Lady Saito informs Ohano that the family must take the mother into the household, obedient Ohano removes herself by committing seppuku. Lady Saito humbly begs Moonlight to return, so when Gonji returns home he finds that he has a son—and Moonlight. One day, a cicada flutters against the wall. To Lady Saito it is a bad omen. But Moonlight cries, "Oh, do you not see—it is Ohano, poor Ohano! She has returned to us in this way" (174).

The Honorable Miss Moonlight, like *Tama,* is a sad story. Winnifred herself was undoubtedly sadder than in earlier years; her circumstances, with her unhappy marriage and the loss of a child, seem to permeate these two strange and somber novels. The themes of a lost baby, a harsh mother-in-law, and a family sacrificing a husband to war had been used before, but here they are melded in a painful drama. The characters' anguish is manifest. Moonlight suffers ("She had remained in this motionless position from the moment they had told her of the loss of her child" [119]); Ohano suffers jealousy and rejection ("Looking into her husband's face, Ohano knew, without questioning, who it was who would make the final precious journey with him" [88]). But perhaps cold Lady Saito, whose domineering causes all this suffering, suffers most poignantly: "Whatever were the thoughts that tormented and haunted the mother-in-law of Ohano . . . her hair turned as white as snow (155). . . . Great tears ran down the stern and furrowed cheeks of the lady, nor could she speak for the sobs that tore her" (157). Permeated with tragedy, disappointment, and loss, the book is as effectively moving as anything Winnifred ever wrote and eloquently reflects the sadness and loss in her own life.

Again, reviews were good. One reviewer called the book unsuitable for the "Rather Young Person" but commented, "There is so much of the spirit of Old Japan interwoven with the delicately written narrative that the Occidental reader fairly loses sight of his own ethical training in his sympathy for the childless wife, doomed, under the old custom, to divorce or suicide."[25]

Another of Winnifred's projects in 1912 was the adaptation of Paul Anthelme's play *L'Honneur Japonais,* which was produced in Paris. The elderly playwright had composed the play years earlier; it was a samurai drama that *Theater Magazine* described as an old-fashioned, masculine story, turning on "an incident which Western minds would consider trivial, while Orientals esteem it of deep consequence." A prince presents another prince with a fan signed by a famous painter; the signature turns out to be a forgery, and honor must be avenged. The story ends with a disemboweling, which *Theater Magazine* gingerly termed "barbaric."[26]

Winnifred's novels were still selling; sales even seemed to be growing, with her later novels doing especially well. With the exception of her one enormous best-seller, *A Japanese Nightingale,* her novels generally sold between 5,000 copies (*The Wooing of Wistaria* and *A Japanese Blossom*) and an estimated 40,000 for *Tama* and *The Honorable Miss Moonlight.*[27] Yet Winnifred was weary of turning out these books and longed for a change. So she turned to diversionary fare.

During the last years of her marriage to Babcock, Winnifred was close to her sister Sara, who also lived in New York with her husband, a German artist named Karl Bosse. A genial couple, much liked by their niece and nephews, the Bosses had a house on Staten Island. Sara and Winnifred's collaborative work came to its culmination in Winnifred's 1916 novel, *Marion,* which was Sara's story as written by Winnifred.

The first of the joint efforts by this pair of sisters was a series of cooking and entertaining articles that appeared in *Harper's Bazaar* and the *Ladies' Home Journal.* The four pieces of domestic novelty fare ran between January and October 1913. They appeared under the sole byline of Sara Bosse, but it can hardly be doubted that Winnifred had a major hand in them—she probably did the actual writing and sold the pieces to the magazines. The reason her name did not appear is obvious: the subject was Chinese cooking, and Japanese Onoto Watanna could not be suspected of knowing about things Chinese.

In 1914 the articles were shaped into book form, and *Chinese-Japanese Cookbook* was published by Rand McNally, the Chicago house that had been Winnifred's first publisher. It was one of the two or three earliest Chinese cookbooks in the United States and possibly the first Japanese one.[28] Both the sisters' names were used, Sara's first, then Onoto Watanna's, cleverly implying that the Chinese recipes were provided by Sara, the Japanese by Onoto Watanna.

With these cookery articles, Winnifred seems to have regained the frivolous, lighthearted touch that characterized her flower garden article. They have more than a touch of outrageous Onoto Watanna fantasy, going to such preposterous lengths to achieve an exotic style of entertainment that it is hard to believe they were meant to be serious. It is easy to imagine that the sisters were having fun and were highly amused by their own extravagant suggestions.

The first article, "Cooking and Serving a Chinese Dinner in America,"[29] illustrates the dawning popularity of Chinese food in an era long before Szechuan takeout was available everywhere. The American public's ignorance of Chinese food in the early decades of the century must have been profound. Yet the article informs us that "the Chinese restaurants have pushed their way out of Chinatown and are now found in all parts of the large cities of America." The article advances the myth that cooking Chinese at home has not caught on because "the average Chinese cook becomes as inscrutable as the Sphinx when asked by a 'foreign devil' for a recipe; and even when, under exceptional circumstances, he is induced to part with one, he generally leaves out a vital ingredient, so that the American seldom really obtains the true Chinese dish. That is why many who have experimented with Chinese cooking at home complain it does not taste the same as the dishes served in the Chinese restaurants" (27).

Decorating, however, came before cookery. A Chinese dinner, according to the Eaton sisters, had to be served in Chinese style. "Chinese decorations should be hung upon the walls and suspended above the tables. The wall decorations consist chiefly of ornamental scrolls, Chinese paintings on silk or gauze (they are inexpensive and very showy), Chinese embroidery, etc. The swinging decorations consist chiefly of bells and gongs, ornamental flowers, and the short Chinese swords" (27).

The recipes include such dishes as "gar grun yung waa" (bird's nest soup), "boo loo gai" (pineapple chicken), and duck chow mein. These "authentic" recipes were not learned at Grace Eaton's knee, for even if she had managed to learn any cookery in her infancy in Shanghai, chop suey did not exist there.

Heavy on the sweet and sticky, with ingredients the hapless reader was instructed to try to find in Chinese groceries, the recipes would not have been easy to produce in a 1913 kitchen. In truth, however, elaborate cookery was nothing new for *Harper's Bazaar* readers, who were in the same issues instructed how to make cakes in the shape of baseballs, custards formed into pails and shovels, and prune whip resembling a haystack.

The March article, "Giving a Chinese Luncheon Party,"[30] features a dramatic, theatrical photograph of Sara in pensive profile, wearing a kimono and cloche and holding a fan. The aim of the piece is to help the guests "become imbued with that quaint far-away feeling." Accordingly, instructions are given to "transform the most ordinary of American rooms into a Chinese dining-room. Of course all furniture should be removed or covered or hidden by screens and draperies," the reader is told. Lamps should be of solid jade, and readers must remember that "the Chinese, when entertaining outdoors, like to have a fountain close at hand, a couple of peacocks, and some Chinese pheasants," though it is noted that "these possibly are not within the means of the average housewife" (135).

The recipes, we are told with a hint of mystery and still more hokum, have never been printed before, "for the very good reason that they are secret recipes handed down from Vo Ling, a worthy descendant of a long line of noted Chinese cooks, and himself head cook to Gow Gai, the highest mandarin of Shanghai. They are all genuine, and were given to me as a special expression of respect by a near relative of the famous family of Chinese cooks" (135).

The last of the *Harper's Bazaar* articles, "Giving a Chinese Tea in America," rises to a fanatic frenzy in its decorative details:

> Chinese roses are always used on festive occasions, and they are inconceivably beautiful . . . as large and brilliant in color as peonies. . . . I attended a Chinese tea given in the studio of a famous French artist. Almost the entire room was decorated with artificial roses. . . . Our host had obtained a number of very large butterflies, and these set loose in the room fluttered gaily about the flowers. The effect was charming, refreshing, and graceful (it was a cold winter day). In China and Japan butterflies, and for outdoor entertainment fireflies, are always used at parties.[31]

The article in the *Ladies' Home Journal,* "A New Dinner for Churches and Clubs," has an ecclesiastical slant.[32] Accordingly, the writers abstained from the more highfalutin decorative fancies and tailored their recipes to a poorer audience. "A Chinese dinner, properly served in the true manner of the Middle Kingdom, would be especially appropriate if given by a missionary society engaged in foreign work," the article imaginatively suggests. Here, decorations are perfunctory, emphasizing cheapness: "ordinary punk sticks" will do for incense, though they decidedly would not have sufficed in the earlier articles. Another churchly touch, revealing a biographical detail, notes that a "most elaborate Chinese dinner was given as a mark of respect to a teacher in a little church in Montreal, Canada, by the grateful Chinese Sunday-school pupils" (113).

Some of the recipes, such as the one for chop suey, may sound mushy and bland. In truth, Winnifred's own Chinese cookery, as remembered in her Calgary home, was a byword for disaster. She boiled everything until it was inedible, and her husband Frank Reeve flatly refused to eat it, insisting on plainer fare. *Chinese-Japanese Cookbook,* however, reassures the reader that its Oriental dishes are so simple and clean, "the Westerner will cease to feel that natural repugnance which assails one when about to taste a strange dish of a new and strange land" (1).

By the time Winnifred and her sister cooked up this cookbook, Winnifred was thoroughly used to presenting a facade that bore little or no relation to the truth. This was her customary method of marketing. She approached the project, like everything else, with an eye for what would sell. Winnifred and Sara were original enough in their thinking to write one of the first Asian cookbooks in the United States, and they were canny enough in their marketing practices to be sure they obtained payments from top magazines first. In so doing, Winnifred succeeded in making some money and helped her sister achieve a little recognition and make money, too. Their conspiratorial fun must have been a welcome diversion in what was a period of family tragedy, and it paved the way for their important collaboration on one of Winnifred's most fascinating novels, *Marion.*

7. Divorce

> I've made up my mind not to bother about men at all—I've cut them out of my life for good and all.
> —Winnifred Eaton, private diary

> You can't tell me you are not going with men. I *know* you! You are a born courtesan and its impossible for you to do without them!
> —Bertrand Babcock, private diary

SEVERAL DEATHS came close together in Winnifred's family, following that of her little son Bertie in 1908. Her eldest brother, Edward Charles, died in Montreal in 1911 at the age of forty-eight; then her sister Edith died on April 7, 1914, at forty-nine; and her father, Edward, died of cancer on February 20, 1915, at seventy-six.

According to his obituary, Winnifred's brother died of "a bullet wound near his heart," from a revolver kept under his pillow. The coroner concluded that there was no reason to suspect suicide and ingeniously suggested "that in turning or twisting in bed the bed clothing or the pillow covering became entangled with the trigger, as a result of which the weapon was discharged, and the bullet entered Mr. Eaton's body." Edward Charles was known as a crack shot at the Montreal Gun Club; once before, however, he had "met with a painful accident" through the accidental discharge of his revolver.[1] If not a suicide, he was the victim of unusually bad luck in suffering two self-inflicted gunshot accidents, one fatal. What effect his death had on Winnifred we do not know; she had most likely not seen him in many years.

In 1913 Winnifred left New York to visit her old home in Montreal, taking Doris with her. It was her final visit with her father. In a last, charming glimpse of the elegant old bohemian, Doris, who was seven at the time, remembered her grandfather as a slight man with a white goatee. "He didn't know what train to meet, so he met *all* of them," she recalled.[2]

Winnifred could not have had much contact with her relatives during this period. Because of her work, her children, and the exigencies of her marriage, she seldom traveled to Montreal, and she may not have seen her sister Edith at all during the last decade of Edith's life. Edith shuttled between Seattle, Los Angeles, Boston, and Montreal, but after an 1896 visit, she did not, apparently, approach New York, Winnifred's terrain.

Edith was in Montreal at the time of a secret visit of the Chinese revolutionary leader Sun Yat-Sen, around 1900, and was one of the few who had entrée to his rooms.[3] Family legend holds that they were engaged to be married, but she broke it off because she did not want to live in China.[4]

Her fate was in her writing, though it was not until the time of her *Globe* interview in May 1912 that Edith announced the publication of her first book, a collection of Chinese American stories, *Mrs. Spring Fragrance.* She added, "I have also written another book which will appear next year, if Providence is kind." But Providence was not kind; not only did this novel not appear, but no trace of it has ever been discovered, and Sui Sin Far is known only for her single volume of stories. Yet her heartfelt joy in her accomplishment is palpable: "My people in Montreal, my mother in particular, my Chinese friends in Boston and also American friends are looking forward to the advent of *Mrs. Spring Fragrance* with, I believe, some enthusiasm. I am myself quite excited over the prospect. Would not any one be who had worked as hard as I have—and waited as long as I have—for a book!"[5]

A. C. McClurg of Chicago published twenty-five hundred copies of *Mrs. Spring Fragrance* in June 1912.[6] This was a small run, compared with the tens of thousands of copies of Winnifred's books. But the *New York Times* was respectful of Edith's achievement. Under the heading of "A New Note in Fiction," the reviewer said, "Miss Eaton has struck a new note in America. She has not struck it very easily or with surpassing skill. But it has taken courage to strike it at all."[7]

In an optimistic spirit, Edith wrote that before long, she hoped to be in China. "When I am West, my heart is East. . . . As my life began in my father's country it may end in my mother's."[8] In fact, her life ended in Montreal. The *Montreal Star* obituary related that years earlier she had suffered from inflammatory rheumatism and was left with permanent heart trouble, which recurred "just when she was really getting into the public eye." She entered the Royal Victorian Hospital for treatment, "and there working to the very end, as much as her condition allowed her, at her tales, she suddenly died at dawn."[9]

It was evidently Winnifred who wrote the *New York Times* obituary that appeared on April 9, 1914, intertwining her own legend with Edith's in confusing and extravagant terms. She noted that Edith was called the "Chinese Lily," but she also claimed that their mother was a "Japanese noblewoman," thus implying that Edith was the poseur, not Winnifred herself. Much of the piece is taken up with inventing wealth and importance for Edward Eaton, instead of concentrating on the facts and achievements of Edith's life. These are brushed off with the comment that "her short stories attracted favorable comment," quickly followed by the assertion that "one of Miss Eaton's sisters, Mrs. Bertrand W. Babcock of New York, is an author, writing under the pen name of 'Onoto Watanna.'"[10]

Amy Ling refers to Winnifred's "continuation of her deception even into the obituary of her older sister," while S. E. Solberg maintains that perhaps "the obituary should be taken as one more proof of the hostility toward Chinese-Americans against which Edith Eaton fought in her lifetime."[11]

Yet whatever Winnifred's motives for shortchanging her sister in death, she wrote more truly, if anonymously, in *Me,* published the following year: "I thought of other sisters . . . the eldest, a girl with more real talent than I, who had been a pitiful invalid all her days. She is dead now, that dear big sister of mine, and a monument marks her grave in commemoration of the work she did for my mother's country" (194).

A striking monument was later erected for Edith in Mount Royal Cemetery, next to the grave of her father, her mother, her infant siblings, and the brother who was drowned. Their low stones are overshadowed by Edith's tall, handsome black obelisk, on which is inscribed, in part, "Erected by her Chinese friends in grateful memory of Edith Eaton, Sui Sin Far." Above these words are Chinese characters meaning "It is right and good that we should remember China." Cemetery records show that permission to pour the foundation for this monument was requested in October 1927, but the identity of the "Chinese friends" responsible is unknown. According to Annette White-Parks, Edith's great-nephew L. Charles Laferrière suggested "the possibility that Winnifred, in her own trickster manner and in an attempt to atone, might have had the monument put up some years later."[12]

Edward Eaton did not long survive his eldest daughter. When he died the following February, Winnifred returned to Montreal and helped in the move, wrenching to the family, of her mother to New York City, where she was to live for the rest of her life with her youngest daughter, Beryl. Winnifred, who had put Beryl through nursing school, continued to contribute to this household financially. Grace lived in New York until she died in 1922, when her body was brought back to lie next to her husband's at the top of Mount Royal.

With this spate of family deaths, and at a time when her own marriage was collapsing, it is not surprising that Winnifred fell ill and was hospitalized, though we only know of this from her friend Jean Webster's introduction to *Me:* "The writing of this book seems to me one of the most astounding literary feats I have ever known. It is one hundred thousand words long; it was started on Thanksgiving day and finished before New Year's. . . . The author had been wrenched from her feverishly busy life to undergo an operation in a hospital; four days later she began the writing of this book." She quotes Winnifred as saying, "It seems to me as though these two weeks I have just passed in the hospital have been the first time in which I have had a chance to think in thirteen years. As I lay on my back and looked at the ceiling, the events of my girlhood came before me, rushed back with such overwhelming vividness that I picked up a pencil and began to write" (n.p.).

Why it was necessary for Jean Webster to play a part in the issuing of *Me* is not entirely clear. Winnifred was a long-established author who could get published on her own. Yet her publishers kept wanting her to write Japanese novels, and the only time she had broken away, with *The Diary of Delia,* they had forced her to use the Watanna pen name against her wishes. Jean might have acted as a go-between, arranging everything so that even the publishers did not know who the author really was. Even writing anonymously, Winnifred did not feel safe enough to reveal her true ethnicity and expose the lie she had been living.

Winnifred admired Jean Webster and looked to her as a mentor, often asking her advice although Jean was a year younger than she. Winnifred's mother-in-law teased her, saying Jean was her "oracle."[13] But Winnifred was not as sure of herself as she may have seemed, despite her successful career. She was not confident of her skills as a businesswoman or negotiator, and conscious of her ragtag upbringing, she often felt at sea about how to behave. In such matters, she turned to Jean, the supremely confident and accomplished daughter of a literary family, very likely the closest woman friend she ever had.

Jean died not long after writing her preface to *Me,* in another of the series of deaths of those close to Winnifred. The book's dedication to Winnifred's friend Lolly "who was" also includes "Jean my friend who is." But not for long.

Jean Webster was born in 1876 in Fredonia, New York. Her mother, Mark Twain's niece, had married Charles Webster, a descendant of Noah Webster, the lexicographer.[14] Twain did not live in Fredonia himself, but he settled his mother and sister there, choosing the town because he had received a pleasant reception there at a lecture he gave, "Savages of the Sandwich Isles." He thereafter made frequent visits to the town, where Bertrand Babcock was also growing up. Winnifred later knew Twain too, and Doris remembered peeping through the banisters at the great man.

Jean—like Winnifred—had early success. At Vassar she wrote a newspaper column, and in 1903, within two years of graduation, she had a best-seller with her first book, *When Patty Went to College*, a charming, high-spirited account of college adventures. Her big best-seller, *Daddy-Long-Legs*, came out in 1912 and later was a hit play. In 1915, Jean married Glenn Ford McKinney, the alcoholic son of the president of Standard Oil, after an engagement kept secret for seven years because of his unhappy first marriage. He sobered up under Jean's positive, bright-spirited influence, and they had a happy year together, which ended in her death in June 1916, the morning after she gave birth to a daughter. She was thirty-nine.

Jean Webster was, not to put too fine a point on it, of a different class than Winnifred. She came from literary aristocracy, was a brighter literary star than Winnifred, and was wealthy to boot. She was definitely privileged and had no need to claw her way to fame. She would not have clawed anyway: she was used to mannerly ways and never really lost her "Fredonia notions of propriety." Part of the easy charm of her writing style was a spirit of mischief that rebelled in the very nicest, most proper way against the rules of conventional behavior. In short, Jean was a lady; Winnifred, by the standards of the day, was not. The only acceptable ladylike occupations in 1900 were teaching, social work, nursing—and writing. Winnifred, not qualified for ladyhood by birth, elevated her social status by becoming a successful author.

Jean's busy writing years roughly corresponded to Winnifred's; between 1908 and 1912 she published four books. She also intensively studied techniques of writing for the theater. An article about Winnifred tells us, "Interested in all theatricals, she would attend the best and the lowest of New York theaters. . . . Jean Webster, author of *Daddy-Long-Legs* and niece of Mark Twain, was her constant companion."[15]

In 1915 Jean was riding high. Her play was a smash hit, and her wedding was celebrated at a friend's Connecticut house (perhaps for the same reason that Winnifred also married her second husband in Connecticut, two years later—New York State did not recognize certain divorces). The grand honeymoon was at Glenn's private game preserve north of Quebec, where Theodore Roosevelt was also vacationing.

Jean's biographer mentions that "Mrs. Babcock had often been helped by Jean and had known her for fifteen years"—in other words, since Winnifred's arrival in New York. "She's quite wonderful," Winnifred is quoted as saying. "I would do anything in the world for her."[16] In a nostalgic piece Winnifred later wrote entitled "You Can't Run Away from Yourself," she looked back on her New York years and her friendship with Jean. She remembered such things as the lights of Broadway, tea in a New York studio, and the fluttery chiffon dresses and silky things that she had once worn:

> I thought of taxicabs and Follies girls, of first nights, of the Opera, of George Cohan, of David Belasco [it's a wonder that she recalled him fondly], of pouring tea in Dan Frohman's rooms above the Lyceum. Of newspapermen with tired faces, so keenly lighting up. I had known many of them. I had indeed married one once. . . . Over and over again my mind would come back to—Jean Webster! She had been my friend for most of those years in New York—and such a friend! I thought of Jean's delicate, lovely, radiant personality and the effect it had upon my whole life. I thought of . . . beautiful things she had done. The convicts she had befriended. Of the ex-burglar with the grip in his hand whom she left waiting awhile for her with the light injunction to "Help yourself—but most of our silver is plated!" . . . Of the day when I rode up and down on the Subway holding a copy of Jean Webster's "Much Ado About Peter" conspicuously before me, my nose buried in it, and audibly chuckling, much to the interest and amusement of fellow passengers. I was a Subway "Ad" that day for Jean's book, and she responded by dropping wrappers of my next book in various prominent places on the El.[17]

The two friends obviously took a mutual glee in their simultaneous, heady success. Winnifred had, indeed, made a sensation, for in 1915 New York billboards as well as subway ads tantalized the public with such captions as "Who is the author of *Me?*"[18]

The mysterious *Me* received mixed reviews. The *Literary Digest* said there was "a compelling charm about the personality of the narrator" and that "the naivete of her actions, the unconventional way she went to meet these thrilling experiences, could be true only of a girl with such a heritage."[19] In contrast, the *New York Times Book Review* found little to praise: "It is a distinctly ungracious task to criticise the personality of a heroine who is asserted to be real."[20] The *Nation* simply stated, "Personal narratives of this type are embarrassing to the reviewer."[21]

On October 10, the *New York Times Book Review* devoted a lengthy, prominent, and witty article to answer the all-important question "Is Onoto Watanna Author of the Anonymous Novel *Me?*"[22] "So many inquiries are made about the identity of anonymous authors that there is little opportunity to reply to them all. So here are a few simple directions by which unknown geniuses may be traced to their respective lairs," the article opens wryly (869). The writer sets out a logical process, based on the geographical principle that "authors in disguising the names of cities follow parallels of latitude." The author of *Me* therefore did not come from Quebec, as was claimed in the book, but from Montreal. Since "the main heart interest" in the story was in Richmond, "the law of literary latitude" must be applied to move this location to Louisville, Ky. "Richmond is up in arms against *Me* because she believes that none of the story could have happened there, and Louisville is disturbed because there are certain of her denizens who do resemble characters in this hide-and-seek autobiography," the article suggests knowingly (870).

Concerning the author's race, the reviewer noted that "she cannot conceal the glow of pride she feels in being half Japanese. *Me,* to drop into a cheerful and ungrammatical manner, was half English and half foreign, through her mother." Nora kisses the sleeve of tall Mr. Hamilton because she is short, and it is the custom of her country. Another indication is that she took seriously the marriage proposal of the Tokyo merchant. Hot on the trail of the secret, the reviewer suggests, "Find then a half Japanese young woman, a friend of Miss Jean Webster's, formerly of Montreal and a frequent visitor in Chicago." Another clue is the reference to a Broadway play:

> That at the time which the book evidently covers no writer who was half Japanese would have neglected Japan for local color is self-evident. This brings on the almost irresistible conclusion that the creator of *Me* is none other than the author of *A Japanese Nightingale,* a novel which in 1903 was dramatized and produced as a play. . . . This gifted authoress . . . is distinctively Japanese in appearance, and in Japanese rather than American costume the charm of her personality is more fully revealed. Her knowledge of newspaper men and their ways is explained by the fact that she was married to one. [870]

This tongue-in-cheek article pretends to employ a deductive method, by talking about parallels and pen names, but the writer (anonymous himself) was probably acquainted with Winnifred or had at least seen her. He thought she looked Japanese; he knew about her friendship with Webster and her marriage, which he refers to in the past tense; and he hints that "Mr. Hamilton" makes the citizens of Louisville nervous.

Of course, with our greater knowledge, this article is a joke on itself, since Winnifred was not Japanese at all. Even though her identity was revealed (as she probably desired), her Japanese facade remained intact. Was the writer a close enough friend to be aware that she was not Japanese, and was he helping her to keep up appearances? Perhaps. By her use of anonymity, Winnifred had created a superbly provocative publicity device.

Shortly after completing *Me,* Winnifred embarked on a project of a kind that was new to her, writing a story for "motion picture serial men." She must have expected this experience to be interesting enough to be worth writing about in itself, for she kept a running diary of events.[23]

This diary was written at a key period of change and turmoil in Winnifred's life, and it provides glimpses of her disintegrating marriage, which ended soon after the diary did. It also reveals a good deal about Winnifred's work methods and her ways of making decisions and dealing with business people. Never a good businesswoman, veering from arrogance to insecurity, she relied on the more confident Jean.

Perhaps the most surprising, and rather endearing, facet of Winnifred's character that we glimpse in the diary is her flirtatious attitude toward the "movie men." With the breakdown of her marriage, Winnifred was a free woman again for the first time in fourteen years. Unaccustomed to being without a man, she was casting about for the next candidate. It is amusing to see that the girl "Nora" in *Me,* who saw every new man as a potential suitor and was born to flirt, is still virtually unchanged in Winnifred, the forty-year-old woman of the world.

At the start of her exciting first encounter with movie people, her hopes were high, as usual, but the enterprise did not pan out in the end, and only about half of the fee she negotiated on Jean's advice ever actually materialized. Her diary, peopled by such comic figures as her farcical collaborator Captain Leslie T. Peacocke, provides an absorbing glimpse of how things were done in early movie business days. "13th May—Had interview with Medill Patterson at woman's university club in regard to doing serial—movie story—went with him to Jean's house—and then to lunch at Knickerbocker Hotel. There was introduced by him to Max Annenberg—who has charge of the matter of engaging an author for this work—Also met Mr. Sheldon of the distributing firm—think they want me," she wrote.

So the adventure began. Winnifred took the precaution of asking her editor at Century if doing this type of work would hurt her "literary prestige." He thought not; many authors were doing it. And he reassured her that orders were coming in for *Me.* "Owe everything to Jean. She is an angel," Winnifred noted gratefully.

However, she anxiously wrote, "Bert is ugly about this matter. He insinuates things about me—and thinks I should not have lunched with men." He was definitely cramping her style, and at a time when she could not afford to be distracted by his nonsense. "Mr. Patterson called me on 'phone & requested me to turn in by tomorrow a scenario of a story—It will mean quick money work I must say," she noted. Luckily, that evening "Bert went out thank heaven, so I had a chance to work."

The next day, Patterson, Annenberg, and Sheldon wanted to see her for a conference, and Winnifred did not know what to do. Jean had gone out of town, and she could not have the movie men in her apartment, with or without Bert. So she arranged to meet them at a friend's studio. Patterson read the scenario she had constructed overnight and gave her one by "Captain

Peacock [*sic*], a professional moving picture scenario writer" to read. Patterson had a contract to use Peacocke's scenario, but he wanted to "try" Winnifred as well. She was asked what her price would be, but did not feel able to answer this question without Jean's advice, so she promised to name her price the next day.

After the meeting, Winnifred dropped the men off at their hotel in a taxi and went on home to face Bert again. "Bert very ugly—Sneers at this kind of work & hints I am flirting with these men," she wrote. She was tired from the excitement and anxious as to how it would all turn out.

The following day, May 15, in a flurry of phone calls, Winnifred plunged into negotiations. She "mentioned" $10,000, and Annenberg said it was too much. He suggested $7,500, but she was not so keen. In the evening they dined at Luchow's and agreed on $8,500—$1,000 down, $6,500 on August 1, and a bonus of another $1,000 if the serial was a success. She was given a contract, to be signed Monday. Annenberg thought she ought to see a serial play, so they saw the latest Vitagraph movie, *The Goddess*, which in Winnifred's judgment was "very poor."

The movie men brought her home late, at a quarter of ten, and a truly terrible scene ensued:

> I saw Bert on steps, so fearing Annenberg would see him I had them let me off at corner. I was so afraid he would do something before these men & I would lose my contract. I ran up the street. Bert—had a taxi at door. He was drunk & wild with rage—tried to force me into taxi. I resisted & he kicked & beat me on the steps. Mrs. Bandelli let me in. My dress torn off my back—He attacked her too—I ran back & locked myself in. He called me all kinds of names—finally he went. It was terrible—I found he had destroyed lots of my things. He had gone to all the boarders and said I was doing this and that!
>
> He was thrown out of the Knickerbocker & Baltimore when he went to seek me there—This is the last—I am *done* with him. He has beaten me for the last time. All the house is in an uproar about it—the men say they'll kill him.

The next day, Sunday, Winnifred was ill all day, "feverish and in an hysterical condition." She had not slept all night; her body was black and blue; and she felt weak, hardly able to stand up. Mrs. Bandelli got a warrant for Babcock. Winnifred's friends Sam Webster (Jean's brother), Charlie Jones, and Billy Morett—all men, and doubtless enthralled by the exciting drama, which Winnifred was at no pains to conceal—came over and "took care" of her all day, in shifts. They brought a doctor to examine her, and she was given a sleeping potion. She made the most of the sympathy and attention.

She vowed again, "I'm done with Bert forever—this is the last straw. I've had fifteen years of hell & my goodness has been rewarded in this way—he is a madman—Oh! I *hope* they did not see him. Suppose it altered the plans & the contract's not signed yet!"

On Monday morning she awoke feeling much better, her energy and joie de vivre fully restored. She signed the contract, and once that was safely done, she could follow her natural exhibitionistic instincts and display her bruises, no longer fearing to lose her assignment. "After it was all signed I *told* them and showed them my arms. They were stunned. They said they would like to kill him," she reported with relish. Gallantly, Annenberg made another contract with her, to do a sequel, twenty chapters at $500 a chapter. She was pleased. "So, you see, I've two contracts instead of one—These men are all good and kind & I think I've made them my staunch friends. When one has lived with a wild fiend *real* men seem pretty good to me."

She dined with all the movie men at Delmonico's, and they went to see one of their serials, *The Diamond in the Sky.* "Tying one on," they went next to the Midnight Follies. "Oh how tired I was—but I humored them and went along," she wrote. Afraid to go home, she took a room at the Knickerbocker.

On Tuesday morning, she joined Annenberg at breakfast, and he and the other men departed for Chicago.[24] Winnifred was left to write eighty thousand words by August 1, two months off. This was to be done under the direction of Captain Peacocke, and they were to start working the next morning at eleven. She noted, "Bert sent me five letters begging forgiveness. I can forgive—but *never* will I live with him again. I've cut him clean out of my life."

The next day, however, Peacocke did not show up. She called his apartment, but he was not there. His wife did not know where he was, but Winnifred had heard that he was apt to drink and disappear for days at a time. Could this be one of the times, just now, when the work was so important? "Oh dear! It would be dreadful if things slipped up now," she agonized. She waited all day, but there was no word from him.

On Thursday, Mrs. Peacocke phoned to say that her husband had been called away to Atlantic City, so Winnifred decided to go visit the farm where her boys were staying. (Perry was then nearly twelve years old, and Charley was almost eight.) Nine-year-old Doris was with her mother, and Winnifred recounted, "Doris went out—on street & told Bert we were going there. I whipped her for that. And we could not go—for I knew he'd go out there. He is in a state of remorse—but it does not touch me now. . . . He has done these things too often." She cheered herself up by buying a pretty new hat and two dresses, sent home twenty dollars "to pay for my sister's new baby," and dined with women friends. The next day, although it was raining, she and Doris went to the farm, where she found the boys looking fine.

On Friday, back in the city, she finally got ahold of Peacocke, and he told her he had been "sick in bed" for several days, contradicting the Atlantic City story. Clearly he was prone to go on benders, and Winnifred was worried. "I don't know what to do," she wrote. "We *must* start work. He says he'll be able to tomorrow. I certainly hope so."

They did start work, for the diary breaks off for a month. "I have been working very hard," Winnifred resumed. "We turn out two installments a week—It is rush work—very rough and bad—I am not happy about it. Inconceivably lurid & wild melodrama—revolting situations—wish I'd never undertaken the work."

The only good part of the business was that the men she worked for were "the salt of the earth." "We have no men in New York like these Chicago fellows—I've met a good many of them—have had lunch—dinner—taken drives with a number of them, & love them all—even Annenberg with his coarse jokes and bold sort of lovemaking. He has a good heart at bottom with all his surface roughness & I don't believe he'd hurt a flea—Great character for some story."

She followed a routine, getting up at 5 A.M., exercising with dumbbells, and having a cold water bath. Then she wrote until noon, when she dictated to her stenographer until Peacocke arrived. "If only I could follow my own synopsis," she complained. "If only they had allowed me to furnish the rest. But—no! They give me this weird crazy synopsis, and from day to day I go almost following the stuff Capt. Peacock plans out for me." She tried to put in material of her own, but in giving the "movie men" what they wanted, she found herself "dropping into a habit of thought along those lines," which she loathed.

The whole story revolted her. "The situations in this story are so screechingly funny & improbable—where they are meant to be the most serious & tragic that all the Irish in me flows to the tiptop & I'm saved from despair by my own laughter," she wrote. As for her co-writer, "Capt. Peacock is a joke. He's very tall & wears impossible waistcoats & noisy panamas with bright bands on them. He has been an actor & looks it! We get on fine together & I could have all kinds of a flirtation with him if I wanted—I can see that—but—no! He's not my 'kind' even if I . . . and then besides we must work and not be diverted. I'm determined to grow up—that's the worst of woman & men—working together—the ever-lasting sex *will* come up."

Certainly, it would come up when the woman was Winnifred; however, there was no danger of her dallying with the ridiculous Captain Peacocke. "Thinks *he* is leading in this work—ahem! I've got the reins in hand just like on a horse," she preened herself. Still, there was no getting away from the "rotten stuff" they were turning out. "He keeps insisting that it is the sort of stuff they want for the movies," she sighed.

At last Jean Webster returned to town. "As she put it, to cast a material eye upon my efforts." They went for an auto trip to Stamford, Connecticut, and Winnifred wrote that she suspected her relations with Glenn McKinney. "Dear little Jean—she deserves only the best of everything." Since Jean had carried on a secret engagement with McKinney for many years and was to marry him three months later, it may seem that her degree of intimacy with Winnifred was not that great; but Jean kept her affair with a married man strictly hidden from the world.

Jean and her friends, not surprisingly, "screamed with laughter" when Winnifred related the story of her movie writing experience. "Well, it is funny, no mistake," she said ruefully.

Captain Peacocke was telling her daily that the serial would never be produced, that serials were "a drug on the market," so they needn't take such pains. He was pessimistic and gloomily said they had better make sure of the money. She was sure the movie men were "all right." One of them, Jimmy Sheldon, was "just about the squarest, dearest man I've met in a long while & I'm half in love with him—only it's in the right way—Here's a man just devoted to his wife & children & yet—brimming over with liking and healthy sentiment for all women. . . . You're safe enough from me however—I may be at the dangerous age—but I'm dangerous only to myself."

Winnifred was still being bombarded by letters from Bert. "Poor fellow—my heart aches for him—but—what *can* I do—he is unbalanced. I can't go back to him. The very fury of his love for me is a sort of madness—I'm really not strong enough to stand all that emotion. I work too hard—my energy and force must go into my work," she concluded.

She then made an extraordinary declaration, hilariously unconvincing: "I've made up my mind not to bother about men at all—I've cut them out of my life for good and all—Anyway—that part of me is dead & it is seventeen years since I loved a man and I guess I'm all through with that now—I did make an honest effort to love Bert & be a good wife to him—but—oh!" "Seventeen years since" was 1898, the Mr. Hamilton era; but there are secrets of Winnifred's heart that we will never know.

The next day she ran into Bert on the street, and he shouted, "You can't tell me you are not going with men. I *know* you! You are a born courtesan and it's impossible for you to do without them!" Winnifred jumped into a taxi and fled. But the incident disturbed her deeply, and she queried her diary anxiously, "Now—*am* I a born 'bad woman.'—I don't know—Perhaps

I am & I think though I'm not *bad* in character—I *am* too easy & free in my talk with men—An unconscious familiarity established at outset between me & men. Perhaps they despise me for that & I don't mean to be coarse."

Bert told her he was having her watched, because "he says my kind of woman *must* have men." Winnifred ruefully admitted, "That's pretty bad. I think about that some, and last night I cried when I went to bed." Surely, Bert was wrong. "I'm not bad. I'm a good woman, fundamentally good," Winnifred assured herself. But she hated living alone; the only thing that kept up her spirits was her work. When discussing her situation with the attractive, married Jimmy Sheldon, she begged him not to judge her by any "ordinary standards." She was still Winnie, sure she was different and special.

Bert begged once more to be forgiven. He realized, now, that for fourteen years he had "entertained an angel unawares." The sweet words won him some sympathy, but she did not change her mind. "Poor Bert—! he has done terrible things but—he is his own worst enemy, & then after all he is the only person in the world who really loves me," Winnifred reflected. But then she thought about someone else. "Sometimes I think that *He* loves me still—And then I won't think about that. . . . That's all dead, that part of my life—*He* thinks I am a happily married woman, the mother of little children. . . !" As it was once asked, "Who is *Me?*" we may ask, "Who was *He?*" but in vain.

Winnifred amused herself by writing descriptions of the men for whom she was working. She saw a good deal of them when they were in town, but she feared that they said flattering things to her merely because she was "their author." "I suppose they think it necessary to 'jolly' me & keep me good-natured," she mused. "Wish they *really* liked me."

J. Medill Patterson was "a long green sort of man," sarcastic, clever, blunt, and a rich socialist, which she thought was "a joke." Still, she liked him and thought it was too bad he was rich; otherwise, he would probably be a successful author. She believed that financial need kept people writing—it was what drove her so feverishly. And she "laughed internally" at lunch when Patterson said he was no longer interested in women and that the "riotous desires of youth" were all quite dead in him. "I wonder if that was a sort of warning to me to 'Keep off the grass'!" she wondered. "Men are funny geese."

Max Annenberg was "a crude mixture of shrewdness & big heartedness, a unique character full of power & energy." It would, she thought, be dangerous to know him too well. "He has a habit of forcing forbidden subjects in conversation. . . . He is no more in love with me than the man in the moon, yet every time he is with me he manages to begin on that. . . . All this is pure *junk.* I string him along & he strings me." Familiar as he was in his speech, she would trust herself anywhere with him. "Some men of his sort think me pretty sharp. I dare say if I was a whaling desirable beauty—which I'm not—alas!—I'd not be quite so safe with Max!" she thought regretfully.

Another of the men, John Burnham, spelled danger. He was her kind, the sort of man she used to get "sweet" on, long ago. "He's what men call 'a good fellow.' A big spender, generous, rather bohemian. There's something lovable about him," she concluded wistfully. "Wish he liked me! What a fool I am!"

As he was about the fourth man she was speculating romantically about, even Winnifred herself suspected that this was excessive. But she was comforted by an artist friend, Charlie Jones, who vowed that if she ever went back to Bert, he would not forgive her. "He understands me like an old grandma," she wrote. "It's queer, I used to think Charlie cared a lot for me—He was always kissing my hands—& made a fuss about Bert &—But no! Charlie is just a queer aesthetic exquisite—interested in me only as he is in his Oriental collections. He once said I was a finishing touch to his studio." Gay male friends were not out in the open in 1915, and Winnifred seems innocent on the subject. "It's queer, I'm not a bit in love with Charlie—yet I go to him about—everything."

But she was describing her "bosses." Who was next? "Ah, Jimmy! The last and best. Lucky Mrs. Jimmy."

This pleasant line of thought was rudely interrupted by what Winnifred proclaimed, "A tragedy! I'm fired! I take back all the nice things I said of these men I was working for! They have hurt me hard. I've got a lump as big as an egg in my throat." In this emergency, she went to see Jean Webster, who "read a lecture" to her. Winnifred also consulted her sister Grace, the lawyer, who advised her to take a firm stand.

Jean's advice was sage: "Above all things be dignified. Don't be so *familiar* in your interviews with men." Winnifred rather endearingly pleaded, "Oh Jean—I can't help it—I don't know why—but—somehow men don't respect me. Gee, they all call me Winny." Jean said haughtily, "Do you suppose any of them would call *me* Jean?" One would rather suppose that, with her engaging girlish charm, people certainly would call her Jean; but evidently in business, Jean's innate propriety came to the fore.

Winnifred recounted, characteristically and amusingly:

> Anyway, I promised to be firm & dignified & armed with this resolve I forthwith went forth for an interview with Mr. Sheldon & I was firm & dignified just about two minutes. Jimmy disarmed me at the outset & there's something peculiarly *honest* and *dear* about him, & I don't know why—(goodness knows I'm not even a speck in *love* with him) but I almost feel like a mother to him. He

> looks like a nice clean chubby blonde boy—They say he was once a famous football player & I can just imagine him playing—Anyway he had hardly begun to talk to me when I realized that Capt. Peacock was wrong. Jimmy was telling me the straight talk—as he said, "All my cards are on the table Winny"—And the truth was that our serial was "*rotten!*"

Hurt in her professionalism, Winnifred reflected, "If I could, I would not accept payment for the work at all." But she quickly turned to self-justification: "It's really not my fault if their scenario was so bad. I tried to tell them that from the first." Anyway, it was over. She cried, partly because of the money and partly because she did not "make good."

Jimmy Sheldon, she thought, was sorry for her. She saw in his face he didn't give a rap about Peacocke; it was *her* he was worrying about. "Damn sentiment anyhow," Winnifred lamented, "if I wasn't a weak mushy fool . . . I could probably make them carry out their contract." Still, the heart was knocked out of her. What if she lost her "prestige as an author of any real worthwhile standing"? She had failed, and she was mortified. "I never failed before! I wish I were dead! I hope they don't despise me for writing all that drivel; oh dear!" she wailed.

Winnifred went to see her "exquisite" friend Charlie, who was sorry for her. "Poor little Winny," he said, "here, I'll make you some Turkish coffee." Then he told her she wasn't to fret a bit; he read her hand (he was a great palmist) and envisaged nothing but good fortune.

Winnifred was cheered by letters from the movie producer Colonel William Selig, and she decided to go to Chicago and try her luck there. On the advice of her sister Grace, she would establish residence in that city, with an eye to divorce. Grace told her that if Bert contested her suit, she should drop it; all the "infernal deviltry" in a man comes up during a divorce action, and Winnifred would be pilloried "however innocent of any wrong."

She met with Colonel Selig, who made her promise to work for only him; perhaps he would produce *Tama*. He, too, showed a protective interest in her and insisted that she move to another hotel, the La Salle, where all the film people stayed. His chief scenario writer, Gilson Willits, reserved her a room next to his. She had known Gilson for eighteen years, since her old Chicago days, but had not seen him for a long time. He hugged her when they met, they dined together, and he would slip notes under her door, with just one eloquent sighed word on them: "Dearie!"

She and this old friend had long talks. He said she was too analytical, "an animated questioning point—that I never can love any man because I have probed down into the whys and wherefores of everything. Little he knows me!! Men are queer! Unless one falls in love with him a man imagines one is cold to other men too." Gilson was a poor old dear, and romance was out of the question. Every day he asked her, "When are you going to give me the 'high sign?'" and she countered with, "What's that?" "Well—you know—Why—a sign that I may make love to you."

Winnifred just laughed at him. Definitely, she had fun in Chicago, where she recalled gay scenes of her youth. "I had a proposal!" she announces, though she is discreet about who made it. This occurred when a man took her out to see his horse farm, and he had to change a tire, which he did with some discomfort, being plump. "It's the only work I think he ever did in his life & I poked fun at him about it—I who have worked all my life," she said. Later, he asked her, "When will you get the divorce?" And she replied, "Quien sabe?"

At this, Winnifred thought better of her indiscretions and tore out the page. "After all this isn't a journal," she reprimanded herself. "I set out just to chronicle my experience writing a movie scenario. Personal affairs are out of place!"

And she added her valedictory, "Goodbye nice Chicago men—I kiss to you tips of my fingers—You're a good lot! May you get a 'corking good' story to recompense you for the disappointment of mine." But she left Jimmy Sheldon a note: "Please don't like this new author better than Me."

"I want to add just one more thing," she earnestly wrote in her diary. "These men lost about $5000 or more on this deal. Nevertheless they lost it like sports—of course as Peacock said it was nothing to them—Still some men might have been mean about it. Instead they were just as nice to me when it was finished as when they were expecting big things of me & I'll not forget something Burnham said to me on the telephone that did much to heal my very sore heart. He said 'We're all in love with you!'" But instead of accepting the compliment, a Winnifred grown cynical commented shrewdly, "Now, that's a safe thing to say. When a man says 'We' instead of 'I' he knows its pretty safe—Nevertheless I was glad he said that."

Seldom does Winnifred reveal herself so artlessly as in this diary about her tragicomic adventure in movie serial writing, written when her life was in a state of flux and uncertainty. Her reflexive, innate flirtatiousness showed how badly she needed, at this transitional period, to be considered attractive and worthwhile. This is the same trait that the girl in *Me,* her younger self, possesses. It would seem that Winnifred had not matured at all; but perhaps a better explanation is that she wrote *Me* when she was freeing herself from her miserable marriage, and her sense of the freedom, adventure, and possibilities in life gave the book its freshness and vigor.

"I know what's the trouble with me," she wrote. "Bert has shut me up for years in a box and I haven't got out & met or mixed with men in years. I feel like a colt let loose—" This is an accurate and shrewd summation of the reason for her regarding all the men she met with exactly the same eye she had when she was twenty, looking on everyone as a potential lover. After years in an abusive marriage, she was desperate for men's approval, validation. In writing about her naive young heroine's susceptibility to men, Winnie was only describing herself—as she still was. To have a Mr. Hamilton, a fairy godfather, a Daddy-Long-Legs, to take care of her and solve all her problems, to nostalgically remember a long-ago lover, must have been a pleasant fantasy in the midst of perplexity; but the strong moral feelings with which Winnifred continually struggled prohibited her heroine from loving an adulterer in *Me* and kept Winnifred continually assailing herself with guilt, even while contemplating the temptations of attractive married men.

The serial Winnifred and Peacocke had been working on had two working titles, *Gold* or *Who Killed Peter Cramp?* The script's heading called it a "Synopsis of Photoplay Serial in 16 Episodes by Captain Leslie T. Peacocke and written into Serial Fiction Form for Newspaper Syndication by Onoto Watanna."

Winnifred's publicity clippings claim that she won a $10,000 prize in a serial contest from the *Chicago Tribune,* though her diary makes no mention of this. Writing about her serial experience much later, she said that she was hired to write twenty-eight installments within two months. "I became a sort of mental machine. . . . The work was not pleasant and violated every literary ideal I possessed." She was given endless conflicting advice by the men concerned, and "my head used to reel with the weird, wildly exciting and lurid incidents that seemed to be the thing desired for a motion picture serial." With some bitterness, she pointed out that the "pretty faced actress" who played the heroine received $150,000, compared with her $10,000.

Elsewhere, Winnifred claimed that she wrote the first two episodes of the early serial film *Gloria's Romance* (1916), filmed with Billie Burke.[25] Her name does not officially appear in connection with this work, but she may have worked uncredited. *Gloria's Romance* was a sensational tale about a hoyden who gets into scrapes in the Everglades, "with their interesting denizens of alligators, crocodiles and Seminoles."[26]

It is not impossible that Winnifred won a contest. Throughout the 1910s and 1920s, new "writing talent" was constantly being discovered. As late as 1922, Goldwyn Pictures and the *Chicago Daily News* ran a contest whose top prize was $10,000; it attracted 27,000 submissions. The winner came out of a screenwriting program whose most successful graduate, C. Gardner Sullivan, was later Winnifred's boss at Universal Studios. Fan magazines heavily touted the freelance screenwriting market. In 1919, Anita Loos and John Emerson, for example, wrote a series of articles offering practical advice on photoplay writing. Thousands of people tried their luck.

Through such means, prospective students were, as Anne Moey put it, "suckered" into "believing that there was room for them in an industry that had actually become, by the early 1920s, hierarchical and closed to the unconnected, untrained, and naive."[27] That did not apply to Winnifred, whose professional talents were inevitably pushing her toward Hollywood.

Even though the serial was not a success, *Me* was, and Winnifred followed it up the next year, 1916, with her second autobiographical novel, *Marion.* A letter from her literary agent Paul R. Reynolds, addressed to her new flat on Riverside Drive, New York,[28] informed her that *Hearst's Magazine* agreed to pay $7,500 for the serial publication of *Marion*—a bonanza.

Since Winnifred had run out of her own early adventures and was particularly close to her sister Sara, it was natural to turn to Sara's own girlhood for subject matter. This contained, if anything, even more daring material than Winnifred's own story. Winnifred also contemplated a sequel to *Marion,* to be entitled *In the Nude,* but this was never written.

Me and *Marion* brought in a comfortable enough sum for Winnifred to go to Reno and finally divorce Bertrand Babcock. She was in Reno when she received the news of Jean Webster's death, and in July 1916 she wrote a sad letter to Jean's sister-in-law. "I don't know if I'll come back now," she wrote, "I really loved Jean more than anyone, and I feel as badly as if I had lost a child of my own." No one would ever know how good Jean had been to her. "I used to wonder why she bothered with me at all, for you know how I used to go to her about nearly all my troubles—most of them I suppose of my own making," she wrote ruefully. "Jean always had such a *sane* little head." She exclaimed, "I had an instinctive *fear* of something like this." With questionable sincerity, she added, "I wish I could have gone in her place."[29]

Instead of dying, Winnifred was starting over. She established residence in Reno with her children, now ages thirteen, ten, and eight. It was in Reno that a photograph of her kneeling on a lawn, wearing a kimono, was taken. There is nothing artificial or Japanese about her pose; she merely looks like a relaxed, fortyish woman with high animal spirits, cheerful and optimistic, as different from the hard-pressed, tense, brittle, anxious novelist-about-New-York as can be imagined.

8. Calgary Writer

"You can't run away from yourself."
—Winnifred Reeve, unpublished manuscript

IN 1916, THE TRAIN journey to Reno took several days. Soon after her arrival, Winnifred rented a house and put her children in the local schools for the duration of their six months' residence. For the children it was a carefree time. Used to the confines of New York City apartment dwelling, along with the tensions of their mother's hard work and their father's abuse, they enjoyed running free and spending happy days on horseback.

Reno also had many attractions to appeal to Winnifred, who was exhilarated by a western landscape and way of life. The change would have been appealing after her fifteen hectic, stormy, exciting but often unhappy years in New York City. A stay in Reno was no hardship; the city was set up to make the stay of divorcing ladies and gentlemen as pleasant as possible. A promotional booklet, *Reno Reveries,* advised the sojourner, "Why mope? Surprise yourself by rising early in the morning and gaze from your hotel window toward the south. Notice the ever-changing colors on the snow-clad mountains and fill your starved, city-cursed lungs with Nevada's life-giving air."[1]

There were bathing resorts—and Winnifred always enjoyed resorts, hot springs, and spas. There were cafes and restaurants, where, as the jolly little booklet full of matrimonial jokes put it, "you will see famous and beautiful women dining with sons of the sagebrush or Eastern gentlemen who also belong to the 'Separation Squad.' . . . Notice new combinations forming all the time. What brings them here to Reno? Why are such attractive women apparently unappreciated? Whom will they marry?" There was no reason to be miserable during one's Reno stay, and the travel guides featured jokes aplenty. (Judge: "How long have you been here?" Haughty "New Yawk" lady on witness stand: "Six months and ten minutes.") Reno prided itself on being a town so cosmopolitan it was impossible to be bored there. Day trips included such jaunts as a "journey to the old camp of Virginia, where over seven hundred millions in gold have been extracted."[2] We may be sure that Winnifred's new swain, Frank Reeve, who was a man of action, spent some of his Reno stay enjoying such activities.

Winnifred would certainly have agreed with the promotional writer who opined that for the student of human nature Reno provided "the most wonderful tangle of human problems that ever existed. There is an undercurrent of intrigue, an element of comedy, a world of tragedy spread for your continued amusement. And the heart interest." All this was on display nightly at the Liberty Cafe, with its "Look 'em over Room," where the men would look through the long window on the front to see if there were any "dolls" newly arrived in town. There was also a dimly lighted "Romance Room."[3]

Winnifred made notes for a sensational story that she projected as "a novel of the divorce colony of Reno," called *City of Restless Love.* But she never finished it, probably because she was "too busy living a romance to write one."[4]

Her divorce decree was granted on February 3, 1917, and Winnifred was awarded custody of the children. Meanwhile, Frank Reeve's own divorce proceeded apace. His wife, Florence, who had left him for another man, was to have their home on Greene Avenue in Brooklyn and a sum of $3,000. They had no children.

Whatever else Winnifred did in Reno—visited hot springs or explored mines—one event was momentous: while she was divorcing her first husband, she met and fell in love with her second. This cozy set of circumstances would have been considered the height of brittle, shocking sophistication at the time.

Her children overwhelmingly approved of Frank. Doris believed that he wanted to marry Winnifred because he loved her children, and Winnifred often told the story of how little Charley blackmailed Frank to promote the marriage with "Gimme ten cents or I won't ask my mother to marry you today." It was hardly any wonder the children begged her to marry the kind, vigorous, genial, generous, fair-minded Frank, who was so utterly unlike their own brutal, drunken father. But despite the children's wishes, Winnifred's decision was not easily made.

A glimpse of the state of flux in her life and mind can be seen in a letter she wrote to Frank, who had gone to Toronto in January.[5] "Now Frank, I'm not going to get married to you or anyone else. I'm going to stay free—for a year anyway, and I'll be satisfied with my Reno decree. I am going to work for those Film men," she told him. Mr. Sheldon was telegraphing her money. "So, you see, I'll have to work for them. I had already put your check through the bank, but I'll pay you back." So Frank was already giving Winnifred money; and she was taking it from two other sources as well, the "movie men" and another lover, John Mercer. Mercer, who was based in New York and worked for South American Mining, was one of her marriage candidates during this period, as was her old friend Tom Steep. When she had gone to Reno, she had thought it might be Steep she would marry after her divorce, but she assured Frank that she was "not in love with him, only grateful for how good he had been" to her. Steep and she had "agreed to consider one another free."

What savings Winnifred had stored up to support her in Reno were dwindling, and she was anxious for security. Now officially single, with three children to support, she was unsure if she wanted work or a husband, but she resisted lapsing into the status of a paid mistress. She told Frank, "I couldn't go on like that. It would kill me. I know you've done everything you could, and all for my best good, but, dear boy, I can't help the situation, and I cannot afford to stay here longer, either as dependent upon you or John Mercer." It was different with the business men: "I can work for them, and earn what they pay me." She was "practically broke," and Babcock was not contributing to the children's support. Her literary agent, Paul Reynolds, had not sold her story about Reno, and it was urgently necessary that she get "into harness" again, taking an executive position "with these men who have already had me, and who want me again."

Winnifred had written to the "movie men" on Frank's account (she said) as much as her own: she did not want to be such a financial strain on him. "It would be madness on your part to marry a woman in my position," she protested. "I wouldn't take a position after I was married, though I would go on with my writing. You will need all your own money, dear Frank, to start again, and I feel like a pig to have already taken some of it—but soon you will have it back, and I'll never forget."

She understood that Frank loved her and wanted to help, but "it would be a poor sort of return on my part to ruin you," she pointed out. "My default decree, as you say, doesn't leave me free to marry in New York. Very well then, I'll work for a time, and then if I decide to marry, will come back here. But I cannot stay any longer. I cannot take people's money and not pay it back—and the people who send it I must work for—do you see? I am almost passionately honest in this way."

When people protest that they are passionately honest, one's antennae go up. Winnifred's behavior, borrowing money from various men to keep her in Reno, may have been somewhat more acceptable at a time when women were accustomed to depending on men and had fewer financial options. A woman's distress brought out the chivalry—and money—in men, and even though accepting money from her gentleman friends might be at odds with her own self-image as a successful independent businesswoman, when pressed and desperate, she took what she needed.

It was only a matter of time before Winnifred, a new divorcée, married someone. For a forty-one-year-old mother of three, which was considered more advanced middle age than it is today, she had an impressive number of potential husbands in reserve. She would not necessarily marry the richest man—she was enough of a romantic that being swept off her feet was a basic requirement—but the decision she made about her future was important. In the end, it was Frank Reeve who was the most determined suitor of all, and he won Winnifred's hand.

Frank wrote from Toronto in February, "I hope that I have the good fortune to finish my mission of finding a ranch soon so that I can be with you at an early date. We do not fully realize what we mean to each other until parted. . . . Darling we have not known one another long but we have had many delightful moments and have come to be very dear and near to each other. I love you more and more as the moments go by."[6]

Frank and Winnifred were married in Greenwich, Connecticut, on March 26, 1917, rather than in New York, because New York did not recognize out-of-state divorces. Frank's age is given as thirty-nine, hers as thirty-eight (a subtraction of three years). He listed his occupation as "Transportation," she gave hers as "Authoress." Unusually, she gave her correct birthplace, Montreal, a sign that the changes in her life would be so sweeping that she need no longer worry about such matters as her Japanese pose.

Her new husband, Francis Fournier Reeve—Winnie's Frank—was born January 31, 1878, at Riverhead, Long Island. His parents were farmers, with eleven children, though only five lived to adulthood. Frank went to sea in the Merchant Marine and began as cook on a tugboat, but being an energetic, enterprising worker, by age twenty-five he had become vice president of the flourishing Red Star Towing and Transportation Company.

Frank also served in the National Guard Cavalry in New York. Later, when he went to Reno, he was one of a group of men who started a National Guard Cavalry to chase Pancho Villa along the border—Villa was sought by General John J. Pershing in 1916, and the whole National Guard was mobilized against him. However, Frank, being a careful man, did not go so far as to leave the state and jeopardize his divorce.

When Winnifred met Frank, he had sold out his interests in the tugboat company in a disagreement with his partners, who he felt were not competitive enough. He decided that after his divorce was settled, he would find something else to do. Once, on a trip to Florida to negotiate contracts, Frank had met Alberta farmers who had impressed him about prospects there. Wheat prices were sky high during World War I, so Frank thought he would try Alberta. He knew how to farm, and he and his nephew Roswell decided to pool their capital and buy a farm there. When Frank sold his tugboat interest, he had about $50,000 (Winnifred exaggerated it into "a couple of hundred thousand"), and he and his new wife went to Calgary together.

Frank and Winnifred were an odd pair. He was tall and blond, she was short and dark. He was methodical and businesslike, with a great deal of common sense and a genius for finance; Winnifred was mercurial and impulsive, had little understanding of business, and had no money sense at all. Their temperaments either complemented each other or clashed, depending on how you looked at it; she liked to tease and goad him, and he would typically clam up and be silent. He was a very quiet man, but generous and genial; he believed in fair play. However, he had a temper and could be stubborn.

Frank might seem an odd choice for Winnifred, with her literary interests; most of the men who had interested her had been journalists or educated university types. But Frank, a self-made, self-educated, contemplative man, was a great reader, who particularly enjoyed reading books about the Civil War. "Both my father and grandfather fought in the Battle of the Wilderness," he liked to recall.[7] He bought all the Harvard Classics and methodically read his way through them. There is no doubt that he was bowled over by Winnifred from the first and that he remained so for the rest of their lives. He was anxious to leave New York, partly on her account, for Winnifred desperately wanted to leave her memories of Babcock behind.

The first winter at the farm in Alberta was difficult. Being housebound in snowy, remote cattle country was like nothing she had ever experienced, and during subsequent winters she remained in Calgary, taking a house there. Roswell did much of the labor on the farm, and the following year, the Reeves bought a ranch, incorporating a company of both the farm and ranch.

These early years were hard, and the ranch ultimately failed because the prices of wheat and beef declined after the war. Frank lost as much as $25,000 in a single shipment going from Calgary to Chicago in 1921. In 1924, he faced foreclosure and had to sell the ranch. Frank then took a job in a stockbrokerage firm on the Calgary Exchange. Later he bought a seat on the exchange and founded the firm F. F. Reeve and Company. He made a small fortune in the boom of the late 1920s, and, foreseeing the stock market crash, he sold off his margin accounts and remained in good shape, keeping his brokerage business open while shifting his attention to the oil business. He and two friends held a lease in the Turner Valley, where major oil was found in 1936, and they sold it to a developer for a large royalty on production. The well was a huge one, the biggest in that field to that date, producing over three thousand barrels a day of high-grade crude. This gave Frank money to buy control of Commonwealth Petroleum Ltd. in 1937 and to establish a drilling company, Commonwealth Drilling, which expanded enormously after the war to become the largest drilling company in Canada and Commonwealth's main revenue producer. Frank, the president of this company, was an enormously wealthy man by the end of his life.

But that was far in the future. In 1917, when Winnifred and Frank first went to Alberta, their fortunes were still uncertain, and they lived simply. The children went to school in Calgary, first to Mount Royal College and then to South Calgary High. The Calgary house was a modest frame house on an unpaved street. The farm house, with its large barn, was fifteen miles northeast of Calgary, while the Bow View Ranch was forty miles west of Calgary, on the Banff road, which was not the bustling highway of today but a remote place, back of beyond.

Winnifred wrote a good deal about the hard work on the farm and ranch, but this was relative—she always had help, including a housekeeper, and the Reeves enjoyed many comforts, even while "roughing it" in their first ranch years. Winnifred always dressed fashionably and had friends from the East to stay in Calgary; photographs show social groups in stylish flapperesque clothing or smart riding outfits, on horseback or relaxing on the porch, clearly having fine times together.

During these early Calgary years of her "first marriage" to Frank, Winnifred, in addition to helping run a farm and a ranch, looking after her lively children, and participating in Frank's business, kept up her writing. Her reminiscent "Starving and Writing in New York" piece, in which she looked back affectionately on the now long-ago days of her youthful travails, dates from this time, and in 1919 she wrote a lengthy two-part story for *MacLean's Magazine*, "Lend Me Your Title."

"Lend Me Your Title" was a stilted and artificial concoction, and it probably was enough to convince her that her writing was not going well. Later she rewrote it as a play, and it enjoyed some success in summer theaters. The story is told solely in dialogue, but with only one side of the conversation—an experiment that does not work at all well. Kitty tells Dick, her sweetheart, why she can't marry him: a cattle-rancher uncle left Kitty's poor family ten million dollars on condition that she marry a man of title. Dick travels to Japan, where his manservant is a Japanese count. On his return, Dick disguises himself as Japanese, uses the count's title, and persuades Kitty to marry him. Her mother is aghast and rails with melodramatic passion: "He has hypnotized you—yes, practised some wicked Oriental art upon you. He is a rat—a snake—to inveigle his way into a Canadian home like this." She refuses to consent to her marriage with "a painted up, lisping, bobbing, hissing little ex-butler like that! You have lost your wits. I shall call in an alienist!" Dick unmasks and explains that the count had sold him his title, so "I am, in fact, the Count Toodle-oodle-oodle, umpty dumpty Ichijo!"[8]

Winnifred's growing dislike of Japan and her own Japanese deception is perfectly obvious in this story. "Other People's Troubles," also written at this period, was more successful. It is the story of a doctor whose method of dealing with patients in trouble is to tell them of others whose troubles are worse. An editor in New York suggested that Winnifred write a "Trouble" column, based on the story, but instead she sold it to *Farm and Ranch Review,* a Canadian magazine, for a price higher than any they had ever before paid. The editors were naively overcome by their own extravagance and introduced the first part, on February 5, 1919, by proudly announcing that they had paid a big sum "to secure such a high class story" because their readers were entitled to the best money could buy. "Mrs. Reeve has written for the very most exclusive of America's leading Magazines and commands a price running almost into five figures."[9]

The story was accompanied by a breathless profile about her "remarkable life" that reads "like a story book." Written by her Calgary friend Elizabeth Bailey Price, the profile added that Winnifred had entered the "Scenario world" and was now visiting New York. Though married less than two years, Winnifred had gone to New York in an attempt to sell some of her writing, as is evidenced by correspondence with John Emerson of Emerson–Anita Loos Productions at Paramount Pictures in New York. Winnifred had taken an apartment at 487 West End Avenue and was making one of her periodic stabs at breaking into the embryonic movie business.

A Japanese Nightingale had been filmed in 1918 by Pathé in a disappointing production, but through this and her serial writing, Winnifred had gained some film experience and had built some contacts. She felt drawn to the business and was convinced that it was the coming thing. Despite the hopeful energy with which she had thrown herself into her new life in Calgary, she still had a divided mind about what she wanted and was keeping her career options open.

In 1921, she received a feature film credit on *False Kisses,* released by Universal Pictures and presented by Carl Laemmle, who was to become a mentor to Winnifred. The director was Paul Scardon, the scenarist was Wallace Clifton, and Winnifred did the adaptation, which meant writing the dialogue titles. The work was probably done in New York. *False Kisses* was a melodrama adapted from a story called "Ropes," by Wilbur Daniel Steele, which had appeared in *Harper's Magazine* earlier that year. The story concerns a schoolteacher who comes between two fishing partners. The one she marries goes blind and suspects his wife of infidelity. Mary Philbin, an actress Winnifred wrote for several times, was the star.

Although Winnifred must have found satisfaction in having this film produced, she was no doubt distracted the following year by the death of her mother at her sister Beryl's home in New York. She accompanied the body back to Montreal and helped settle family affairs.[10] She may have had a hand in writing her mother's obituary, which gives an account of the "Anglo-Chinese" woman's missionary career and church work and mentions a serial story she wrote about the Shanghai she remembered.[11]

In 1922, Winnifred had been settled in Calgary for five years, less the time spent in New York. Now she produced her first major novel since *Marion* in 1916—*Sunny-San.*[12] Probably Frank's business reverses plunged her into anxiety, and nothing stimulated her writing projects like financial worry.

Sunny-San was her first Japanese novel to appear in ten years, and it was the last "Japanese" novel she ever wrote. She had lost touch with her market and with her publishers, and the book was published by a new firm, McClelland and Stewart, in Toronto and by the George H. Doran Company in New York. The book was also brought out by Hutchinson's in London.

In *Sunny-San,* the dancer Madame Many Smiles dies, and the geisha house owner insists that her fourteen-year-old daughter, Sunny, dance in her stead, stripped of her mourning robes, in skin tights. An American student, Jerry, and his friends save her from a whipping. "She's not a Japanese girl, she's as white as we are," Jerry declares (18). Sunny's white father left when she was a child, and Madame Many Smiles was a half-caste, so Sunny is three-quarters white. "I are white on my face and my honorable body, but I are Japanese on my honorable insides," she says (34).

The boys form a syndicate to take care of her, and when they go home to the United States, they leave her with a minister to train as a missionary. Years later, Jerry gets an unexpected message: "Miss Sindicutt" has arrived in New York. The young men are charmed with her, and all propose except Jerry. He is engaged, a prearranged match. But he breaks it off, and his mother inspects Sunny. "You do not look like a Japanese to me, unless you have been peroxiding your hair. In my opinion you are just an ordinary everyday bad girl," she declares, turning Sunny out (194).

When Jerry finds Sunny gone, he is appalled by his mother's explanation and exclaims, "*Sunny!* Bad! She didn't know what the word meant!" (205).

Sunny walks the street until Katy, a poor Irish shop girl, takes her in and gets her a job. Katy can't believe she is Japanese: "*You* ain't no Chink" (230). In the end, Sunny is reunited with her rich senator father and marries Jerry.

This novel, with its formula romance elements, contains several themes that Winnifred had used earlier. The theme of a girl running away was first used in *Miss Numè of Japan.* The American young men visiting in Japan are seen in many of her books, and the pretty little pidgin-talking Japanese heroine is the same girl as ever. The missionary who believes he has converted Sunny echoes the minister in *A Japanese Blossom.* The kind, comic, Irish working girl is a staple in Winnifred's fiction, and the mother and the fiancée are characters used in "The Unexpected Grandchild"—though in that case, the white girl wins the man.

This novel has a perky charm, despite its recycled themes, but it is not the work of a young writer just starting out. Winnifred was forty-six and comfortably settled at some remove from the pressures of New York. She had grown away from her Japanese material, and no doubt wrote another Japanese book solely in hopes of making some money based on her former reputation. But even in her return to former themes, this novel is moving away from Japan as fast as it can. Her last Japanese novels are less "Japanese" than the earlier ones, and this one least of any. The language is not so stylized, the settings are less steeped in Japanese atmosphere, and the heroines grow whiter. Tama is a blonde fox woman, and Sunny is the least Asian of all Winnifred's Japanese heroines. She is blond, fair, blue-eyed, and only one-quarter Japanese, less Asian than Winnifred herself.

Sunny-San may open in Japan, but the scene swiftly moves to the United States, and it becomes a very American story indeed, with a New York City setting and characters. Soon, the only Japanese in sight is Sunny, who is barely Japanese at all. She comes to the United States dressed reassuringly as an American girl, and she displays many traits that Winnifred had herself. She lives off men, in an innocent, childlike way, until she is told point-blank that this is immoral behavior. Then she shows herself willing to work as a shop girl, in a passage strikingly reminiscent of stories of Winnifred's own youth. The appearance of Sunny's rich father to save her from a fate worse than death—being a poor working-girl, for which the frivolous Sunny is plainly not cut out—is melodramatic but enjoyable nonetheless.

The story is oddly reminiscent of Yone Noguchi's 1902 "Diary of a Japanese Girl in America," which concerns a clever, charming Japanese precursor of Sunny, who gives her quaint impressions of the United States and Americans. Sunny is the most self-consciously adorable of Winnifred's heroines, bolder, less modest, less tragic. But Sunny's active, calculated charm is no borrowing from another writer's twenty-year-old story; the resemblance is a byproduct of her being the only one of Winnifred's Japanese novel heroines to come to the United States. Sunny does not hark back to the past but is emphatically a creature of 1922. She has an artificial, studied appeal that is supposed to be artless, and she is a blonde bombshell who devastates men with her calculatedly babyish ways—perhaps influenced by Mary Pickford or who knows what golden-haired heroine of the early Hollywood.

Being Japanese, in this book, is distinctly something to be ashamed of, to minimize; being American is desirable. Sunny's highest aim is to turn herself into an American girl, "to acquire the American point of view, and in fact unlearn much of the useless knowledge she had acquired of things Japanese" (45). Yet Winnifred nostalgically recalled the charm of the Japanese, from the period when she adored such things; and Sunny's bewitching ways reveal the Japanese as dear, harmless little people. In this last of Winnifred's "Japanese" novels, Japan itself fades almost to the vanishing point. The vigorous American setting punches its way through, to be elaborated with still more energy in her next two books.

Linda Moser points out that Winnifred's "renewal of a Japanese theme seems peculiar especially in the light of growing hostility toward Japanese immigrants at the time,"[13] and she cites such contemporary works as Gene Stratton Porter's *Her Father's Daughter,* in which Japanese students learn about American culture to be able to take over the U.S. government. Moser also underlines Sunny's sexuality and her "Japanese" lack of modesty. Sunny's sexuality is acceptable because of its innocence—but despite the Japanese guise, she is an artificial, glittering, babylike, Hollywood-style blonde creation. Winnifred recognized this Hollywood quality in Sunny and strove mightily to sell the movie rights for *Sunny-San.* To the end of her life she believed that the book was ideal movie material.

The theatrical rights to *Sunny-San* were bought by H. L. Amster in June 1922. Carl Brandt, an agent, showed the book to a writer called Cosmo Hamilton, but he declined to develop it on the grounds that the story was similar to *East Is West,* a book which Winnifred herself later adapted as a film.

With Mr. Amster, Winnifred had a cordial correspondence, and he would compliment her ("The enormous amount of energy a little woman like you has, is a marvel").[14] He took a stuffy interest in her children, particularly Doris, who was now seventeen and stage-struck, and he advised Winnifred not to let her act until she was mature enough to understand "the glitter of stage life."[15]

Amster and Winnifred eventually settled on a writer named Hobart, who had written and staged the Broadway success *Greenwich Village Follies,* to dramatize *Sunny-San.* Amster was pleased that Hobart "left intact all the sweet little expressions and actions of Sunny San."[16] The play eventually found a producer and in 1924 had a modest New York production.

About this time, Winnifred's interest in the theater led her to establish the Little Theatre Association in Calgary. She formed a committee of thirty-five "prominent residents"; proposed that the Prince of Wales, who owned land in Alberta, be invited to be patron; and was unanimously elected honorary president.[17]

In the publicity flurry following the publication of *Sunny-San,* Elizabeth Bailey Price again interviewed Winnifred, describing her "rosy cheeks of her father's people, and the dark, almond shaped eyes of her mother's."[18]

"First of all," Winnifred said earnestly, "I am American before anything else. I live in America. But I cannot forget that it was America who first set my mother's people on the road they are now traveling. Commodore Perry opened the door."

"Don't you think," the interviewer suggested (while Onoto Watanna attacked a neglected chicken patty), "that both East and West have things to teach each other?" Winnifred could safely agree to that. "A decidedly Occidental sparkle came into Onoto Watanna's Oriental eyes—one can't get used to seeing a smart navy blue toque above them, instead of a pile of shining black hair stuck with many fantastic pins."

Winnifred rattled on about the differences between East and West. The Eastern woman was brave but needed to develop savoir faire. The Western woman could teach the Eastern woman personal ambition. She added strangely, "One thing Western women have, which they can never teach the East. It is beauty—personal beauty. The Oriental woman is charming. But the Occidental woman—preeminently the Anglo-Saxon type—is beautiful." "The thing for us all to do," she concluded earnestly, "is just to remember that we belong to the same human family, and that, as good brothers and sisters, we ought to help each other whenever and wherever we can—instead of talking about Yellow Perils!"

In 1924, Winnifred wrote a revealing piece of self-analysis about her life's dilemma. Ruefully entitled "You Can't Run Away from Yourself,"[19] this manuscript shows what was in Winnifred's mind when she pulled up stakes yet again and left her husband and Calgary for New York. She began by reminiscing about how she came to marry Frank: "I was tired of writing and sick of New York. I felt like a human fly caught in the cogs of its mighty machinery. . . . Writing became a sort of torment—something I had literally to drive myself to. Many a time I have laid my head down among my papers and pencils and cried—hopelessly, for there seemed no escape for me. There were many dependent upon me."

It is not surprising that Winnifred felt this way during the pressured years of her New York life. She summarized the writing she had done up to that time, exaggerating the number of novels (it only felt like eighteen) and probably the number of copies sold of *A Japanese Nightingale,* though this did go through three editions and was translated into Swedish, Hungarian, and German, while *Tama,* bizarrely, made it into Finnish: "I had written hundreds of short stories and eighteen novels—all concerned with Japan. I was 'labeled' Japanese. The little oriental blood in me did not make me a real 'Jap' any more than the drop of French in me made me a Frenchwoman." This is a strange disavowal, considering that Winnifred did not have a "little oriental blood" but was half Chinese. It is true that her "oriental blood" could not make her "a real 'Jap'" (nothing could); but what is striking is that this misrepresentation appears in a private, unpublished, diary-like document, entitled, with hilarious irony, "You Can't Run Away from Yourself." It is remarkable to see Winnifred in the very act of lying to herself; perpetuating her false identity had become so habitual she did not drop it even in a discourse going on in her own mind. Perhaps she intended to publish this autobiographical piece eventually—she wrote virtually everything with that in mind—but it is revealing that she did not separate fact from fantasy even in her own private ruminations.

"I dreamed of the day when I could escape from the treadmill of writing about a subject I did not love," she wrote, explaining that "vogues are transient things and my readers probably were as tired of reading about little Japanese women as I was of writing about them." She went on, "Came a day when publishers no longer made me tempting offers of large advance royalties; when editors ceased to solicit stories by me. I said to myself: 'I can write another type of story. This is my opportunity to get away from Japanese tales.' So I wrote three anonymous stories" (*The Diary of Delia, Me,* and *Marion*). Then, she related, a curious phase came over her:

> I was like one who had been running for a long time in a race. Mentally, I was breathless. I found myself unable to write. Previously, writing to me had always been accomplished with facility. I did my best work writing very swiftly, while the plot was still hot in my mind. Now though my brain teemed with plots, when I sat down to write it refused to function. Only the baldest, coldest phrases, stilted and uninspired, came. A terror possessed me that I was done for—written out. I had lost my single talent. And I was still, comparatively speaking, a young woman!

If this attack of writers' block came after the writing of *Marion,* at the time of her divorce, it was not surprising that during such emotional turmoil, she was temporarily unable to write. In her narrative, however, she coyly omits mention of her divorce:

> During this period, someone was saying to me almost daily:
>
> "Why write love stories. Live one. Let's cut all this out. Marry me, and we will go out west—northwest—out to some big country—a country in the making! What do you say?"
>
> He was a big fellow, the kind one calls a man's man. His personality emanated a dominating, fine, clean sort of strength. He had steady, keen, kind blue eyes and a strong chin, hair of a nondescript blond color and one of those fine, straight noses that are somehow typically English.

Frank sounded like just the ticket, the rescuer, the knight in shining armor—and with an English nose to boot. How could she resist? So often the knight does not turn out as dreamed of, but in this case, Winnifred chose both wisely and well. According to this account, she hesitated "to dump my troublesome progeny upon him" and forthrightly told him what it meant to have "three wild, husky, noisy children in a house." She painted her own defects, too, "in black colors." But Frank only said, "I'll take a chance on you, and as for the kids, I love them. Haven't any of my own and it's fine to have a ready made family."

She liked Frank's attitude and was confident he would succeed. As for herself, after years of city life, she found farm life a revelation. "Sometimes I felt like one in a dream. It seemed incredible that it was actually I, used to the teeming, seething throngs of a great city, who was living now on an Alberta ranch." She wrote lyrically of "the great distances . . . the mirages and the phenomenon of sky and earth merged into one great brooding haze. . . . All I saw was rolling prairie, dim brown under a sky that was eternally gilded with sun. . . . In certain months in Alberta daylight stays till nearly eleven o'clock at night and a great moon hangs above the waving, golden grain, seeming like an immense artificial balloon, orange colored as if its interior were all fire."

Seeing the crop going in was a great sight; Winnifred enjoyed watching the men on the land, and it gave her fine and comfortable thoughts of equality. "Our men were of a type I had never come into contact before—overall men. I had always been inclined toward socialism. That is to say, I believed that all men should have been born equal. . . . In a ranching country like Alberta there really is no such thing as 'caste.' I liked this. We were a little democracy in ourselves."

Their 640 acres turned out to be a "drop in the bucket" in Alberta, however; if the Reeves wanted to stay in cattle they had to have more land. So they bought Bow View Ranch in the foothills. "We had ten thousand acres under fence and shared a government lease of Forest Reserve which ran to about 200,000 acres with two other cattlemen. We put a competent foreman in charge of the grain ranch, and took up our residence at Bow View."

It was a beautiful place, the Ghost River flowing down the canyon, in the fall bearing the hundreds of logs of the Eau Claire Lumber Camp. On another side was the Blue Bow River. "Wherever we looked were sungilt hills, and beyond them . . . the jagged, marvelous outline of the snow crowned Rockies, silhouetted against a sky whose iridescent colors were like a sea of opal and mother of pearl. This was my home."

She was happy, galloping over hills and into woods, "where the long searchlights of the sun pierce through to the flowering carpet of every conceivable color," picnicking with friends, neighboring ranchers, and people from Calgary. But "something beat like an aching pulse away back in my mind and deep in my heart. Letters from New York thrilled me to the bone. I could have hugged a stranger from out of my old world. And then my work—my writing!" She had plenty of time to reflect that "love alone does not make life wholly joyful."

Winter came, and Winnifred felt isolated. The children were at boarding school in Calgary, and Frank was away on ranch business for days at a time. During one three-week period they were cut off by a vast storm, and Winnifred never left the house. The Swedish cook sat rocking and moaning. She was homesick, and so was Winnifred. "I awoke to a sudden piercing realization of what I had done in cutting myself off from all my old friends and associates and isolating myself on an Alberta ranch."

The house could not have been more comfortable. There were twenty-five hundred books in the great living room, the floor was bright with Navajo rugs, and she could play music on the piano player and pile logs on the fire. But she couldn't write. "What could I write? Little fairy-like, delicate romances of Japan?"

Her New York life seemed glamorous in retrospect, and she felt like "an exile in Siberia." But there was no hope of change; Frank's money was tied up in cattle and land. They couldn't pull up stakes and quit, even if Frank had been willing to do so, which he was not; he loved his work. At times, she too loved the life, which seemed so fine and big. Distances meant nothing; the ranchers all had cars and horses and went back and forth to one another's place. Some were English, which Winnifred relished—a peer's grandson kept a roadhouse, where they had Friday dances; two Italian princes had a great horse ranch and came to call in overalls. She wrote a feature article in the *Montreal Daily Star,* "Royal and Titled Ranchers in Alberta," about the aristocrats she found on the prairie.[20]

She knew the Indians, too, "well enough to call them by name." There were six hundred on the Indian reserve on one side of the ranch, and Winnifred wrote about them in a lady-of-the-manor fashion. She brought sweetmeats and cakes and "things Indians love" for the "squaws and papooses." Hearing about the death of a papoose, she brought the mother brown sugar candy. "I left the little squaw waving to me, with a smile coming through her tears and her fat cheeks full of candy." But the sheriff's wife said, "Mustn't do that, Mrs. Reeve. You'll have a dead Indian baby every day on your hands if you do."

She "acquired quite a reputation" as a doctor, and she portrayed herself ministering to sick Indians, curing scalds with baking soda, so that "one Indian after another would come to Missis Boss" for treatment. This sounds uncomfortably like a plantation owner's wife going around as an angel of mercy, but we may charitably consider that Winnifred was undoubtedly, with her customary genial good nature, doing her best in a strange land.

In another piece of local color, she wrote about the "motor hoboes" who sought relief at the ranch. It is a vivid glimpse of life on the road before motels studded the Calgary-Banff highway, before it was a highway. Tents were set up by the river, but the ranchers' patience wore thin at all the "applicants for shelter, meals, milk, eggs, tools, horses, vegetables, use of telephone, use of verandah for picnic, gasoline, and berries." Winnifred recollected "one woman with a great giddy car, that was brim full of chattering and bevelled sister adventurers," who thought she was doing the Reeves "a mighty favor" by asking for dinner. She called them "rubes" and haughtily "stated that she understood it was the custom of the country for the farmers to take in people who were on the road. . . . Not the mere motor hobo!"[21]

Winnifred grew increasingly dissatisfied, as she wrote in "You Can't Run Away from Yourself": "It wasn't that I wanted so much to return to New York and my friends—but deep inside me was the overpowering urge—to write! I realized that when I went down to Calgary, shut myself in a room for two weeks, and it seemed as if I had turned on a mental faucet. Everything wanted to come tumbling out of me at once!"

Despite her protestations at not having written for years, the truth is that writing was a constant in Winnifred's life. Her daughter remembered living on the ranch with her writer mother: "We had to be absolutely quiet. My mother would read to us what she had written and this more than compensated for the rules she had imposed. We all sat at her feet like admiring little slaves."[22]

Another of Elizabeth Bailey Price's post–*Sunny-San* interviews with Winnifred appeared, which describes the visit of a group of literary men on a Canadian Authors Association trip. "Just to think," said John Murray Gibbon, the president of the group, "that in the foothills of the Rockies, buried on an Alberta ranch, we discovered one of our greatest Canadian authors, one that has had the distinction of having the largest sale of any of us."[23] The party included Winnifred's old friend Arthur Stringer, author of a trilogy of prairie novels, who lavishly praised *Sunny-San.*

Still another Elizabeth Bailey Price interview, in *MacLean's Magazine,* October 15, 1922, was flatteringly entitled "Onoto Watanna, An Amazing Author." This article gushingly observes, "To have reached that pinnacle of success of an author in the U.S. . . . then to leave suddenly and bury yourself for five years on an Alberta ranch, is the experience of Mrs. Frank Reeve. . . . Now that she has been reclaimed from her long residence in the States, she is desirous to be known henceforth as a Canadian" (64). Winnifred was now playing the "Canadian" identity for all it was worth. She declared that her future work would be that of her native Canada; she would write five novels set in Canada.

Asked in another interview what she liked best to do, she said, "Work among my flowers and cook a bit." She remembered that her friends used to tell her that her literary work had two formidable rivals—her babies and her garden.[24] In truth, though she would not admit it, the latter two could never compete with her writing.

The Canadiana went patriotically on and on. Another Price piece detailed how seven of Winnifred's nephews served in the late war, one of them, Lt. Eaton, an aviator, giving his life in the service of his country. During the war years, but before the United States entered, the Reeves came to Alberta, to do "their bit," producing grain. "Since the war, the Reeves' outfit have employed only veterans." Every possible Canadian link was related:

> Mrs. Reeve's New York publisher, George H. Doran, is a Canadian; Willard Mack, who is to do the dramatization of her novel, is Canadian; Tyrone Power, who is to star in one of her plays, has long been a resident of Canada, though born in England; and Madame Tamaki Muira, who will produce the operatic version of her *Japanese Nightingale,* though Japanese by birth, was educated by the Canadian prima donna, Madame Albani. She has requested that the illustrator of her novel shall also be Canadian. Mrs. Reeve is vice-chairman of the Calgary branch of the Canadian Authors League.[25]

That clinched it: Winnifred was Canadian. Most of these claims, however, never came to fruition; Tyrone Power never starred in any film by Winnifred, nor did *A Japanese Nightingale* opera come to pass.

Despite her ranch life, Winnifred's writing powers were undimmed, and in 1923 one of her most polished and accomplished stories, "Elspeth," was published in a Canadian short story magazine.[26] The widowed Mrs. Maitland works as a stenographer to support herself and her sixteen-year-old daughter, Elspeth, who threatens to elope with a young McGill student. Her "Muzzie" lectures the girl, but Elspeth does not listen. Mrs. Maitland tells her boss she must quit her job to stay home and take care of her daughter, but it is too late: Elspeth elopes. When the boy's father, a rich senator, calls Mrs. Maitland a schemer, she tells her boss she is coming back to work so she can put her son-in-law through college. Her boss tells her that it is fine if she wants to come back to work but that she must marry him first.

This story is unusually natural and realistic; the interaction between the patient, tired mother and the willful daughter has such a ring of truth that it is easy to imagine it may be partly inspired by Winnifred's relationship with her own daughter. The mother's exasperation and the girl's petty determination have a convincing universality. And the story has an unexpected ending—it is true that a romantic interest for the mother pops up, in line with the conventions of magazine fiction, but nothing is done to stop the teenage girl's marriage: it is allowed to happen, as it might have in real life, with the mother's making the best of it. This piece shows Winnifred in her writing maturity, a confident master of the short story form, using her acquired wisdom about life to good, not false, effect, while obeying the rules of commercial fiction.

By this time, Winnifred had enough experience of life in the West to feel she had material for a real, rawboned, earthy, pioneer Canadian novel. Perhaps she was inspired by such writers as her contemporary Willa Cather, whose *My Antonia* came out in 1918. *Cattle,* Winnifred's "Alberta" novel, was to be a complete departure from anything she had ever written before.

For this project, she used Winnifred Eaton as her pen name for the first time in many years. She reflected that her work had "been chiefly noted for its delicate and even poetic quality. . . . But I was not going to write with a delicate pen now":

> The first publisher to whom I sent my Alberta novel returned it to me with the statement that it was the most brutal manuscript that had ever come into his office, but that it had gripped him so that, jaded reader of fiction though he was, he had not put it down until he had read every word. Strangely enough this verdict gave me a singular pride. I said to myself: "Now I am writing with a man's pen. I am going back East. I am going to come back as a writer, not this time as a writer of fairy-like stories of Japan, but tales of things and people I had known.[27]

Winnifred had done some serious thinking about her new endeavor. In an article entitled "The Canadian Spirit in Our Literature," published in the *Calgary Daily Herald* on March 24, 1923, which she also presented as a radio address before the Canadian Club of Calgary, she put her thoughts into words: "With a very few and rare exceptions, there has come out of Canada, thus far, no important literary production in which a typical Canadian spirit is revealed." The Canadian author was "forced to go outside of Canada to find a market for his work."

Winnifred now asserted that it was "of vital importance to Canada that its authors should remain at home." She herself, of course, had left Canada for the United States at the first possible moment, returning to her native land only when her markets dried up. But now, seeing things as a Canadian, she complained, "Our country has been and is flooded with magazines and books from the United States and England."

She hoped that the Canadian Authors Association might make the writer's position more independent. Winnifred was consistently involved in the association's affairs; she had been a charter member of the American Authors' League in New York and was the founder and first president of the Canadian Authors Association in Calgary, as well as being vice president of the national organization. Recently she had gone to Ottawa as a delegate to the association's convention, working to reform the copyright law.[28] She concluded her article by asking, "Would it not be fine if a Canadian author of great talent should cunningly weave into a tale something of the fascinating glamor, the exciting spirit of adventure, the wonder and beauty and charm of this land of ours. . . . A strong, hot pen might unfold the epic of our grain fields." She intended, of course, that this author would be none other than herself. So Winnifred wielded the strong, hot pen and created *Cattle*.[29]

Big "Bull" Langdon owns the huge Bar Q cattle ranch. Nearby is the humble "Dan Day Dump," where poor widowed Dan lives with his ten children. The oldest, Nettie, fifteen, is "a big girl, with milk-white skin . . . hair as gold as the Alberta sun . . . a slow-moving, slow-thinking girl, simple-minded and totally ignorant of the world" (10). The young homesteader Cyril Stanley is in love with her. When she asks what he's building, he replies with a grin, "A *home*, girl!" (27). He thinks how she will light up the place.

Dan dies, and the younger children are put up for adoption. Bull asks Nettie to work for his sickly, gentle wife, who spends her time reading tracts that "deny the existence of evil, pain or illness" (54). Then Bull sends his wife on a holiday, and alone with Nettie, he brutally rapes her. Nettie miserably tells Cyril that she "ain't the same" (115). He assumes she has another fellow and storms off. When Bull assails her again, he is interrupted by his wife, whereupon poor Mrs. Langdon collapses and dies of shock.

Nettie's baby boy is born, but she can hardly look at it, and it is cared for by Angella, an Englishwoman whom neighbors call "the man-woman" because she works her own land. Angella keeps Bull off with a gun. Disease ravages the countryside, and Nettie helps the good Scottish Dr. McDermott care for sick hands at the lumber camp. Bull snatches her baby away and tosses him to ranch hands, saying the baby has his brand on him. The child dies, and Bull is gored to death by his own prize bull. Cyril and Nettie marry, as do Angella and the doctor.

This stark and brutal novel certainly constitutes Winnifred's break away from charming, delicate little Japanese tales. Brimming with raw power, at times her story of rape and brutality on the big, rough prairie landscape is overdone and overstated. The portrait of the brutish tyrant is crude: he is a caveman, who considers rape a perfectly satisfying relationship; even his name—that Bull of a man—is anything but subtle. With his overbearing, uncontrollable presence, the emotion that permeates the book is a sharp fear and hatred of masculine force. There are good, decent male characters, such as the doctor and Cyril; but they, like everyone else, are powerless to protect a helpless girl from the brutal man-monster. Only the ambiguous figure of the "man-woman" is strong enough to stand up to Bull and threaten him with a gun. Other women are weak and passive—feeble Mrs. Langdon and Nettie, the beautiful victim.

Is *Cattle* her best book, her masterpiece? Winnifred cannot be said to have ever written a masterpiece. If she wanted to be a Willa Cather, she lacked the beautiful spare prose style to accomplish such an apotheosis. She was a popular middlebrow commercial writer, whose best quality was an extraordinary flair for compelling storytelling. She could spin a breathless tale and keep her readers literally on the edge of their seats, waiting to discover, for instance, what would happen when Mrs. Langdon learned about her husband's rape of Nettie or what Cyril's reaction would be. Some of Winnifred's descriptions of Alberta are vivid, even beautiful; and she strongly conveys her feeling for the larger-than-life, harsh country, as when she writes, "Alberta is, in a way, a land of sanctuary, and upon its rough bosom the derelicts of the world, the fugitives, the hunted, the sick and the dying have sought asylum and cure" (34).

In *Cattle,* Winnifred could not completely rid herself of threadbare writing conventions, even when most consciously trying to make a daring break away from her usual materials. The doctor and Angella have to marry, to make a rosy, double-couple happy ending. Well-aware of the tricks of commercial fiction, she made some attempt to break away from them in *Cattle,* though. In spinning this strong, harsh tale, melodramatic as it is, she did achieve qualities of forcefulness and originality.

Although Winnifred's stories usually devolved into predictable, pat, happy endings, they skirted and veered off from the familiar and were not completely convention-bound. Unlike many women writers of her day, she never hesitated to allow truly appalling things to happen to her characters. These tragic, unexpected occurrences can evoke a powerful response and keep the reader surprised and off balance, and they make Winnifred's work much more interesting than a strictly formulaic writer's work. She reveled in delivering thunderbolts of fate down onto the heads of her hapless characters. She allowed her Japanese heroines to wander around as mendicants, lose their children, be abandoned. She allowed Nora in *Me* to find a career, but not true love; and she allowed Nettie to bear a child as the result of a rape.

Cattle was at least partly written and submitted several years before it was published. Internal evidence of this includes the devastating flu epidemic featured in the book, which actually occurred in 1919, after the war years of bumper crops. Similarly, there is the general shock at Angella's mannish attire and short hair—which might have seemed revolutionary in 1919 but already much less so by 1924.

Reviews were positive, though *Cattle* did not equal the sales of Winnifred's Japanese novels. A reviewer in the *Saturday Night Magazine* called the book "a strong, if somewhat crude, story of ranching, in Western Canada. It is a story of action—clear-cut and convincing. . . . I recommend the novel as vivid and readable, but warn you not to look for subtlety in it, or shadings or overtones, because they are not there."[30] Another reviewer, Stephen Leacock, writing for a Canadian publication, summed up the situation succinctly, "At last, Mrs. Reeve has given up writing for Sunday school libraries."[31]

Winnifred tried to sell an early version of the book to the movies some four years before publication, but a letter of rejection from Paramount Pictures, dated July 6, 1920, to Winnifred at Bow View, declared that *Cattle* was not well suited for movies: "We do not like to put on the screen—and our exhibitors like it less than we do—a heroine who has been betrayed and whom we watch looking after her illegitimate child."[32] Despite Paramount's negative response, once the book was published, D. W. Griffith's partner, Elmer Clifton, bought the motion picture rights for $1,200. He created a sensation by visiting the Bow View Ranch, was eager to see everything, and was thrilled by the spectacular Alberta scenery. This visit from "movie men" surely contributed to

Winnifred's growing desire to get back into the world of big-city writing and movie making.

She wrote a breathless and witty description of Elmer Clifton's visit, noting that when she went to the station to meet him and his cameraman, Penrod, she had no idea what they might look like.[33] Clifton, producer of *Down to the Sea in Ships* and *The Warrens of Virginia,* turned out to be a youngish man with a clean-cut, boyish face, who might have been in college.

"This is great! The air's literally alive! Let's get right off to the ranches!" he exclaimed. Winnifred noted that he would not even stop in Cochrane for a drink. "What, and you've lived in Hollywood and are movie men!" she cried. "Sad, but true," he grinned, "I'm afraid you'll find us a dull bunch. We hasn't any wices." When they approached Bow View Ranch, he cried, "Stop the car! This is immense! Immense!"

Winnifred's final novel was *His Royal Nibs,* which she wrote under the name Winifred Eaton Reeve (oddly, with only one *n*) and was published by W. J. Watt and Company in 1925. When the book came out, Winnifred had already gone to New York to work with Carl Laemmle, and she dedicated the book to him: "To CARL LAEMMLE, for whom the author has the sincerest admiration." An amusing story is told about what happened when Winnifred asked Laemmle if she might dedicate the book to him. The movie mogul agreed and asked when the dedication would be. Seeing that he expected a formal event, Winnifred got up a party for the occasion and presented the "dedication" to him, with full ceremony.[34]

His Royal Nibs takes place in the same landscape as *Cattle.* The story opens at a time of year when tramps and veterans and men from across the sea are walking from Calgary out to lumber camps and ranches, looking for work. An Englishman, miraculously neat after the forty-four-mile walk from Calgary, arrives at the O Bar O Ranch and is promptly knocked over by a steer. When the foreman helps him up, he exclaims, "Ch-cheerio!" in a stuttering English accent and timidly asks for a job on the "rawnch" (15).

The hands and ranch owner P. D. McPherson's two children, spunky, dark-eyed Hilda, who is eighteen, and her younger brother, Sandy, laugh at "Cheerio." He is given all the worst (or impossible) jobs to do—steers to milk, foolish errands to run—but he is willing and cheerful. He gamely rides a bucking bronco and shows himself a first-rate rider. Also an artist, he makes an art studio in a cave above the river and paints not only the Indians but also Hilda.

Roughneck Holy Smoke causes trouble, picks fights with Cheerio, and attacks Hilda, but Cheerio vanquishes him. A curious reporter reveals the Englishman as a war hero, the missing son of a lord. But he has no wish to leave Canada—he marries Hilda and is satisfied to be "Cheerio, Duke of the O Bar O," and Hilda becomes "the darling Duchess!" (318).

The ranch setting of *His Royal Nibs* is similar to that of *Cattle*, an even more faithful description of Winnifred and Frank's own Bow View Ranch. Even the Chinese cook from *Cattle* appears for a second time. But the atmosphere is very different: it is not malign. No Bull bawls and strides and dominates this second cattle ranch story. There is a Bull type in the bullying Holy Smoke, another male caveman who tries to rape the heroine, but he is much smaller in scale than his predecessor and is only a minor character and minor annoyance. Slim, delicate-seeming Cheerio puts him away with ease.

Far from a brawling Bull, this story's male protagonist is very much an Englishman of the 1920s. Cheerio is amiable, cultivated, and sensitive; despite having his origins in Winnifred's English snobbery, he is a modest and pleasant hero. Though her attitudes toward Japan and the Japanese changed, her attraction to England and the English remained constant and are reflected in this, her final novel, written when she was nearly fifty. In some idealized way, Cheerio seems to have represented her father, Edward Eaton. He even has the same name, in a titled version—"Edward Eaton Charlesmore of Macclesfield and Coventry" (317)—his talent for painting, and his gentle manner.

This stuttering gentleman is not the most dashingly romantic figure, and his romance with the headstrong Hilda is never quite convincing. There is no strong narrative; the plot consists of the very thinnest tissue of misunderstandings. Cheerio and Hilda meet, and she takes a dislike to him based on a series of petty misconceptions, all of which are inevitably sorted out so that Cheerio stands forth as a flawless hero. There is some repetition, in description and events, so that essentially *His Royal Nibs* may be seen as a defanged, neutered, and tamer revisit to the world of *Cattle*.

Yet that world is subtly changed: the mood has become one not of brutality but of charm. The situational appeal of the Englishman in the rugged West is fresh and piquant; we are exhilarated by the ranch, the free life, the riding, the painting, the scenic beauty, seen through Cheerio's eyes. In a way it is an idyllic Alberta novel and can be enjoyed as a nostalgic, affectionate, and very vivid depiction of the Canadian cattle ranch life between the wars.

The character of Cheerio was at least partly based on a real individual, the cowboy painter Roland Gissing, a neighbor of Winnifred and Frank, who knew him well. Gissing was born in England in 1895 and would have been about thirty at the time *His Royal Nibs* was written. He came from a talented family; his uncle George Gissing was the famous Victorian novelist, author of *New Grub Street*. Roland Gissing studied art in Edinburgh, where he first saw "moving pictures" and was seized with a dream of the cowboy life, which led to his emigrating to Canada. In the spring of 1924, he took out a homestead and built a cabin on the Ghost River, forty miles west of Calgary.

In 1929, four years after *His Royal Nibs* was published, Gissing had his first exhibition at the Calgary Public Library and was launched as a popular painter. Like Winnifred, Gissing never wanted to be "the classic artist starving in an attic," and he painted for the popular taste. He loved to paint mountain lakes, such as Lake O'Hara.[35] Winnifred and Frank owned several paintings by Gissing. One was a water color of their ranch, another a pastel of their woods in the autumn. These Winnifred's grandson, Tim Rooney, gave to the Glenbow Museum at the time of his mother's death.

Gissing occasionally worked on the Reeve ranch, though probably only as an additional hand at busy times. Tim Rooney remembers often visiting the Gissings with Winnifred, Frank, and Doris. In 1944, Gissing's home burned to the ground, with some of his best paintings and his rare book collection. Frank Reeve loaned Gissing money to help him rebuild, and in return Gissing gave him a picture of a cowboy on a bucking bronco. Gissing died in 1967. His lovely landscapes and paintings of cowboy life are beloved in Canada and fetch high prices today.

Winnifred published no more novels after *His Royal Nibs,* though her writing output, far from slowing down, was about to reach the most frenetic pitch of her life. Over the next seven years, she churned out dozens of screenplays, screen treatments, synopses, story ideas, and articles, as well as manuscripts for several novels that never were published. She did not stop publishing novels because she was "written out," or felt she had nothing left to say, or was tired. Her energies simply went into another kind of writing. With fifteen books to her credit, she went to work in the movie business at the age of fifty. It was not the easiest time in life to begin a new career in an entirely new environment, and this change in her life has all the markings of another one of Winnifred's bolts from difficult circumstances. The ranch was doing poorly, income was down, and the Reeves' finances were at their lowest ebb. Perhaps most important, Winnifred had long been restless in Calgary and yearned for New York. So, in 1924, with Frank's reluctant blessing, off she went to New York, taking all three children with her.

A series of letters from her old friend Frank Putnam, who years ago had written poetry about his dear Onoto, helps illuminate the circumstances. Putnam wrote from his home in Milwaukee, sending her a copy of his poetry book *Love Lyrics,* which she had asked for. He describes his son who "like your Perry, is planning to take an engineering course when he finishes high school.

He, like Perry, is a radio fan."[36] Commonplace enough, but this is among the few mentions of Perry's having normal interests and leading a normal life, before his mental illness overwhelmed him only a few years later.

Putnam complimented "dear Winnie" on her writing and commented on her plans to leave Calgary: "Why should I blame you for striking out alone once more? Far from it. Exactly what one *must* do, when the choice is freedom or stagnation. You'll come through, all right. . . . You are about the youngest individual I know, except myself, and I can't seem to grow up at all."[37]

Now middle-aged, Putnam loved to remember the old days, and he confided in Winnifred about his marital problems ("My wife is not clever") and his extramarital dalliances: "The good laugh I got from your comment on my latest love lunacy brought me out of it OK. . . . May the little gods permit me at least a few more renewals of it. . . . You are having such a perfectly corking stiff adventure of your own right now. You and the plucky boys and lovely little Doris—all destined to win through."[38]

Before going to New York, Winnifred was, somewhat surprisingly, up to her old tricks of cadging money from male friends. After all, she was still married and living with Frank Reeve, who was certainly not indigent; however, he may have refused to pay for her adventure, since he did not really want her to leave him. In February 1924, Putnam wrote, "I should like to be able to provide the entire thousand you say you will need for the removal back to your market, but other demands on my income make it for the present impossible." He soon changed his mind, however, and wrote cheerily, encouraging Winnifred and supporting her daughter's plans to try for an acting career: "Hurray for Doris, the bright young muse of the dramatic stage! . . . I went to the bank this morning and borrowed five hundred for you. . . . I owe you the five hundred for laughing me out of my latest lunacy. . . ."[39] Later, Putnam wrote that he was "eager to have a bound copy of Cheerio . . . Lately I reread *Miss Nume* . . . Your own youth in it."[40]

He has more to say about Doris: "'Unhappy, restless and rebellious'—of course she is; she wouldn't have much spirit if she wasn't at her age. . . . That stored up restlessness will be her guaranty of energy and courage, when she gets going. Tell her I said she shouldn't marry at 18. . . . The woman I married is the woman whose photo you saw on a mantel in my room at the NY hotel the day you and Doris came to dine with me. You said, 'She won't let go easily.' Good prophet!"[41]

Winnifred consulted Putnam about her plans while awaiting Elmer Clifton's visit, and he tried to help her sort out her thoughts. When Clifton arrived in Calgary, Winnifred was better able to judge whether she should remain there to work with him or go to New York or Hollywood. Putnam's advice had been that she should "adopt a course which I never have had the hardiness to adopt, namely, let the folk dependent on you sink or swim on their own efforts until you have achieved, unburdened, your own task of establishing a new business footing." He thought her boys would do well on their own; Perry planned to drive to Hollywood, and this showed spirit.[42]

Soon after this, Winnifred headed for New York and energetically started looking into work possibilities. Arthur Stringer wrote to Paramount asking them to hire her, and she had several interviews with the producer Walter Wanger. Frank kept writing letters imploring her to come home, but in November, she wrote to him, at length and decisively, from an apartment she had taken at 127 West Seventy-ninth Street. She would have liked to have her cake and eat it too; but if the choice was between having Frank in Calgary and having a career in New York, her choice was made:

> I am very likely to sign up with the Famous Players . . . they are talking terms now with my agent, Miss Marbury. . . . my dear Frank, what are we to do? I will undoubtedly have a large salary, but my time will be theirs. I am told that I will probably be retained right here in NY and not be sent just yet at all events to the Pacific coast—more likely to Long Island.
>
> Now Frank, look here, dear man, don't you see that unless you can arrange to come to me that it looks as if we will not be together? How could I live in Alberta and go on with my work? Today most women work—married or single, and in adjusting their matrimonial affairs, that has to be borne in mind. . . . My business is as important as yours and yours as important as mine, and neither of us can sacrifice his interests for the other. I did it for seven and a half years, as you know, and you demonstrated that in Alberta, at all events, you could not take care of me. So here I am back in the arena, and I must go on. My work as an author is too much like a seesaw and it is far better for me to take a regular position as I now propose to do, but I don't want to lose my husband in doing it. I want you to stand by me, and be with me like a good sport. . . . If you sell out—if you leave Alberta, after all, it will not matter much where you go. Why not here, where your wife's work is. . . . I believe moreover, I will soon have considerable influence and power, and I might very well be able to help you into something that would lead to big things. . . . The children would have a separate place to live, except Doris. They are all doing fine. Charley, from copy boy on the Mirror, within one week, has been made Bronx reporter, and his pay raised from $18 a week to $25. Perry got raised from $22 to $25. Now that looks well for the kids, doesn't it?[43]

The next news was the clincher:

> Oh just think Frank I've signed the most wonderful contract. I start work on Monday. I've a great staff under me—it's a very important position. I will be

> in New York for 6 months. Then go on to coast. I get $200 a week first six months. Then $250—then $300 and up to $400—3 year contract. I get $3000 to $5000 for every original scenario I write tho' the first few months I will be rushed with the work of the department. Its no lazy job believe me. I've got to get out and hustle but I don't mind as long as my health holds out. I have a great longing to see you dear. Do come if you can. Heaps of love. . . .[44]

Frank had lost her.

9. Hollywood Screenwriter

> Hollywood had about broken my heart and nerve, and a woman alone is like a ship adrift.
>
> —Winnifred Reeve, letter to Colonel William Selig

> Twinkle, twinkle, Movie Star!
> Who in the heck do you think you are?
> Just a year ago, sweet Mable,
> You were waiting on a table.
>
> —Winnifred Reeve

THE JOB THAT Winnifred had described to Frank so excitedly, with Walter Wanger at Famous Players, did not materialize, but within a couple of weeks she did win the plum she sought. On December 12, 1924, she signed a contract with the Universal Pictures Corporation, New York. Winnifred had an office at Universal's New York headquarters at 730 Fifth Avenue, a staff, assistants, secretaries, and an important, prestigious title and position. Now she was part of the glamorous movie business, as typified in a news item about one "Ora Teague, heroine of a modern fairy tale. A few weeks ago she was a waitress in a Los Angeles coffee shop. Then Mrs. Winifred Eaton Reeve, Universal's eastern scenario editor, saw her and now she is on the road to movie fame."[1] This was the world Winnifred had entered.

Winnifred was a protégée of the Laemmles, who had taken a liking to the hardworking, personable writer with a nose for commercial taste and the ability to turn out scripts rapidly and to order. Carl Laemmle, an immigrant clothing dealer from Russia, had founded the Universal Pictures empire; his son, Carl Jr., was a progressive young dynamo coming to power even though he was not yet out of his teens. Carl Sr. specialized in B movies and short two-reelers, while Carl Jr., who had more expensive tastes, was moving the studio toward larger pictures and first-class productions, changing Universal's image as a supplier of "short stuff."[2] At the time Winnifred joined Universal, the movies she worked on were silent five-reelers, a type she herself labeled "slushy." The cost of these short features was usually between $17,000 and $28,000, but by the end of Winnifred's movie business stint in 1931, Carl Jr. was preparing a lucrative cycle of long, big-budget movies. *Dracula,* for example, was filmed at a cost of $355,050. Winnifred's own *East Is West* (1930) cost as much as $428,040. An even more revolutionary change came about while Winnifred was in Hollywood: the shift from silent pictures to talkies.

Winnifred made a splashy beginning as East Coast scenario editor, impressing Carl Laemmle Sr. mightily. In June, he shot off a memo to the West Coast: "I think it desirable to send Mrs. Reeve to Coast to go over with you all stories. Have confidence in Mrs. Reeve consider she has shown greatest ability any editor yet. If Coast does not cooperate with her we will do the deciding on all stories."[3]

An item in the *Universal Weekly* in September 1925 reports on the visit of "Mrs. Winnifred Eaton Reeve" to the West Coast, "where she was in daily conference for two weeks with Raymond L. Schrock, general manager of Universal City, and the production and scenario departments."[4] Winnifred's visit and the powers bestowed upon her by Laemmle aroused the ire of a number of people on the West Coast, as can be seen in letters Edward J. Montagne, the West Coast scenario editor, wrote to her.

In October, Montagne expressed his exasperation with the new executive, whom he clearly perceived as an annoyance and a threat: "I received your letter of the 5th inst. and frankly do not like the spirit of the same. You say what is the use of your attempting to write or do anything for us when you know that I will bash it or find some reason for blocking its acceptance at the coast."[5]

Montagne complained that Winnifred's powers were enhanced because the West Coast reading department had been shut down; he had no readers, and agents were told to submit their stories to New York. Montagne himself was reading nights, Sundays, and holidays. It was too difficult to refer everything to New York, and it meant a diminution of his own influence. "Authors do not like to do business 3,000 miles away. . . . If you haven't the time or the authority, he goes to the next studio, and there are twenty-five or thirty of them out here," he pointed out.[6]

Immediately after Montagne had fired off his complaints, Winnifred was transferred to the West Coast, no doubt to his chagrin. Her New York secretary, Eda Galantiere, wrote her chatty letters that convey the flavor of work and politics in a 1920s scenario department. "The place is dead without you," she said. Winnifred's former assistant, Phelps Decker, was in charge of the scenario office during her absence, but Eda thought Winnifred should retain the title of editor, because "nobody will ever take your place."[7]

Phelps Decker wrote her in humble mode, assuring her that everyone missed her terribly and that he would not dream of usurping her title: "There is no need of sticking my name in a vaunting position. . . . to everyone that has inquired who the editor is, I have stated that you are the Editor and that you have simply gone to the coast in an advisory capacity for an indefinite period."[8]

Two months later, now officially the eastern scenario editor, Decker, addressing Winnifred cheerfully as "Dear Lady," told her that it was with "a sigh of relief" that her old friends learned that things looked "more cheerful and bright" for her. "We all agree with you that it is greater for you to stick it out and not let them have the laff on you and say that they drove you back to New York," he assured her. Everyone knew it was a "hot-bed of intrigue" on the West Coast. He summed up the confusing situation that existed during the shift of activity from the East Coast story department to the West Coast: "I can't for the life of me understand what in H—— is the use of maintaining a department in New York City—reading like mad and discovering wonderful stuff for them out there if they have never even taken the trouble to read what we send them. This undoubtedly will all change now under the new regime—at least let us hope so."[9]

Winnifred was the new regime, but she was to prove no match for the political competition of such rivals as Montagne. From New York, Decker, knowing where her real talents lay, tried to persuade her that she should not be concentrating on the routine business of running a story department. He knew her well enough to stress the things she most desired: money and status as a writer. "To H—— with the routine work for you—what the deuce do you want to be reading and having to do a lot of drudgery for? Get onto the creative writing end of the work—that is what you have wanted to do—now go to it. . . . Get in the Frances Marion and Sada Cowan class," he wrote.[10]

Phelps Decker's suggestion to Winnifred that she stay away from office matters and concentrate on writing may have been disingenuous and aimed at getting rid of an obstacle to his own rise. In 1928, Eda wrote to Winnifred, probably after Decker lost his job, "I am sorry for Phelps Decker but if I were you I wouldn't waste any sympathy on him. He wasn't your friend, I can tell you that."[11] Yet in advising Winnifred to get into the Frances Marion class, Decker was very likely feeding back to her a desire she herself expressed. In any event, Winnifred did follow this advice, if not necessarily by choice: her tenure at Universal was not long, and during the remainder of her Hollywood stay she worked principally as a screenwriter, for MGM and Twentieth Century–Fox as well as Universal.

Frances Marion, who was perhaps the top woman screenwriter of the day, made her name by writing the Mary Pickford movies at MGM and went on to write such sophisticated classic masterpieces as *Dinner at Eight* and *Camille.* Marion's biographer points out that during the silent picture era:

> over a quarter of the scenario writers were women and many of them were already friends, including June Mathis, Agnes Christine Johnson, Dorothy Farnum, Gladys Unger, and Winnifred Eaton Reeve. Most had entered the business at a time when a one-page synopsis of action could be turned into a two-reeler, but they had grown with the industry and were now well paid and highly valued for their abilities. The women were as likely to write jungle films or swashbucklers as tales of female angst and Thalberg maintained that his preference for women writers was a commercial one.[12]

In the 1920s, there was a higher proportion of women writers in the movie business than there is today. Some specialized in writing for certain stars—Frances Marion wrote for Mary Pickford, and Anita Loos wrote for Lillian Gish.[13] Winnifred's own "stars" were two blondes, Mary Philbin, star of the 1925 Lon Chaney version of *Phantom of the Opera* (which Winnifred worked on without credit), and Mary Nolan. Most of these women writers were younger than Winnifred; her friend Sonya Levien, for example, was born in 1888 in Russia, although she altered her birthdate to 1898, as was standard practice (Marion also changed her age).[14] In the movie business, then as now, youth was everything, and Winnifred got a late start.

Like Winnifred, Levien started as a New York scenario editor for Samuel Goldwyn Pictures, and in 1925 her scenario department was moved to Hollywood, just as Universal's was. Levien said of her screenwriting work, "I never knew what work meant (although I have been a wage-slave for years) until I hit the motion picture profession. The overlords pay well but demand every ounce of flesh and blood. . . . There is nothing in the screenwriting profession for a woman who wants a quiet, peaceful life or for a writer who is ambitious for literary fame."[15]

Perhaps Winnifred's closest woman screenwriter friend was Lois Weber, with whom she kept in touch even after returning to Calgary. Born in 1881, Weber was closest in age to Winnifred. She started her writing, acting, and directing career as early as 1912 and directed the 1918 *Tarzan of the Apes.*[16]

According to Wendy Holliday's "Hollywood's Modern Women: Screenwriting, World Culture and Feminism, 1910–1940," in the mid-1920s, nearly half of the writers on staff at the studios were women. In 1922, there were four men and three women at Metro; in 1925, both Fox and Warner Brothers employed six men and four women; and Cecil B. De Mille's staff at Metro in

1926 included an even number of men and women, at seven apiece.[17] One of these was Winnifred, who worked at Metro that year.

The successful screenwriter received a very high salary. Between 1931 and 1933, the annual compensation of the regularly employed writer averaged around $14,000. This was approximately what Winnifred earned. A salary of $200–$300 a week was an excellent wage at a time when a secretary might earn $30 a week. Top writers made considerably more; Anita Loos earned $100,000 in 1924.[18]

Some of these writers were highly visible through much publicity, almost like movie stars themselves. Jeanne MacPherson, for example, wore puttees and riding boots in imitation of Cecil B. De Mille's famous costume. Dress for female screenwriters was often masculine, with trousers and tie. Fan magazines wrote about these women's style, homes, and earning capacity, and star writers invented new backgrounds for themselves. Winnifred was not particularly flamboyant by Hollywood standards. For once in her life, she hardly stood out at all.

Although there were many women in Hollywood (the American Film Institute catalogues for silent feature films list 461 women writers in the 1920s),[19] all the full-time professional screenwriters of the period were white. "Racial minorities were either turned down for such positions when they were summoned to Hollywood's door, or they never showed up," says Holliday.[20] Winnifred may not have been the first or most successful woman in Hollywood, but she was unquestionably one of the earliest Asian American screenwriters. It is tempting to focus on this aspect of her career, but with Winnifred's characteristic pragmatism in playing the role that would best benefit her, she did not emphasize her Asian heritage or appear in Hollywood as the kimono-wearing Onoto Watanna. She obtained jobs not because the industry needed a resident Asian for ethnic projects but because she was a capable, hard-working professional. She presented herself as an ordinary white businesswoman, used a Western name ("Mrs. Winnifred Reeve"), and dressed in Western business clothing. Yet she did not conceal the fact that she was Eurasian. It was no secret that she had written "Japanese" novels and had "Oriental" blood—her success as a novelist had secured her employment in the first place, and her books were widely known and commercially respected.

Not unnaturally, when there was an "exotic" story in the works, she tended to be assigned to it. Two of her six credited features (*Shanghai Lady* and *East Is West*) had Asian themes, while perhaps a quarter of her projects—scripts, partial scripts, treatments, assignments, collaborative pieces, ideas she conceived, or stories she was assigned to—had either Asian or otherwise "exotic" themes. She was never pigeonholed, however. The range of stories she worked on was extremely diverse. Winnifred was not confined to ethnic themes or ghettoized.

Although she won few of the very top assignments, it is unlikely that the way her ethnicity was perceived had much to do with her employment as a screenwriter. The environment in which she worked was so geared to churning out commercial productions that a writer's sex and ethnicity were not of paramount importance. Being a woman was no barrier to employment at the time Winnifred was hired, and she obviously played her ethnicity just right for the time. She secured Hollywood employment earlier than other minority writers because she was already well established as a writer. No doubt, her chameleon nature helped—she could turn out whatever was wanted, and she could also be whoever was wanted.

This was one time in Winnifred's career that she did not pretend to be anything other than what she was. An early MGM publicity release features a photograph of her looking like an ordinary Western businesswoman. Yet her former nom de plume, Onoto Watanna, is prominently mentioned. Despite all the pressures on her to perform during this period, at least she no longer had to live a life of pretense. In this respect, she had come into her full maturity.

Interestingly, it was in her Hollywood period that, for the first time in her life, the flirtatious Winnifred was gone. Until then, in her dealings with men, it had been second nature for her to consider their romantic potential. For all the tough-mindedness that a career woman of her era needed to cultivate, Winnifred was what would have been called "all woman" or "man crazy." Yet this facet of her personality seems to have completely dried up during her Hollywood phase.

It did not dry up permanently. As will be seen, she performed a remarkable feminine feat at the age of fifty-six, winning back her long-estranged husband Frank and making short work of his mistress, in one of the most passionate and startling episodes of her life. Winnifred had lost none of her female force and allure. But in her Hollywood years, there is nothing to indicate that she ever looked at a man in anything other than a businesslike, cut-and-dried way. There is not the slightest indication that she was ever unfaithful to Frank during the seven years of their separation, and her interactions with other men were signally lacking in any flirtatious element.

There was little time in her life for romantic fantasies. Busy as she had been in former years, she never worked as hard in her entire life as she did in Hollywood. Her output was phenomenal—whatever the quality, she worked obsessively, with a desperate edge. She was frantic to "make good," not to disgrace herself, to keep afloat. There was nothing frivolous about her time in the dream factory.

When she broke with the Laemmles and Universal over her assignments, Winnifred lost another asset—she had no "rabbi" or powerful mentor who would look out for her, so essential to a Hollywood career, then as now. Without a protector, whom she might have attracted had she been younger, she had to fight for herself and battle alliances and social networks against which she stood no chance.

One writer recalled that during the 1930s "the competition was very great—you couldn't make mistakes because there were other writers waiting to step in and fix your script up the way you were fixing somebody else's."[21] With competition for assignments what it was, an aging woman, by her own admission tactless and blunt, inept at politics, and not such a stellar talent, was sure to be cut right out of power by the more cunning. The hotly contested spoils of Hollywood would be wrested from her. It is no wonder that Winnifred eventually gave up the struggle, in her mid-fifties, and went home to a man who still thought she was the greatest little woman who ever came along.

It may also be that Winnifred dropped the flirtatious approach because there was simply no place for it in the hustle of a busy story department. The casting couch was not usually a hurdle for the screenwriter; coming across with the product was what mattered. Nor does it seem to have been the case that women screenwriters of the silent era were subjected to much in the way of sexual discrimination or harassment. "If they [women] delivered good scripts, they were treated as good writers. They [producers] did not ask if it was a woman or a man . . . but what was the last credit? Was it any good? How did it do? . . . Nobody asked you to take your pants down," said one writer.[22]

As a scarcity of professionals to write the increasing number of films became apparent, a campaign was launched to lure "real" authors to Hollywood. In 1919, Samuel Goldwyn came up with his Eminent Authors' Program and hired a number of famous writers to write original stories, including Gertrude Atherton, a California novelist and friend of Winnifred; Rex Beach; Mary Roberts Rinehart; Elinor Glyn; and Somerset Maugham. The plan was not notably successful, as the writers complained that they were not allowed to supervise their productions and were merely used as publicity for Goldwyn.[23]

Holliday notes that many silent screenwriters had once been authors, mostly of magazine fiction. In a survey cited, "of 183 writers, 85 had backgrounds in fiction, drama or journalism. Both fields were open to women. Writing popular fiction had been one of the few career outlets for educated women in the nineteenth century and continued to be so in the twentieth."[24] This may explain why Winnifred was recruited so readily by Universal in the first place. With her solid career as a popular writer, she was part of the "Famous Writers" movement.

According to Holliday, the women who wrote the silent scenarios "did not see themselves as path-breaking women; they possessed the consciousness of highly skilled craftspeople."[25] Frances Marion recalled their reaction to the arrival of Goldwyn's "Eminent Authors": "All of us who had been schooled in writing directly for the screen grew a little fearful of being undermined by so much talent, yet we knew that sooner or later these authors would find out that the screen was not an easy medium to write for. It entailed many special aspects of which they could have no previous knowledge."[26]

The number of women screenwriters dwindled after the advent of talkies. Benjamin Hampton provides an explanation for this: "Though a handful of women made the transition . . . the greater number fell by the wayside. When asked why, Lenore Coffee, who flourished in both epochs, commented, 'A silent film was like writing a novel, and a script was like writing a play. That's why women dropped out. Women had been good novelists, but in talking pictures women were not predominant, because there were few prominent female playwrights.'"[27]

One aspect of Winnifred's screenwriting career becomes clear when it is realized that, as Hampton points out, "few final shooting scripts in the studio era came from the pen or typewriter of one writer. The vast majority of scripts, produced and unproduced, resulted from the collaboration of anywhere from four to fourteen writers." A producer at Twentieth Century–Fox recalled that he supervised writing on fifty-two stories, written by a total of ninety writers. At MGM in the 1930s, each script averaged seven writers.[28] That is why it is not surprising that Winnifred worked on hundreds of stories, scripts, and treatments, yet she is formally credited with only six finished films, even though we know, from her correspondence and actual scripts, that she worked on others that were produced and many more that were not.

The success of the "talkies" following *The Jazz Singer* in 1927 was so great that, in Hampton's words, the "already prosperous industry . . . was almost immune to the chaotic aftermath of the Wall Street crash of 1929."[29] This was not a prosperity in which Winnifred participated. With her glib dialogue skills, she weathered the initial transition but soon fell on hard times and left Hollywood when the number of women writers was rapidly shrinking.

Where did Winnifred fit in this array of early women screenwriters? With no major hit or great classic film to her credit, she was not one of the great ones, nor was she the highest paid. She started her film-writing career when she was older than most writers, with a long novel-writing career behind her.

She was clearly flummoxed by big-gun politics, which may have held her back instead of promoting her screenwriting career. Yet even though her performance may be considered average at the studios, she achieved no small measure of success. She was steadily employed, turning out hundreds of pieces of work to exacting specifications in a cutthroat industry, and she managed to survive in the industry for seven years.

She began those years in high spirits and came out of them a noticeably more cynical, discouraged, and disillusioned woman. But in 1925, early in her adventure, she had a blithe feeling of her new power, and she celebrated her good fortune with some humorous verse about her screenplay, *A Savage in Silk*. It conveys her good-natured, if queenly concept of her place in the office:

> Winnifred Reeve one good day,
> To her Scenarists assembled did say—
> "Behold, it is my royal intent
> To stage a scene of merriment,
> For a Savage in Silk has duly been sold,
> Its story in movies soon to be told." . . .
> Doris in red, gave us all a wee peep
> At her 'dorable babe in his cot fast asleep . . .
> Now, Sir Charlie Babcock I honestly think,
> Was smitten in heart by a Lady in Pink.
> Perry, I'll aver is a good natured scout,
> Said he'd chauffeur all home, tho distant the route.
> Our Hostess most charming, brimmed o'er with elation—
> Verily the affair was a gala celebration![30]

A Savage in Silk, a script about a gypsy in high society, had just received an offer from Paramount for $10,000. As it turned out, Winnifred could not take the offer because she was under contract to Universal. Universal paid her only $2,500, and the script was never filmed. In a friendly letter, producer Alfred A. Cohn gave Winnifred some wise advice—not to sell her stories to Universal while in charge of the scenario department but to hold back her work. "If the stories are good, they will keep. . . . I know the history of scenario editors pretty well and why so many of them have fallen by the wayside," he observed.[31]

By the end of 1926, Winnifred's relations with Universal had cooled. It was announced in publicity releases that Winnifred would do the adaptation of *Show Boat,* an Edna Ferber novel with a Mississippi River setting. She was supposed to have a month to do the job. Trouble set in almost immediately. She wrote an earnest memo to Carl Laemmle Sr. on November 12, 1926, discussing the problems of the piece.[32]

The studio had paid $65,000 for this best-selling novel by a famous author, but the story had little plot. "It is practically just a record or history of an itinerant troupe of actors on a show boat. . . . There are no big dramatic situations or episodes," Winnifred wrote in her memo. She could see how to develop a thrilling story, with dramatic punch, but here she got to the core of the problem: she was not getting "*intelligent* supervision." "If a writer is heckled and destructive criticism hurled at his work, he loses his enthusiasm and ability to create," she reasoned. "A fine ability of the success of *trusting the writer* is shown at Metro Goldwyn Mayer. Miss Dorothy Farnum, chief scenario writer for Irving Thalberg, told me that conferences on a story while in writing are confined merely to the supervisor, the writer and the director."

Winnifred's pleas to be allowed to work on the adaptation as she wished were for naught, and two months later she quit her job in exasperation. Her memo to Laemmle Sr., dated December 7,[33] gives the details of this split, in which she proudly advised her employers that she had signed up with MGM for a salary three times what Universal was paying her and that her services were "competed for" by three other companies. "I am writing this," she said, "mainly to express to you my real sorrow at leaving your employ. I admire, love and respect you, and I am just Oriental enough never to forget a kindness. You gave me my start in pictures, and it is not your fault that I was despicably treated at the coast. From the day I arrived I was a marked woman. Stories without the slightest basis in fact were circulated about me to the effect that I was impossible to get on with."

In an attempt at self-justification, she irrelevantly insisted that everyone who ever worked with her was her friend; that she had in her employ two servants, one of whom followed her from New York; and that she had the same friends today that she had when she was a girl. "Does this look as if I was a troublemaker or a woman hard to get on with?" she asked. "John Emerson, with whom I collaborated on two plays said I had the most pliable mind and disposition of any person he had ever worked with. I am merely another example of Universal picking an original mind and unique personality, training them, and then . . . [letting them be] immediately picked up by another company."

After a panegyric to her own competence and honesty, she pointed out that very few authors stayed in the industry any length of time and that she was "a unique exception inasmuch as I did not despise motion pictures but came in and learned the work from the sales, scenario, story and executive end, and am still in love with the work and intend to stay."

Another side of the story turned up seventy-five years later, when the screenwriter Frederica Sagor Maas, age one hundred, wrote her memoirs.

Winnifred had replaced her as Universal's story editor in 1924, and Maas wrote, "They had been expecting me to quit and now wanted me to break in my successor. . . a sixtyish Japanese lady. I was told she had no association with the motion picture business and knew nothing about it. She lasted six months and almost wrecked the story department in that time."[34] Interviewed later, Maas softened the story. "I remember a woman who was very scared, and putting on a bold front," she said diplomatically.[35]

At New Year's, Eda wrote to Winnifred sympathetically, saying, "I don't believe even you are praying as hard as I am that you get a chance to show what you've got in you at Metro."[36] Winnifred, however, did not remain at Metro long and made no important sales while she was there, though she had hopes that producer David Selznick would buy her novel *Tama*.

Her major work in motion pictures was still to come. Her credited features were all released in 1929 and 1930, and the bulk of her writing dates from those years. In 1927, she made ends meet by doing ghostwriting. The following year, she was back at Universal, this time solely as screenwriter, not story editor.

After she had returned to Calgary, she summed up that period for Colonel William Selig, then her agent:

> Both Goldstein and Mr. Laemmle thought the world of me—so much so that within 3 months after I took the job on, they closed the western story department, and I was made editor in chief. . . . I was instructed by Mr. Cochrane and Mr. Goldstein to investigate certain things, and this I tried to do. Mr. Montagne resented my being sent there (he was western scenario editor), I'll not go into the mean politics. . . . I left Universal and went to Metro. Dave Selznick was a great friend of Montagne. Montagne had been buying for Universal old Selznick properties. Anyway . . . it makes my head ache to think of it all. For a long time the meanest propaganda to keep me out of the business ensued.[37]

At about the same time (1933), she wrote to her old friend Louis Whicher about the experience, which still rankled:

> I ran amuck of studio politics. When they sent me out from New York, I went into a seething maelstrom of politics. They resented a woman being put at the head of them. . . . I had one unfailing friend in Mr. Laemmle, but he went abroad, and I did not know how to handle my problem. . . . I made enemies and was wrathful and independent, and then befell the tragedy of tragedies in my life—the long illnesses of my children. . . . I was forced to do ghost writing . . . for other writers who could not write, but who had all the pull and brass in the world. I had to swallow my pride and eat dirt. Well I'm up here now.[38]

There had been signs of trouble with Winnifred's children even before she left Canada; Charley, already a handful, had been expelled from Mount Royal

College. When Winnifred moved to New York, they came with her—Perry was twenty-one, Doris eighteen, and Charley seventeen. Bizarrely, all three children believed that they were two years younger than they really were. In falsifying her own age, Winnifred had long ago altered her children's ages too, and Doris and Charley learned their true ages only after her death, when it was a considerable shock to them both.

It was after Winnifred left New York for Hollywood that her family really fell apart. As soon as she departed, Charley decamped for a bohemian life in Greenwich Village. Later he joined his mother, who tried to find him work in California. He was extremely handsome, and glossy head shots were taken; he probably obtained some extra work, as Doris did. Charley was always highly attractive to women. At one time during his stay in Hollywood, he had an affair with a married woman whose composer husband came to see Winnie, declaring, "I won't be a cuckold!" It was an incident about which both she and Doris giggled.[39]

Charley flitted between Los Angeles and New York and in 1928 hitchhiked across the country, showing up in Hollywood so "appallingly thin" that Winnifred sent him to Santa Fe to recover. He enjoyed life in "a colony of artists and writers, headed by Mary Austin." Winnifred wrote, "He writes wonderfully . . . but not popular stuff. Imagine Charley as a poet! Yet his poetry has appeared in Paris Transition, Contemporary Verse, Free Verse, Greenwich Village Quill and other very exclusive journals, and one of the publishers here said she considered him the foremost of the promising young poets of America."[40]

Winnifred exerted herself to get Charley some assignments in Hollywood. He worked on a few stories with her and on original scripts of his own. While in Hollywood, he was erratic and never given to steady employment, but his drinking was not yet so severe as to alarm his mother. During this period, she probably thought of him as a charming, lovable, talented scapegrace, who would pull out of his instability and turn out a success. It was not to be.

Doris, the stable one of Winnifred's children, eloped at the age of eighteen in 1924, with a young man Winnifred disapproved of, very soon after Winnifred's arrival in New York. Doris's marriage lasted until shortly after her baby was born—Paul George Rooney, always known as Tim, was born on July 14, 1925. When Tim was four months old, Winnifred, who by that time had moved to Hollywood, journeyed back to New York and took Doris and the baby to California, a five-day train journey in those days. After this, Doris and little Tim were a permanent part of Winnifred's ménage.

Doris's husband, Geoffrey Rooney, a photographer, had contracted tuberculosis in the army during the war, and by the time his son was born and his marriage had ended, he was in a sanitarium, unable to provide for his family. He remained there for years. Doris later spent many months in a sanitarium herself, with tuberculosis she had probably contracted from her husband. During this time, little Tim was put in a boarding kindergarten, but his grandmother saw him often. In Hollywood, Winnifred and Doris lived in rented houses or apartments, with servants and a nurse to look after Tim while Doris worked. They often moved, as was Winnifred's habit. Tim still remembers her at work, her typewriter clicking and her voice excitedly talking out the dialogue she was writing; sometimes gales of laughter issued from her room.

After Doris got out of the sanitarium, Tim stayed at the kindergarten as a day pupil, later going to Grant School at Wilton Place. Winnifred had a car, which Doris usually drove, to take him to school. Sometimes Winnifred would be working at a studio, sometimes at home. She often took Tim to Universal with her and sometimes to the birthday parties of studio executives' and stars' kids, events that he disliked because he seldom knew the other children.

Doris, to support herself and her son, worked as a stenographer, remaining in Hollywood with Tim after Winnifred left. By then, the Great Depression had set in, and Doris had a hard time getting work. She had little success at acting—a director friend, Robert Florey, got her a few bit parts (she played a nurse in the 1934 film *Bedside*) and some extra work. Winnifred sent her money but was limited as to what she could send out of Canada. So Doris and Tim moved back to Calgary in 1934. Doris then went to work for Frank and worked for him without interruption for the next twenty-two years, becoming a director and vice president of Commonweath Petroleum.

But if Winnifred worried during her Hollywood years about Charley and Doris, their problems were nothing compared with her oldest son Perry's situation, surely the worst tragedy of her life. Perry, by all accounts, was a normal, healthy young man when he accompanied his mother to Hollywood, but he developed a severe mental illness, perhaps schizophrenia, in 1926, when he was twenty-three years old. Many years later, on his death in 1964, Doris wrote about his sad life: "Perry was 61, the oldest of the family; and like [Charley] his life was full of tragedy. His tragedy however, was not of his own choosing." As a child, Perry had had spinal meningitis. His eyesight and hearing were affected, and he wore leg braces. Gradually he became physically stronger and did very well in school, especially in mathematics. Interested in mechanics, he entered technical college after high school, and the family was very proud when in the early days of radio, he made one of the first crystal sets in Calgary and won a prize at a local exhibition. Perry also loved music and played the piano. "In personality, he was sensitive and rather shy, but very lovable," Doris remembered. Then came dark times. "Perry had his first nervous breakdown at 23, followed by many others, and . . . was finally committed to a State Hospital. There were several years when he was able to work in a radio factory in Hollywood; and he also took flying lessons with the objective of becoming a 'crop duster.' My mother and I went to see Perry at least twice a week after his final committal and while Mamma was still living in Hollywood," Doris wrote.[41]

That sums up the sad story of Winnifred's oldest son. After Winnifred returned to Canada, she made visits to Perry in California in 1936 and 1938, then yearly after the war. A photograph of the two of them together when she visited Camarillo in 1938 speaks for itself; the look on her face is tragic. Once, when old friends from Calgary were visiting at the ranch and were looking at pictures, Winnifred burst into tears: "That's my Perry."

Tim Rooney remembers how, when he was a child of three or four, his uncle Perry came home from the asylum and was "very strange. He'd wander around and take all the knives and put them under his bed."[42] Tim found his toys in the waste basket—Perry had urinated on them. Back he went to the asylum. First he was in Patton, beyond San Bernardino; then in Camarillo, where he remained for the rest of his life. Two sad little undated letters from him exist, written in a childlike style: "Dear Mother, I want to apologize to you if I was rude to you. I don't mean to be that way at all, but my nerves were kind of wrought up today, and I will be much better after this. Please please try and forgive me if I've been trouble. I will be much better next time. With love always, Your son Perry." In the second letter, he begs Doris to come to visit him and to bring him some new shoes. He tells her that some of her friends have come to see him "and they are also my friends."[43]

Despite the tragedy of Perry, Winnifred and Doris managed to have many friends and a cheerful social life in Hollywood. They were happy in their household, and they both doted on little Tim. Robert and Aileen Florey were perhaps their closest friends; Aileen had been Doris's school friend in Calgary. Another friend was the actress Ann Dvorak, who appeared in *Barbary Coast,* a movie Winnifred worked on. Other "names" who were friends of the mother and daughter were the actresses Anna May Wong, Mary Martin, and Loretta Young. Yola D'Avril, another of Doris's close friends, was originally from Belgium but had immigrated to Calgary. She went to Hollywood with her mother and appeared in such films as *All Quiet on the Western Front.* Yola married a composer, Eddie Ward, who wrote music for films, and Tim Rooney remembered staying with the Wards at their house in Laurel Canyon while his mother was ill. Other friends were the pretty blonde actress

Carol Tevis, the voice of Minnie Mouse, and Ida Mayer, Louis B. Mayer's socially prominent sister, who stayed in touch with Winnifred for some years after her return to Canada.

In 1928 and 1929, Winnifred supplemented her uncertain income by writing for movie magazines. Her stories reveal her attitudes about the industry. In an unpublished article entitled "Movie Relatives," she thoroughly enjoyed herself venting her spleen about people who obtained jobs easily through nepotism. "Movie relatives," she quotes an executive as saying, "are like our skin. They stick to us." And she observes, "Probably fifty per cent of the employees on a Motion picture studio lot are relatives of some executive. . . . It is in fact a rare achievement to obtain a position in a studio without the necessary 'pull.' . . . It is but human nature to take care of one's own first." At Universal, the Laemmle relatives were said to be like "Heinz Pickles. There are fifty-seven varieties, all edible." Winnifred gives a character sketch of "the crown prince," Carl Jr.: "A slight, delicate boy of 19 or 20, undersized, nervous, excitable. Does everything on the run. . . . He has a good brain, restless, imaginative, creative, shrewd. Surefire box office sense. . . . He is a poker fiend. He likes the ladies."[44]

Her article "Butchering Brains: An Author in Hollywood Is as a Lamb in an Abattoir," which appeared in *Motion Picture Magazine* in September 1928, is another lively and revealing view of the industry:

> The train from NY is due. Hollywood prepares to make one of its typical publicity gestures . . . a nice, refined little hullabaloo. After all, it is only an Eminent Author who is arriving in Hollywood.
>
> For a few days at least our Eminent Author . . . is wined and dined, photographed, touted, exploited, interviewed, quoted, misquoted. . . . He has a remarkable contract in his pocket. $500 a week for the first 3 months. . . . Small wonder that he gives forth an interview to the effect that he is charmed with Hollywood and intends to devote the rest of his literary life to the Great Art of motion pictures.
>
> Like fun he is! At the end of the 3 months he will get a little note to the effect that the option on his contract is not to be exercised. . . . The inspirational writer, however big his dreams and production, cannot hope to compete with those possessed of sharp wits, craft, salesmanship, pull, politics and the thousand and one petty tricks that contribute to one's influence in this game. (28)

Winnifred was immensely more cynical now than the starry-eyed girl who had clutched her bag of manuscripts on the threshold of New York, twenty-five years earlier. Remembering her own reactions, she describes what the "Eminent Author" is presented with, once parked in an "ugly little office in a noisy rackety-packetty building":

> He sits in his office and scans, with bulging eyes, his first assignment. He is presently either convulsed with wild mirth or is stricken dumb with incoherent wrath. He has been assigned to adapt and treat an "original" by one Susy Swipes or Davy Jones of Hollywood. It is an amazing, an incredible document. Its language is almost beyond credence. It is a nightmare patchwork that contains incidents and characters and gags and plots of a hundred or more stories that are horribly reminiscent to the Eminent Author. (29)

As for the supervisors, the "dese and dose and dem boys" are the big guns that the author must propitiate.

In other articles, she wrote about the casting couch. In one, she interviewed an actress called Camilla Horn, who proclaimed, "I could get any woman's husband!"[45] In June 1929, she interviewed Maurice Chevalier for an article entitled "How Frenchmen Make Love." The interview was not a success. Winnifred greeted him with "bon jour," and an "electrical change" swept across the star's face. "Ah-h-h-h! Vous parlez français?" Unfortunately, the greeting had used up her entire French vocabulary. (Even as a child in Montreal, it never exceeded "Wee, wee, wee!") "When finally Chevalier comprehended the limitations of my vocabulary, he regarded me with an element of regret and reproach. 'You don't like interviews?' I asked. 'In France, I am no longer interviewed. My fame is established.'"[46]

Chevalier was considered an exotic in Hollywood, and that may be why she was assigned to interview him. Not surprisingly, she got all the assignments to interview Asian gentlemen. She interviewed Sessue Hayakawa for *Motion Picture Magazine* in January 1929.[47] The question was why Hayakawa, once a star of the first magnitude, "comparable to Valentino," had dropped out of pictures. "He spoke suddenly and almost roughly. 'I will tell you the true reason. It was something deep. It *strike* me inside!' Hayakawa smote his chest hard. His dark eyes were smouldering like black coals. 'It was something said to me that no true man should speak, and no true man can hear . . . it was, you understand, not decent.'" Some men owed him $90,000, and they picked a quarrel; Hayakawa was called a name, an unpardonable insult to his nationality:

> "Only an ignorant coward throws up to a man that he does not like his race. I come of a proud people—a man of my quality could not endure such an insult. Still I did not speak. I stare at his face, but I say nothing. He say then: 'People in this country have no use for *Chinks.*' I am not *Chink.* I am Japanese gentleman, and the word *Chink* is not fit to be spoke. I continue merely to stare at him, and speak no word. Every man in that room look uncomfortable. Then I bow with politeness to all and I leave the room."

Winnifred recounted this story with sympathy and feeling. Hayakawa settled the claim and sailed for Japan; three years later, on returning to Hollywood, he found "'a broader, friendlier feeling. Prejudices vanish like smoke. There is even a marked desire for Oriental pictures.'"

When Winnifred interviewed another Japanese actor, Sojin Kamijima, for *Motion Picture Classics* in March 1928,[48] she used her pen name Onoto Watanna and her own Japanese pretense for one of the last times:

> "Please to welcome to my house!" The words and the voice, with its fascinating accent, took me back, in thought at least, to a country far across the sea. . . . But no! I was not in Japan. I was entering a very ordinary little American house. At the door, smiling and bowing, were Mr. and Mrs. Sojin Kamijima.
>
> All the world that goes to the movies has seen Sojin; for, since Doug Fairbanks "discovered" the Japanese actor and engaged him to play the Mongolian Prince in The Thief of Bagdad, Sojin has supported the most prominent of the stars. He will be recalled as the toothless Jewish jeweler in The Wanderer. . . . I had never been sure of Sojin's nationality.

The article is accompanied by a photo of Sojin with an artificially big-toothed caricature look.

It was to one of these movie magazines, *Screen Secrets,* that Winnifred sold her novel *Movie Madness,* as a serial.[49] This netted her only $300, which seems a pity, for Winnifred's two novel manuscripts about the movie business are bright and bubbly. They mined much material from her own early work experiences, but the Hollywood setting and adventures are appealingly genuine as well as glamorous and are as entertaining as anything she wrote. It is surprising that she could not get a book sale for them, but she was far away from her New York book publishing market.

Movie Madness is the story of Jane Mercer, a young woman in Hollywood who shares a room at the Studio Club with three other young women. As Winnifred did in her own young roommate days, the young women sleep in one bed and eat frankfurters and crackers. One roommate, Joybelle, is a "tired blonde girl with a glittering peroxided head that made Jane think of a large yellow dandelion" (17). Another roommate "is slaving on the von Stroheim set" (18), and a third gets all the extra work she wants because she "sexes her way in every studio" (22). Jane wants to be a writer and gets a job as stenographer at Filmo. She suffers many travails, such as going on location with a director who steals her story and makes a pass at her. "Nothing doing, birdie. I got you trapped," he says. She retorts, "I'm a very strong young person and you're a flabby, fat middle aged man. You can't imagine how hideous you look" (177).

"Hollywood Melody," another bouncy picture of life in Hollywood, is one of Winnifred's liveliest novels, but it was never published.[50] A story of female extras, it was optioned by Howard Hughes, but he never exercised the option. Winnifred again draws on her "starving and writing" days in New York, but some of the book's realism and sparkle come from Winnifred's observations of Doris and her friends, who did extra work.

Among the young women who aspire to "extra" duty in Filmo City are Adeline, Mavis, and Anita, and the statuesque Anna appears yet again. The writing is some of Winnie's most skillful and vivid: "Slim bodies, slim limbs, white arms, faces vivid with rouge, shrill or raucous voices, smell of cosmetics, perspiration, perfume, listerine. Everywhere lingerie. Cold critical glances, admiring flattering ones . . . " (12).

There are sketches of a set where a dead-tired crew works to re-create the Jungle of Wahiti, and the director is "a wild eyed human dynamo, who for three days and nights had not touched his bed. Alternately he called the players: 'My precious children!' 'My dear darlings!' or 'Dummies!' 'Morons!' 'Lunatics!'" (19). Heroine Mavis catches the eye of the hardboiled associate producer Nicholas Bagley, whose "eyes were as dull and inscrutable as a Chinaman's" (22), and he orders a screen test for her. She is also courted by a handsome young composer.

Not much money was forthcoming from stories or from movie-magazine writing, and in October 1929 Winnifred was forced to ask for an advance on her salary from the studio. This was coldly turned down, with the advice that she apply to the employee organization on the lot that handled loans.

Winnifred was tempted to approach Frank for money again since he was starting to do better financially. After she had been away from him for two years, he had stopped sending her aid and the tone of his letters had become detached. In February 1927 he made it clear he wanted to cut things off between them completely: "Because some magistrate tells you and I that we were man and wife twelve years ago does not say that we are today in any sense of the word. I do not consider that I have any obligation to send you money after your four years absence. . . . I have no hatred in my heart toward you but it is beyond the power of my mind to forget. I will give you five hundred dollars and a full release from further financial obligations."[51]

But Winnifred's sister Rose de Rouville was working for Frank, and her letters, evidently written with the intent of bringing the separated couple back together again, gave Winnifred encouragement. Frank had hired Rose to set up a branch of his brokerage business in Edmonton, and she reported, "I was in Calgary for about four days, saw your Frank, who is looking extremely well and who is almost the busiest man there. He is working night and day in his office, since the oil boom there started, about a month ago, and is making lots of money."[52]

Rose was proud that she and her partner, another woman, were the first woman brokers to start running an office in Edmonton. It was being run on a commission basis, with Frank getting half. "You would be quite excited if you were in Calgary at the present time. Everybody is buying oil stocks," she wrote, adding that Frank was "something of a wizard in the business." She assured Winnifred, "He was lovely to me, and of course talked ever so much about you. He is living as of course you know, at the Empress Hotel. Is comfortable there—has his books, your photographs and Doris' about the room, and I can assure, has no other woman in his mind or eyes. . . . One of you, either Frank or you, will have to take a holiday and visit one or the other."[53]

A later letter from Rose showed that her venture had not turned out as well as she hoped. "I did start off not too badly in July—but it died out. . . . So you see, I have not made *my* pile in oil," she wrote ruefully.[54]

In September 1929, Winnifred wrote a confidential letter to a friend, the American vice-consul Samuel Reat, to find out exactly what Frank's situation was, for her letters to him had elicited no replies, and Rose was no longer on the spot. "I would be very much obliged indeed, if you would kindly let me know whether Mr. Reeve is still in Calgary," she wrote. She went on to self-importantly list her own projects: "Now I'm on an original story for Mary Nolan. Keeps me hustling, but I love it."[55] By this time, Winnifred had completed work on what were to be her main credits in Hollywood.

The Mississippi Gambler was her first released Hollywood picture, opening on November 3, 1929. It was presented by Carl Laemmle and directed by Reginald Barker, the scenarist was Edward T. Lowe Jr., and Winnifred was credited with the dialogue. The story concerns Morgan (Joseph Schildkraut), a Mississippi riverboat gambler who cheats the elderly father of pretty Lucy (Joan Bennett). The *New York Times* review was not entirely approving: "It would appear that Joseph Schildkraut had a Southern accent left over when he completed his work on *Showboat* and Universal Pictures had a Mississippi steamboat on their hands, so the two were put together in another talkie, along with the personable young Joan Bennett, to make the hybrid *Mississippi Gambler.*"[56]

Shanghai Lady, released by Universal at about the same time (November 17, 1929), was also presented by Carl Laemmle but directed by John S. Robertson. Scenario and dialogue credit were shared by Winnifred and Houston Branch. The story was adapted from a 1910 play, *Drifting,* in which the sluttish blonde Cassie Cook (Mary Nolan), late of Polly Voo's Shanghai brothel, meets the derelict McKinney, on the run from the half-breed detective Repen, on a train. Each thinks the other is respectable, and when the truth comes out, they start life anew in the United States. Much of the *Shanghai Lady* dialogue sounds like Winnifred's Japanese stories at their worst, written at top speed: "Take your hands off me, you half-caste ape!" "Go lay an egg for yourself!" "Laugh, you hyena, I do love him—so much that I'd rather die than tell him what kind of girl I am!"

Winnifred and Edward T. Lowe Jr. shared the adaptation/dialogue credit for *Undertow,* released by Universal on February 16, 1930, which was presented by Carl Laemmle and directed by Harry Pollard. This was another Mary Nolan film, adapted from Wilbur Daniel Steele's story "Ropes," published in *Harper's Monthly,* and was a reworking of Winnifred's first picture, the 1921 *False Kisses.* Sally marries Paul, a lighthouse keeper, who goes blind. He recovers his sight to find her kissing her former fiancé, but he realizes it is not her fault.

Young Desire, released by Universal on June 8, 1930, was presented by Carl Laemmle and directed by Lew Collins, with adaptation and dialogue shared by Winnifred and Matt Taylor. Another Mary Nolan vehicle, this was adapted from the 1924 play *Carnival* by William R. Doyle. Helen, a former dancer in a carnival sideshow, kills herself by jumping from a balloon rather than shame her fiancé with her past.

Winnifred's final feature film, *East Is West,* was released by Universal on October 23, 1930. Presented by Carl Laemmle, the dialogue was credited to Tom Reed and the adaptation to Winnifred Eaton—the first time she had used her maiden name in Hollywood, an indication that she was contemplating divorcing Frank at that time. The film featured Lupe Velez, Lew Ayres, and Tetsu Komai and was adapted from a 1924 New York play by Samuel Shipman and John B. Hymer. It was also a reworking of a 1922 Constance Talmadge film, written by Frances Marion. Pretty Ming Toy is saved from being "auctioned." Sent to the United States, she attracts the powerful Chinatown figure Charley Yong, but he gives her up when he learns that she was kidnapped from American parents as a baby.

The *New York Times* reviewer called it "an intricately plotted and quite implausible affair which runs its tedious length for an hour and 20 minutes. . . . Edward G. Robinson appears in his first talkie as Charlie Yong, the chop suey 'king' of San Francisco's Chinatown, and provides most of the entertainment with his amusing characterization of an egocentric half-caste."[57]

If these were the only films on which Winnifred officially received credit, she nevertheless worked on many films that were released without her name and on dozens of other screenplays, treatments, and projects that came to nothing. Sometimes it seemed as if much of her work involved arguing and begging for credit, which usually she was not given.

On November 26, 1929, for example, she wrote a memo to her superior, C. Gardner Sullivan, asking for original story and dialogue credit on *Barbary Coast,* to be shared with writer Charley Logue, as well as full credit for the story and dialogue of *Carnival,* which she wrote in its entirety. She told Sullivan:

> After reading the continuity of *Barbary Coast* I am so depressed I am going to beg you to have some other writer do the continuity of *Carnival.* The original story of *Barbary* had flame in it—it was real and the characters were vivid and natural. . . . The story that has been substituted is mechanical and wooden. . . . I really feel sick about it but it seemed to me to be nothing short of movie vandalism. . . . I don't see what I can do in the way of doctoring up this dialogue, the fact is, I feel as if I don't want my name on this.[58]

She respectfully importuned Sullivan again, asking for a bonus for her work on *Barbary Coast.* She reminded him that she had delivered her scripts in record time, yet was "receiving the lowest salary of any of the scenario writers here with one exception." And she tried flattery: "You are the one person in this industry who was able to bring out my capabilities."[59]

On the same day, she wrote to Carl Laemmle Jr. in the same desperate tone. She opened by arguing that the socialite romance *What Men Want* was not a good story and would not "talk well." It would almost be necessary to write an original story:

> Before writing an original story one needs to be in the right frame of mind and come in the proper mood. I don't mind frankly telling you that certain things have been rankling in my mind. . . . Lowest paid writer on the scenario staff, etc. . . . I have been approached by several agents and by two companies for my services, and that two writers, very well known and highly paid, have asked me repeatedly to team with them. . . . To every proposition made me I have replied that I was under contract to Universal and especially obligated to you and your father.[60]

The *Universal Weekly* announced on January 4, 1930, that Winnifred was adapting *What Men Want,* a magazine story by Warner Fabian. It was to be "one of Universal's big specials" for Mary Nolan. Despite all the wrangling, Winnifred did not receive final credit. Her contract was renewed for another six months at this time, but her salary was actually lowered, to $175 a week.[61] That same month, she was trying to help her son Charley—whom she now called by his new pen name, Paul—by writing to Junior Laemmle and other executives, explaining that the young man had worked as a newspaper reporter, writer, and actor and would be glad to go into any department as writer, reader, or publicist.

Far from taking her son on, however, Universal was about to lay Winnifred off. The business manager, Stern, wrote to her formally, "Please be advised that the undersigned elects to and does hereby lay you off without pay for a period commencing Feb. 25, 1930 and continuing thereafter until further notice from us but in no event exceeding 2 weeks."[62]

Winnifred protested to Junior Laemmle, "At the time I signed my contract both you and Mr. Sullivan told me not to worry about the layoff clause." They were aware of her circumstances. "Later on I would not feel it as I would now, and had intended to ask for a leave for a few weeks to finish revision of my novel."[63] But Laemmle replied inexorably: "We have no alternative but to exercise the lay-off clause just now."[64]

On March 5, in an attempt to drum up work, she wrote to Laemmle persuasively about *East Is West:*

> If we have bought this play, as the newspapers say, may I be assigned to the adaptation? This is the sort of thing I do best, and I could turn you out a corking treatment. I have any number of lyrics and jingles—Japanese—which could easily be transposed for a Chinese picture, and if Lupe Velez were to do the picture, she could sing them charmingly and cutely. I think you know that I have written a great many oriental novels. . . . if we do an oriental picture I'd like to work on it . . . when of course—I am back on the pay roll.[65]

It must have rankled Winnifred at this date to have to play the "Japanese" card to secure an assignment, though the confusion of Chinese, Japanese, and Mexican ethnic components was par for the course in Hollywood. However, her plea worked; she was deemed the right writer for *East Is West,* and her layoff ended. It was to be her last credited feature film assignment.

Winnifred's old friend H. L. Amster, who had bought the rights to *Sunny-San,* wrote to her at the time of her lay-off, mentioning that he had heard that she had signed a five-year contract. This was not true; Winnifred was barely hanging on at this point. Amster had sponsored Paul's trip to New Mexico and was not pleased by a visit from the young man in New York. Paul talked about getting married, and Amster felt that this would "retard his development as an artist," though if Paul wanted to go out west Amster would pay expenses.[66] Winnifred had not entirely lost her ability to charm money out of men friends.

Meanwhile, the issue of divorcing Frank was coming to a head. Gossip was circulating in Calgary that he had a mistress, and on February 10 he wrote to Winnifred, for the first time sounding her out about divorce: "You have written me several times that you would give me my freedom if I wished. I think it would be best for both that you did this; then we would each be able to go our own way."[67]

That was not what Winnifred wanted at all, and she wrote back stiffly, saying that she would need to review with her attorney a property settlement. "I have known for some time that I have grounds for divorce against you, both in the United States and Canada. . . . I will add that I would bitterly contest any action on your part, having never given you cause even for a legal separation, since I left Calgary with your full consent and have letters from you attesting to that."[68]

Things at the studio did not improve. In June, Winnifred was miserably anxious again, working hard, in constant fear of being laid off. She was doing a detailed treatment of *The Oregon Trail* and begged to be allowed to finish it. She wrote to studio manager Henry Henigson, "I get panicky if I try to hurry and cannot concentrate so well. After all, I've taken less time than other writers . . . but when harassed or worried lose my head; and this has been the case when I've been told from time to time that you were planning to lay me off."[69]

At this precarious time, Winnifred did not want to face a divorce. Rose wrote from Edmonton in October saying that she had seen a notice in the *Edmonton Journal* in August that Winnifred had filed suit against Frank Reeve, which was to have come up in September, so perhaps things—meaning a divorce—were settled between them. Rose had information on "the other woman," which she had gleaned from Winnifred's Calgary friends, Mabel Reat and Edith Price, who were visiting in Edmonton. They corroborated all the Calgary gossip about Frank and his mistress, "although they believe that Mrs. Hill exaggerates in regard to Frank's presents to her," Rose reported. "Mrs. Reat dislikes her exceedingly, and the last thing she said to me when she was going out of my office, was, 'Don't let Winnie divorce him so Mrs. Hill can have him!' From what they both tell me, Mrs. Hill is babyish and indiscreet in the way she talks. She has a very nice house, and evidently pets and flatters and makes him lonesome for a home. . . . I'm sorry for Frank if he does marry her. . . . Mrs. Hill is a parasite . . . he'd better marry some other sort of woman."[70]

Winnifred engaged solicitors to follow Frank's movements and to find if he was going to Reno. They reported to her on May 9, 1931: "If he does this and then marries Mrs. Hill we will have him on toast as the divorce will be invalid under Alberta Law."[71]

Two weeks later, Frank wrote to her from Reno, saying that he had given up his residence in Alberta and was residing in Nevada. He downplayed his finances. "I realize that you may make more trouble but even that can come to an end. . . . I purpose to make this my home unless I am driven out. I have had a hard struggle for the past eighteen months. Most of the large brokerage firms in Calgary have gone broke."[72]

Winnifred's own situation was depressingly bad. She had no contract and few options. She was ready to do battle for Frank; rather than try to get a settlement from him, she would win him back. The truth was that her Hollywood career was over, and she knew it.

Space does not permit a complete survey of all the writing Winnifred did during her Hollywood years, but an examination of even a few of her projects gives an idea of the extent and range of the work. There are many stories that she unquestionably worked on—both her notes and the actual scripts survive—but credit was given to someone else, for any number of reasons. A sampling of the screenplays and script material held at the University of Calgary Library includes:

What Men Want. Winnifred wrote a full-length screenplay for this project about a peppy, blonde gold digger, one of her most sparkling and entertaining pieces of film writing. It was filmed by Universal in 1930, but she did not receive credit.

Separate Maintenance. Winnifred described this as a "censorable 3 act play" about a senator who keeps a mistress. It was staged at the Jean Muir Theater in Hollywood in 1938.[73]

The Wolf of Wall Street. Winnifred wrote a treatment for this film about a jailbird turned financial wizard.

The Atlantic Cable. An assignment given Winnifred at Metro, for which she wrote a novel outline and screenplay.

Ourang. The story was by Fred de Gresac, the screenplay by Winnifred and Isadore Bernstein. A horror story about an immense jungle beast, it was later filmed as *East of Borneo.*

Winnifred also wrote full-length screenplays of her own novels: *Tama, Sunny-San,* and *Wild Seed* (a version of *Cattle*).

In addition to all her writing, as we have seen, Winnifred constantly had to defend her own work, seek assignments, beg to be kept on, and otherwise fight for survival, all of which had been enormously draining. Winnifred wryly contemplated writing "The Love Affairs of a Middle Aged Woman" about "the only well known writer to go into pictures and remain without being disillusioned." But she was. It was time to abandon Hollywood.[74]

For a long time after leaving Hollywood, Winnifred had the ill-founded hope that Hollywood would come back looking for her. On a return trip in 1938, she tried to make useful contacts, but without success. Her day was over.

The literary agent H. N. Swanson regretted that his list was so large, he could not help her.[75]

She summed up her experience in the industry in a letter to Colonel Selig, written not long after she left Hollywood:

> When I was in Hollywood, my own personality reacted against me. I found myself holding an executive position in a world of seething politics. I was constitutionally unable to handle my problem and made enemies. Later my boy's illness put me at the mercy of some of these men; that is to say, I had to come to their terms on my stories and my work. You know in the movie game they despise you when you are not at the top—their idea of the top. I had in fact everything that should have made me valuable to a film company. They needed story brains—and I had them. They needed imagination, and that I had; but I did not have a pinch of tact and I was victim of an unforeseen siege of illness in my family. . . . So that desperate and alienated from my husband, I sold my things for anything I could get immediately.[76]

Long afterward, when she was back in Canada, on a visit to Vancouver, she was interviewed by the *Daily Province* about her movie career. "Mrs. Francis Reeve, jovial dark-haired Vancouver visitor, declared she had 'no story to tell' when interviewed. . . . 'Mine is a quiet, uneventful life,' she said modestly. Reminded of her six active years as scenario editor in chief for Universal, Mrs. Reeve gazed reminiscently into space. 'Yes, I made something of a name for myself in Hollywood, but the fame of a film writer is very ephemeral.'"[77]

10. Vanquishing Mrs. Hill

> I've been out in a man's world of work the major part of my life. I have a professional woman's contempt for the weak clinging vine parasitic type of my sex. . . .
> —Winnifred Reeve, "Second Honeymoon"

> You never can understand me. I am a Chinese puzzle as far as you are concerned.
> —Winnifred Reeve, "Second Honeymoon"

In the summer of 1931, a discouraged Winnifred, exhausted by her Hollywood work, thrown out of a contract, and broke, made a final bolt, one that could not be bettered for high romantic style. She breathlessly related her story to her sister Rose in a long letter: "What I am going to tell you is very confidential—for a week or two anyway. You will understand in a minute! Frank and I have become reconciled—and what a reconciliation! I am so happy about it Rose, that I scarcely know what to do—feel as if I were in a sort of dream."[1]

Frank had gone to Reno to establish residence for a divorce. After a few weeks, he came to Hollywood, meaning to sound out Winnifred in person about the divorce. Her landlady met her in the hall and told her he was waiting. She told Rose:

> I was so frightened I nearly fainted. Well—I went in, and there he was. He stood up—we looked at each other—he half lifted his arms. I held back. I couldn't speak, and his eyes filled up with tears. So I said:
>
> "I know why you are here. You want to marry Mrs. Hill."
>
> He replied:
>
> "Winnie—will you go out with me somewhere. My car's outside."
>
> Well, Rose, we drove for miles and miles—away out beyond Long Beach—almost to San Diego. We scarcely spoke, and the day was beautiful. Then I asked him:
>
> "Do you love Mrs. Hill?"

> He said:
> "I think a lot of her."
> I said:
> "You haven't answered me. Do you love her?"
> He replied in a low voice:
> "No."
> After that it seemed as if something was lifted, and I felt almost lighthearted. So I said, after we had ridden awhile:
> "Well, anyway, even if you marry her, we will have had these few hours together."
> He put his arm around me and drew me close up to him, and I *knew*!

When they returned to her apartment, he told her he had never stopped loving her and had fallen in love with her all over again. "That when I came in—the very instant, he wanted then and there to take me in his arms and hug me and that he kept saying to himself: 'Winnie needs me.' He cried Rose! He told me how lonesome he had been—and—Oh—all the rest! Well, I held back for awhile, but the next day I went with him to his hotel at Santa Monica, and then he moved into our place the following day."

She took him to meet all her friends. "Everyone was tickled to death. I'm quite well liked here and have some darling and very important friends among scenarists, directors and others," she told Rose. She clearly enjoyed showing off her handsome Canadian husband.

Then Winnifred and Frank, in a state of delirious bliss, drove to Lake Tahoe and spent a week together, which was like a second honeymoon ("I lived literally in my silk pajamas—lay in them on the beach, and went on long tramps in them"), after which she returned to Hollywood by train. The plan was for her to join him in Calgary in a few weeks' time. They would vacation in the Rockies, and then Frank would return to Calgary, where people owed him money—in particular, Jo Price, the husband of Elizabeth Bailey Price, and Mrs. Hill's lawyer, J. McKinley Cameron. He meant to sue them, but Winnifred, after venturing this indiscretion to Rose, added virtuously that she would not go into details, because "Frank considers matters of business confidential."

Of course, everything was not perfect. The fly in the ointment was, no surprise, money. Frank had unwisely put into Mrs. Hill's safety deposit vault thousands of dollars worth of bonds and securities. He had her receipt and her agreement to return them upon demand, but, as Winnifred revealed to Rose, "it is going to be a sensitive thing for him to handle, and that's why, for the present, be careful not to let anything leak out."

Winnifred went on to Rose, "Frank told me everything about his relations with her. For about a year she has been his mistress. That is to say, no one knew—but she gave herself to him at regular intervals. She is waiting for him to return and marry her."

Waiting in vain, as it turned out. In living with Winnifred again, Frank was nullifying any charge of desertion for a divorce action. Winnifred declared that what "towered above" everything was that he loved her. "And I love him Rose! I never realized how much till we were together again. All the old sores and grievances passed away. He says we must be together alone—he will make a home for me—but the children will not be with us. You can't imagine how lovely he was to me at Lake Tahoe, and to prove his love, he made a will, leaving me everything and appointing Mr. Reat as executor."

For Winnifred, the girl who once wrote that she sincerely wanted to be rich, what more proof of true love than a will, a real will, tangible, and held fast in one's hand? Now she felt free to indulge in a highly pleasurable bit of gloating:

> I have all her letters to him. Not that he gave them to me. I just took them. He would not even read or unseal them when they came in the mail. I said: "I'll take these," and he agreed. And what letters, Rose! Dynamite! The woman's a silly fool. She wrote him yards of slush, all about birds that sing, and elm trees where the wind whistles through, and a lot of stuff she seems to have taken from books, and he laughed about it—saying, that I would be entertained!
>
> Don't feel sorry for her Rose. Do you know what she wrote Frank: "Get rid of her—get rid of her—at any cost!" meaning me. And she discussed my financial status, and what he should give me, and she said: "Don't see her alone ever—she might poison you!"

Little as she cared to think so, Winnifred had to admit that Frank must have liked Edith Hill. But, as she wrote to Rose, he explained that he was "powerfully lonely, and met her at a time when he needed some sympathy and companionship and over six years is a long time for a man and wife to be separated."

Frank, whose brokerage company had done well, was now solvent enough to be a real prize for Calgary women to contend for, and he naturally attracted other people needing money as well. Sensibly, he downplayed his success to Winnifred at first: "Frank tells me he has enough to retire on, provided I am content to live on the income, which will not be big, but enough to keep us comfortably. Meanwhile I'll go on with my writing. He has over $10,000 owing him," she told Rose. "Everyone here says I look ten years younger," she added comfortably. There was another bit of strange news—the whole thing was "Funny, too, because the same week Bert Babcock wrote me saying he heard I was going to be divorced, and would I marry him again! Isn't this a funny old world—and romantic too at that."

Even so, she was desperately worried about Mrs. Hill. Frank had promised to deal with her. "He says he will tell her that he knows he has done wrong, but that he would be doing her a greater wrong if he continued his relations with her or married her, when he loved another." But would he keep his promise? Or would Mrs. Hill be too much for him? "Oh Rose! I hope she will let him alone. I dread any further stuff between them and you know what devils women can be."

Winnifred should know. Rose wrote enthusiastically in response to her sister's news: "Of all the surprises! But I'm delighted—and Frank [Rose's husband]—why he is jubilant! All along he has been mad about it, that Mrs. Hill had wormed her way so insidiously into Frank. . . . After I read him your letter, he hoorayed, and said, 'Write Winnie right away and congratulate her on winning out. She and Frank were never meant to live apart!' "[2]

Telling Rose her secret was not enough for Winnifred. She longed to tell the world—she especially wanted her rival to know of her triumph. So she wrote to Rose, "Will you do me a favor. I want Mrs. Hill to *know.*"[3]

At the same time, Frank and Winnifred concocted a wire together, telling Mrs. Hill that Winnifred was to get the divorce rather than Frank. The purpose of this deception was so that Mrs. Hill might not suspect their reconciliation, because if she did, "he would have had a heck of a time getting his bonds back." Frank warned Winnifred that his task would be difficult, for he would "have to play a part—until he got his securities."[4]

Once Frank was back in Calgary, he was businesslike and uncommunicative in his letters, and Winnifred began to worry. She feared the camping trip Frank wanted to take in the Rockies; was her health up to it? "Rose, I am not sure whether I could stand for long the high altitude of Banff and Lake Louise. I don't know whether I have told you yet that my heart is not good. It is what you call a slow heart and I am supposed but do not take digitalis; but I get very breathless spells," she explained.[5] This breathlessness must have come from living life like a character in a romantic novel; Winnifred was in fact as healthy as a horse in middle life and lived another twenty-three vigorous years.

Back in Hollywood with no work, Winnifred had nothing to do but fret. She had alarming visions of what might be happening between Frank and Mrs. Hill, when she was not there to prevent the temptress from gaining sway over him again. There was some relief in reminding herself of her superiority over her rival as a writer, if not as a woman, by giving in to the irresistible, delicious temptation to make fun of her letters: "Excerpts—slush and gush—from Mrs. Hill's letters, with sinister inferences and references to me. . . . All the stuff about birds and trees etc. are a queer hodgepodge lifted from books and twisted into her own gaga talk. 'At flush of dawn with joy I hear the Robin's early morning lay. . . . This is Mother's Day and at church our preacher said . . . Gagagagagagagagaga . . . To be a poet, artist or musician is to be artistic.' Oh my God! That is the blahest statement ever made."[6]

There is a good deal more in this vein, and Winnifred worked herself up to such a degree that she began to imagine murder threats. She told Rose "that the woman was actually inciting my husband to murder me was self evident in that last letter." But her imagination was running away with her; all that Mrs. Hill actually said in the letter is a fervent and (from her viewpoint) understandable, "I hope we will be finished with her for good."[7]

In August 1931, all Calgary was talking about Frank, Winnifred, and Mrs. Hill. The full-blown marital scandal sent the residents into jubilant ecstasies, spreading the news. Elizabeth Bailey Price, signing herself "Baby" and writing to her friend "Flos Beloved" from Vancouver, where she was working on a story, gave the "'low down' to the amazing case of Frank Reeve." She had heard the whole story from Rose:

> Frank stuck it out four weeks at Reno, then went to see Winnie and "they literally fell into each other's arms." Winnie held out for a day (clever isn't she?) and Frank begged and coaxed and then away they went. . . . What an orgy of sex with all the latest Hollywood ideas—methinks! . . . Aileen Dee had written her mother and said Frank had to return to Calgary to get the $150,000.00 securities held by Mrs. Hill. . . . Don't you hope Mrs. Hill keeps the securities? And to think our last words were that this winter we would be good to poor spurned Frank Reeve.[8]

Price went on lusciously about somebody's suicide and somebody else's drug overdose. How this catty letter found its way into Winnifred's papers is anybody's guess.

Winnifred had made a good beginning, but Mrs. Hill was not vanquished yet. There was always the danger that Winnifred's enthusiastic, not to say venomous, broadcasting of the situation might get Mrs. Hill up in arms. This was a delicate, difficult time, and Frank had a highly dangerous game to play. He had to return to Calgary and retrieve his money and possessions from Mrs. Hill, while not letting her suspect that he was breaking with her and at the same time not being unfaithful to Winnifred. This was a fine line to walk, almost beyond the capacities of mortal man to perform, and poor Frank Reeve was not endowed with any abnormal sense of guile and double dealing. No one knew better than Winnifred how difficult his task was and what the dangers were. So she wrung her hands and endured overwrought agonies. At the same time, she could hardly have failed to enjoy the drama of such a gloriously scandalous, adulterous, marital triangle.

We can re-create her feelings to a nicety, for Winnifred, characteristically, kept a diary—a frantic account, rife with lurid conversations, illustrating the infinite stickiness of the situation.[9] We can hardly help feeling sorry for the man in the middle, well-intentioned but no match for two women such as Winnifred and Mrs. Hill.

The dialogue in this account is luxuriantly rendered, with Winnifred in her natural element, able as last to indite such melodramatic lines as "To hell with you and your paramour!" and have them fit the situation. Not for the first time, her life imitated her writing style. The wonder is that a woman fifty-six years old, by her own description somewhat overweight and with a mild heart condition, should be up to such youthful, stressful, tempestuous happenings. How many women of fifty-six even today, with improved fitness methods and plastic surgery, find themselves in such a situation, passionately tortured by their romantic feelings? But Winnifred, "almost hysterically alive" as a girl, never entirely lost her youthful passion; her feelings were as strong as ever, and they kept her vital and young.

In a dramatized scene, she sets down a telephone conversation between herself in Hollywood and Frank in Calgary:

> "Did you get your bonds back?"
> "Oh yes."
> "Are you seeing her still?"
> "Yes."
> This is a shock.
> "You shouldn't—you can't do that."
> "There's still some stocks to be attended to."
> "Have you told her about me? You promised to."
> "No."
> I begin to sob—I am shaken and hysterical. I cry:
> "I'll tell her then—I'll write her!"
> "If you do you'll ruin everything."
> "Now I understand—now I understand why you didn't write—didn't wire. You've been with her."
> "Be careful—give me a little time—a few days."
> . . . "You'll spend the week end with her."
> He doesn't deny it. I am getting incoherent. I say savagely:
> "You can't resume intimate relations with her."
> He answers swiftly:
> "Nothing like that!"
> I hang up. Just as if I didn't know what happens between a man and a woman, who have for a year or more been on intimate terms. Just as if I didn't know! I send a long, wild wire.

If people thought Frank and Mrs. Hill were together again, it would be humiliating for Winnifred to return to Calgary. "She had better keep hands off now—or I'm going to do something that will just about slay her in that town," she raged in her diary.

Instead, Winnifred now signed with a new literary agent, Theo Lightner, who thought she could find work for her at the studios. Yet Winnifred felt deeply ambivalent. "What do I care for studios," she confided to her diary. "I can't think of anything, but my husband and that woman!"

She reread Mrs. Hill's letters over and over. "What a shallow, silly soul. Yet she must have been clever and scheming, the way she manipulated you," Winnifred told Frank in her diary. "She made a sucker out of you! You gave her everything—or rather put all in her hands. And that will! Drawn carefully in a lawyer's office—leaving her everything but the income from a mean third to your wife! And she financially independent—and I, without a cent, save what I earn."

Winnifred writhed with jealousy over the difference in Mrs. Hill's financial situation and her own. She comforted herself with, "Well, darling, you did make another will in *my* favor. I won't forget that, even if Irvine, the lawyer, says it couldn't be probated and is improperly drawn. . . . What a mess!"

Frank's letters continued businesslike, and Winnifred was hurt. "A cold, cruel letter, without a word of love in it. . . . Did you feel differently once you were back with her? You could not be so weak and base to deceive us both. If so, you are playing a dangerous game—for women are more deadly and inflammable than dynamite. . . . To hell with you and your paramour!"

Feeling rejected, she saw her agent and then worried that she might get a contract at Fox—what would she do about Frank then? She found some distraction in writing and noted, "I'm rather thrilled by a story I am writing. It's about our own drama—Frank's and mine! It makes a corking story and I've got a new twist to it." Still, she continued to suffer. "We all have our Calvary I suppose. Maybe I deserve mine. Maybe. Was I wholly to blame? True I was gone so long—but I wanted to go back, begged you to let me come back—but you had developed other interests—another love! In the days of your success and affluence, you forgot the poor little wife you had taken out of New York and plumped down on the rough farm. I had the rough years—she the years of plenty."

Her agent obtained a check for a hundred dollars from someone at Fox, and Winnifred noted, "I will pick it up tomorrow. Wonder if it will be N.G. [no good]." She was having to scrounge around for money, while the suspense was becoming unendurable. There were no letters from Frank, and in her worst moments she wondered, "You wouldn't do anything so base. You could not come and make love to me and induce me to sign away my rights—and then scheme to deceive me. If ever a man looked and acted honestly you did."

During this period of her Calvary, as she called it, the last days in which Winnifred would ever have to cadge checks from men and wonder if they would be "N.G.," she wrote her story about the affair, "with a twist."

The twist was unusual, true enough; in fact Winnifred now did one of the strangest things in her strange life, one almost unprecedented in literary history. She wrote the story of her, Frank, and Mrs. Hill—but from the viewpoint of the Other Woman. This piece, published in *True Story Magazine* more than a year later, was entitled "Because We Were Lonely" and was unsigned.[10] The prose is Winnie at her purplest (as suited *True Story,* to be sure) and quite riveting to anyone acquainted with the real situation, starting with the opening line: "I schemed and plotted to win another woman's husband" (28).

The narrator explains that she is a widow of a year, possessed of beauty, charm, and a good social position. Her husband had been "slavishly devoted" to her, and after his death she "envied and resented other women with their husbands in attendance." She determines not to be a widow long, but there are few eligible men in town. Winnifred jealously describes her rival's "orchid existence": "I lay abed till noon, when my maid prepared my bath and brought me my breakfast. I played bridge or mahjong all afternoon, and danced all evening." In spite of such pleasures, the woman was in a "pathological condition," missing her husband "as a husband" (28).

"Ethel" meets "Jerry" at a dance, and a friend tells her that his wife's in California: "Been gone three years now. Fancy leaving a man like that!" (28). (Of course, Winnifred is downplaying her defection; she was gone not three years but more than seven.) Ethel resents Jerry's wife: "What sort of woman was she to leave her husband, to follow the career of a writer?" So she uses her wiles to fascinate and court him, plans her campaign "with care and craft," even gets his financial rating through Bradstreets (29). Winnifred does her best to paint Mrs. Hill as a cold-blooded schemer, but of course it is just as likely that Frank, deserted for so long, deliberately sought a mistress. Winnifred did not like to think this; it would have implied that she deserved blame for abandoning him.

She piled on the passion, as *True Story*'s readers liked it: "The mere presence of this man had the power to obsess me with an almost overpowering sensuousness. The first time he put his arms around me, I nearly lost my senses." The description of the man's loneliness has the ring of truth, however. "We were both lonely. He was the loneliest man I had ever met. He was like a child, literally craving and hungering for affection and attention" (30). The subject of his wife is taboo, though Ethel has a morbid interest in her, out in California amusing herself with her "silly writing." She asks, "I hear she's very clever—is she?" His eyes light for a moment, and he replies evasively, "Cleverness is not everything." Her heart leaps, but he goes on to say, "She had everything a man wants in a woman" (92).

Ethel lives by an unabashed philosophy of man-pleasing, but she is discreet: "People never suspected that my lover had a latchkey, and that he came back to my house after my boys were abed" (92). Inevitably, the day comes when the man tells her it's all over: "You attracted me immensely, but your attraction was mainly sexual, and no woman can hold a man purely through sex" (95). When she begs him to kiss her for the last time, he tells her, "No! Apart from the fact that it would not be fair to my wife, it would be odious to me" (96).

After all, the story is Winnifred's fantasy, and no doubt she hoped that Frank behaved exactly that way. She also delights in having her rival punished and publicly ostracized. Ethel wails, "I am paying the penalty—the price exacted of a woman who breaks the Seventh Commandment!" (96).

Winnifred returned to her home ground triumphant, having vanquished Mrs. Hill in both fact and fiction, but there were still some pesky details to tidy up. As soon as she was installed in Calgary, she wrote to J. McKinley Cameron, the barrister representing Mrs. Hill—and also a man greatly in debt to Frank Reeve. On her highest horse, Winnifred demanded the return of possessions that Frank had stored at Mrs. Hill's house and insisted that she herself be allowed to make a search.

Mrs. Hill agreed that Frank could pick some things up, but Winnifred forbade this, "unless I was with him." Her wish list of articles included oil paintings, Oriental rugs, a black ebony chair, brass pieces, and what she imaginatively described as a "priceless old silver tray and tea service," a "huge soup tureen from pantry of George Washington," and a "blue platter given me by daughter of President Grant."[11]

Most of all she wanted her books, especially her prized copy of Mark Twain's *Connecticut Yankee,* an autographed first edition given to her by his wife, Olivia Clemens. Having won Frank back again, she was not going to be satisfied until she retrieved every scrap of her worldly goods that might still be in her rival's possession.

Cameron wrote back in pompous style, advising Winnifred that "Mr. Reeve would be the best person to apply to for information."[12] Apparently Frank had entered Mrs. Hill's house while she was away and had removed some of the goods. It is hardly surprising that Frank, bumbling about in "the other woman's" house, might not have located all of Winnifred's belongings.

Cameron also accused Winnifred of causing Mrs. Hill "petty annoyances" since her return to Canada. "Most of these matters were so puerile that I advised her to overlook them, but, of course, there is a limit to that sort of thing," said the lawyer. Her request to search the house was "quite impertinent," and he added that Mrs. Hill "is, as Mr. Reeve no doubt informed you, a lady of refinement and culture, and is rather particular of the persons she allows in her home." Cameron accused Winnifred of going to Mrs. Hill's home during her absence and making "vile and utterly unfounded accusations against her and Mr. Reeve to her young son," conduct that made it "unthinkable that she should ever be permitted to enter the house under any circumstances."

If Winnifred actually visited Mrs. Hill's home in her absence and made "vile" accusations to her young son, she certainly was not taking the high road. But she immediately fired off another missive, denying the behavior and adding, "Allow me to thank you for a real laugh, when you give me the gratuitous information that Mrs. Hill is 'a refined and cultured lady' and particular as to who enters her house, to which my husband (as per your letter) possesses a latchkey!"[13]

In the end, this correspondence did her no good; not one of the items she desired was ever seen again among her possessions. Frustrated, Winnifred had no other recourse than to turn to fiction for satisfaction. In a novella-length story "Second Honeymoon," she went over the whole saga yet again, step by step, richly relishing every detail.[14] She evidently meant to publish this fictionalized version, for she changed numerous details and made herself and Frank twenty years younger.

"And so they were divorced, and lived happily ever afterwards!" the story begins, arrestingly. In this version of the several-times-told tale, she again makes fun of her rival's letters and portrays the husband's hangdog reaction: "I burst out laughing. Your head droops; your shoulders droop. You look intensely weary." He takes her face in his hands and says tenderly, "How long are you going to keep this up?"

The other woman writes in a beautiful hand. "Mine is a scrawl!" the wife rails (with perfect truth; Winnifred's writing *was* a scrawl). "She has had the advantage of a finishing school! I've been out in a man's world of work the major part of my life. I have a professional woman's contempt for the weak clinging vine parasitic type of my sex." Winnifred reverts again to her childhood's sense of inferiority: "I'm kind of freaky. I never was 'brought up' properly. I just 'growed' like Topsy. My mother once told me my first bed was a drawer in a wardrobe trunk. She was playing one night stands!"

When the reconciled couple has a romantic dinner at Lake Tahoe, the wife is recognized by a Universal scenarist:

> She stares at me in amazement, almost unable to believe her eyes. I look back at her guiltily. I know a humble $35 a week studio reader has no right to be staying at the same luxurious hotel where a $500 a week scenarist is sojourning.
>
> What are *you* doing here? she asks.
>
> Just what you are, I reply.
>
> She stares hard. My husband is approaching and she glances from you to me. Her voice lowers:
>
> Who's your good looking male?
>
> My husband.
>
> Oh ye-eh! She twinkles her finger at me. You don't have to fib to me. I'm too good a sport to tell on you, she avers. Besides even you are entitled to your affinity I suppose.
>
> That's pretty crass. Even I!

Once Mrs. Hill was properly vanquished, and Winnifred got the residue of jealousy out of her system and safely into fiction form, she thankfully settled down to Calgary life as if she had never been away. Her Hollywood fling was over; she was the wife of one of Calgary's richest citizens. With her background as author and celebrity, she was a big fish in a little pond, and she could play the enjoyable part of distinguished doyenne of the arts. She busied herself with Calgary's Little Theatre, she was president of the Calgary Women's Press Club, and she wrote articles on ways to improve Calgary's art scene.

Edith Hill remained in Calgary, too, and retained her supporters, such as McKinley Cameron, who was at swords' point with Winnifred for the rest of their lives. Tim Rooney remembers once, in the 1930s, sitting in a car with his mother, waiting for Winnifred to finish shopping. A tall, blonde woman came out of another shop. Doris stiffened. "*That's Mrs. Hill,*" she said. He remembered the moment sixty-five years later.

Even in her comfortable new life, Winnifred was still doing some writing. She made notes for a novel to be entitled *Boom City,* about Calgary social life. Another rehash of the Mrs. Hill affair, it has a young "Doris" bullied by fictional Mrs. Hill's friends, "ambitious publicity haunting dames who govern the club, themselves mediocrities." The heroine, a married woman, fears her husband is seeing his mistress again. When the town is threatened by a breaking dam, the husband abandons the mistress to save his wife, in best Winnifred fantasy style.

Evidently Winnifred still had some fears about Mrs. Hill to work through, but this story seems to have done the trick, for she had no further doubts about Frank's love. Fully satisfied, she had no more to say; as she grew more contented, her fiction writing petered out. She sold a story to *Collier's* in 1934 for $85,[15] but it hardly seemed worthwhile: what was the use of writing if she could only make such small sums as that? Passion for writing no longer seemed to enter into it.

In 1933, she became involved in a mild dispute with her old friends Louis Whicher and H. L. Amster about rights to *Sunny-San.* Whicher wanted to buy the dramatic rights,[16] but Amster owned the film rights. Winnifred still thought something could be done and remembered that the producer Ernest G. Shipman was so crazy about it that "he walked into Universal's N.Y. office and said 'I want to kiss the lady who wrote that story.'"[17]

She insisted that talking rights were not included in motion picture rights, and she demanded a payment—even if it was only a hundred dollars—that Amster could send to Doris, who was still in Hollywood at that time and was ill, and it was difficult for Winnifred to get money to her. Winnifred's tenacity on this minor point is surprising, but it was probably because Frank always held her finances on a tight rein. She had a tendency to be extravagant (her grandson, Tim, remembers walking down a city street with her and how she exuberantly exclaimed over every new dress and hat she saw; had Frank not restrained her, she would have bought the lot). Then, too, Frank had lost her once and may have thought that limiting her financially would keep her from flying off again. Winnifred had lost all her savings in the 1929 crash, another factor that made her last two Hollywood years precarious. She also adored gambling, especially in private parties—and she always lost. Finally, there was the danger that she would give too much money to her ne'er-do-well son, Charley. For all these reasons, Frank kept her to a budget.

So she kept trying to glean sums of money from old projects. During one attempt, she admitted to Colonel Selig, "I have done little writing since coming up here, for I have a large house and a social position that takes up a lot of my time, and then I am very much a pal of my husband's and go with him on his trips to the wells and the mines and out hunting, etc. You will like to know that I am far happier than I was in Hollywood. My husband is a fine big fellow who strangely enough thinks I am pretty nice."[18]

Throughout the 1930s, Winnifred made visits to California to see her son Perry at Camarillo. In 1938, Winnifred's sister Grace Harte wrote to her, gently criticizing her for leaving Perry in a California institution.[19] But Tim Rooney points out that there was little Winnifred could have done about this situation: as a mentally ill person and an American citizen, Perry would not have been permitted to enter Canada.

If Perry's condition was Winnifred's greatest grief in life, it was soon to be equalled, if not surpassed, by the misery brought to her by her youngest son, Charley.

11. Poetic Ends

He is a fugitive from friends
Unfriendly to poetic ends
—Winnifred Reeve, "Portrait of a Poet"

Poor little Mamma! So much more alive than anyone else!
—Paul Eaton Reeve to Doris Rooney, n.d.

WINNIFRED'S SON Charley—who by now always used his poetic nom de plume, Paul Eaton Reeve—had found intermittent work in Hollywood. He had written a few scripts and stories and had done some reading and possibly some ghostwriting, but his only real success was as a Greenwich Village poet. Throughout the 1930s and 1940s, his poems appeared in small literary magazines, such as *Briarcliff Quarterly* and *Pegasus,* and in anthologies, such as Parker Tyler's *Modern Things. Designed for Reading,* a 1934 anthology of poets published in the *Saturday Review of Literature,* reprinted his best-known poem, "Auto-da-Fe." Winnifred, who had always adored poetry though she had no gift for writing it, was very proud of her son's talent.

An early letter of Paul's, written in 1929 when he was in Santa Fe, reported that he was sending her several chapters of a book he was writing and grandly announced, "I will be perfectly happy if I do this as near as possible as I vision it, and take a year or more to do it. . . . I have in mind some things of Dostoieffsky's."[1]

Naive and unrealistic about his own work, Paul was more shrewd about hers. His advice sheds light on her attitudes about writing: "Be critical, be analytical; for which you have an amazing gift. . . . You speak of household and family trouble. Yet you are writing a book. Don't write it unless it's going to be good. You don't want another book that will bring in a few hundred from some magazine. You want something that will get a good publisher, and attract some attention."[2]

In 1938, Paul was in Hollywood with his wife, Fayette Avalar. They had met while he briefly taught poetry at Bennington, and she had left her professor husband for him. Paul's marriage soon broke up, and he returned east and moved in with another woman, Margaret Moseby, who boasted, incorrectly, that she had helped him conquer his drinking.

As World War II broke out, Paul avoided the army by convincing the doctors that he was "too neurotic for army discipline."[3] Although he served briefly in the Merchant Marine, Winnifred was displeased by his attitude. She told him, "If you are called in the draft, take it as a man." Commenting on his complaints that it was hard to write, she said, "When I was writing I wrote anywhere—I had no choice."[4]

Paul's life only worsened. He was arrested while drinking and sent to the Tombs. She implored him, "Charley, lay off all drinking, won't you—It's hard I know—but in the end you'll not be sorry—it is nothing but sheer poison and in the Babcock family—it simply slays."[5]

It was a bitter thing for a mother with Winnifred's staunch work ethic to have a son who would not, could not work. Her letters to Paul display a teasing pattern of wealth and poverty, bragging about her and Frank's riches and then lamenting that her limited budget prevented her from sharing the wealth with Paul.

In June 1944, Winnifred responded to the sudden news of Paul's remarriage. She was "thrilled and happy" and asked his wife's maiden name, which he had "omitted" to mention.[6] Paul had not told Winnifred his wife's name because it was Finkelstein. Helen ("Bunny") Finkelstein was a twenty-year-old Mt. Holyoke student, the daughter of a law professor at St. John's University Law School; her mother was a teacher and the national president of Women's American ORT (Organization for Rehabilitation and Training), a Jewish refugee organization. But Jewish relatives were not good news to the Calgary household. When the engraved wedding announcement was finally received, someone—perhaps Doris—carefully excised the name "Finkelstein" with scissors.

So Paul kept his secret a little while longer. Winnifred wrote to "Charley and Helen," prudently taking a cordial tone to ensure good relations with her new daughter-in-law and mentioning the possibility of Paul's working. "Paul has a great brain, but he needs direction and in many ways is unbalanced."[7]

Despite the end of war restrictions, Paul and Helen did not visit Canada. A baby was coming, and Paul, of course, wanted more money. Winnifred suggested that he might get a job as a foreign correspondent. Or perhaps his father-in-law could get him a post in some embassy? He did step in and help Paul obtain a position teaching English at the private Normandie School in Miami Beach. Winnifred's only granddaughter was born in Miami in December of 1945. Although the baby was named Winifred Diana Reeve, this attempt to please Winnifred failed; she did not like the name. Paul and Helen called their daughter Diana or Denny.

A brief cheerful period followed, and in the summer Winnifred wrote Paul that, despite experiencing the first signs of diabetes, she was able to ride horseback to Lake O'Hara in the Lake Louise region, "17 miles in all, so you see your mother is still alive and kicking!"[8] She was now seventy-one.

Things with Paul, however, did not prosper for long. When he was fired from his teaching job after a few months, his father-in-law, Maurice, wrote cordially, offering a home in his own comfortable eight-room apartment on East Eighty-sixth Street. But Paul's drinking did not set well with the Finkelstein clan, and in January 1948 Maurice desperately wrote and begged Winnifred to help devise a way to "save the marriage and prevent the baby from growing up fatherless."[9]

In this emergency, Winnifred and Frank made an epochal visit to New York City, staying at the Plaza Hotel. The situation turned into a tragic farce in which each set of in-laws tried to persuade the other to assume the burden.

Since Winnifred had not seen Paul in several years, perhaps not since 1938, this was her first real opportunity to assess his mental condition. On arrival, she wrote to Doris, describing the situation as she found it. "About Charley, I honestly don't know what to do or say. He is not mental. Has a humorous and quite sane state of mind," she reported. "Maurice nearly out of his wits with these two helpless parasites." Maurice declared that he would cut off all help to the couple; he was willing to support Bunny and the baby, but not Paul. "Now Doris I tell you, no matter what, I intend to stand by Charley," wrote Winnie heatedly. "The beautiful suggestion that he be cast out, poor and penniless, without a cent, does not appeal to his mother."[10]

Winnifred never seemed to understand what her own role might have been in molding her son. An alcoholic father who disappeared from his life; a mother who called him a genius but had little time to attend to him and left him on his own in New York as a teenager; a stern stepfather who insisted that he work, while his mother secretly gave him an allowance. Paul never could achieve the grandiose success he thought he owed Winnifred, and no one was more miserable and frustrated about it than he.

Psychiatry was tried, much to Winnifred's disgust. "Maurice brought Dr. Hawkins, a woman psychiatrist—there was a miserable scene—Maurice shouting and denouncing Charley. Dr. Hawkins tried to deliver a sort of speech, but stopped when I asked her how she knew about Charley and how she could diagnose him. She admitted she was going purely by what Maurice told her, had met Charley just once."[11]

Winnifred's anguished bulletins to Doris are noticeably different from the romanticized, semifictionalized versions of her other personal experiences, such as the reconciliation with Frank or the vanquishing of Edith Hill. Here she is talking straight, shaken with worry, hoping against hope that Paul might hold down a job. Her earnest narrative is utterly devoid of art: "Last night I prayed Charley was at work. Useless, vain! None the less I believe he went to pieces mainly because they took his wife and baby from him and the only home they had. . . . You should have seen him when he . . . rushed in shouting, 'I got a job, I got a job!' . . . There is so much that is good and fine about him. . . . I implored Frank to take him back with us. No dice." She was in despair over Frank's attitude. "Frank says if I encourage or give him anything he'll not only cut down my allowance but cut off what he sends to 'your people.' . . . Anyway, he went for a walk, came back all grins, chucked me under chin and kissed me—I said 'What did you mean threatening me like that?' He said, 'Just teasing you.' Doris, he's a stinker, with all his cheerful ways and jolly temperament."[12]

She wished the young couple could come to Canada and work. Bunny was "a clever little girl, writes and designs. She'd get something." Winnifred wrote despairingly, "I wish I were completely independent—as by God! I intend to be. . . . Charley—that's all I can think of. Pity me."[13]

Doris, the level-headed, wrote to Maurice, "I have been terribly upset and worried about Paul's situation, but chiefly fearful of the effect it would have on my mother. . . . Her letters are pitiful, greatly disturbed and heartbreaking to read, for it is her boy who is concerned."[14]

Doris also wrote to Bunny that she thought it best for her and Paul to separate. "Paul must work (and if possible, you too), and he *must not drink,* for I feel that he cannot any longer go on being dependent on your father." She tried to close off any idea in Bunny's mind about Canada. Frank would not allow it, "for the very reasons you have given me, that your father made Paul seem to be too difficult a person to have around."[15]

Maurice, seeing that he had overplayed his hand and failed in his aim to have the Reeves take their son back to Canada, wrote to Doris, in some exasperation: "I find it difficult to convince your folks, and even you, that Paul is a very sick boy. I have my own problems with Bunny, who is also not entirely right. . . . I think often of little Diana and wonder what effect parents like that will have upon her. I wish it were possible for her to be given to some younger person, like yourself, who would have time to give her the kind of upbringing you give to your son Tim."[16]

And so continued the discussion of where fate would place the child—in New York City with the psychiatry-loving Finkelsteins or in Calgary, under the eye of Doris and the former Onoto Watanna? Doris tried to persuade Maurice that her parents were not people of wealth. "Frank is in comfortable circumstances, but we are not millionaires, or anything like it." And she stood up for her mother: "As for Mamma, she is not, as you put it, incapable of understanding or admitting that Paul is ill, but she is *terrified* of the whole situation."[17]

Paul tried to explain his feelings to his mother. "I do not need hospitalization . . . despite the clever propaganda sowed in your minds by Maurice. BUT—and it's a big BUT—I *do* need to be taken care of. My life has been so difficult (to say the least) so streaked with hardships. . . . That is where Bunny comes in. She takes excellent care of me and likes doing it."[18]

Finally, Winnifred decided that she was secretly going to give Paul a set allowance, twenty-five dollars a week. "I didn't ask Frank, but will do it on my own money," she told Doris. "I've *got* to or die." She ruefully admitted, "Frank says the main reason why he would not want Charley in Calgary is because he has to put up with you and I fighting and wrangling and he won't add another!" She begged Doris not to take Frank's side. "He likes to pose as this bighearted genial jovial Santa Claus, but not to me or mine. . . . His treatment of me is despicable—loving before strangers, but silent when alone with me. I'm through. I'll find a way to solve my problem when I get back but I'll never again feel the same to him. I will not forget—or forgive."[19]

She declared that she was a changed woman, that she planned to do some writing again and perhaps go back to the West Coast. But in the end she relented, and her only outlet was to pen a sentimental poem about her persecuted son:

PORTRAIT OF A POET

He is a fugitive from friends
And relatives and grim inlaws
O is there none who comprehends
He is a fugitive from friends
Unfriendly to poetic ends[20]

The allowance solved nothing. Paul was arrested for being drunk and disorderly, and Winnifred, at her very angriest, wrote about the resultant bills. "I am contributing to your criminal delinquencies when I send you money. Every time you have used it not for the purpose sent but to pour liquor down your greedy throat. You are following exactly in your father's footsteps." She accused him of choosing liquor over his wife and child and asked what he planned to live on. ("Not me.") "I have no more to say. For an old woman I have taken a heavy licking and I am through."[21]

The Reeves returned home, and that winter Doris wrote to Paul to tell him that Winnifred had had a hysterectomy. She was recovering well. "Of course, surgery in a woman of her age is drastic. . . . Yesterday was a bad one for her as she had considerable pain and she was quite bewildered, like a child, and didn't understand what was being done for her or to her. . . . When we left she was feeling very bright and perky and was reading the evening newspaper."[22]

Once she was better, Winnifred could write calmly and kindly to Paul. Perhaps she would even visit him in New York again. "I am torn between two things. I feel I ought to see Perry. I feel I ought to see you," she wrote. She encouraged him about his writing: "Keep up your courage and assurance and you know I have faith in your star. I have always believed in your inherent genius, which merely has been in abeyance. I even love to read those published poems. . . . Always remember that your mother loves you." She wished he, Bunny, and the baby could visit her someday. "I wish you and Perry could have had some of the luxury and comforts of a beautiful home," she said sadly.[23]

Having had major surgery, Winnifred was thinking about her mortality and arranging her affairs. She wrote Paul telling him that he would be provided for by an income rather than a lump sum, so that his in-laws could not take action against him.

In mid-1949, Winnifred and Frank went to California again to see Perry. They also enjoyed seeing old friends, including Ethel Barrymore. Winnifred had known her and John Barrymore years ago, and she wrote to Doris describing a party at which Ethel "looked lovely with her dark hair sprinkled with stardust—she introduced me to a score of people as my best friends from Canada." Winnifred also reported to Doris about Perry: "He's in a dream-world of his own." The doctor, a nice Hungarian man, reassured her that she need not worry about the treatment Perry was receiving. "He said no one would be hard on Perry because he never gave any trouble and was *clean* and nice about himself."[24]

She wrote again to Paul about writing. He had suggested that she try to get into the new medium, television, and her response was, "I daresay I could, but the fact is I have no inclination to *work* again. . . . That's a young person's game. . . . My brain teems with plots, but I have not the vitality or energy to write these days, and probably not the incentive or inspiration."[25]

The tragedy of her sons did not by any means keep Winnifred from considerable enjoyment in her old age. She, Doris, and Frank were all enormously proud of Tim, who in 1950 married a beautiful Canadian, Mary Carlisle. After his marriage, he completed his doctorate in mathematics at Caltech in 1952, and the young couple's first child was born while they were in California. Tim and Mary eventually had five beautiful children, and Winnifred knew and adored the two oldest, Frank and Elizabeth. As a university professor, Tim taught at the University of Alberta and later at the University of Toronto. There was much visiting back and forth between grandparents and grandchildren. When Elizabeth was born in July 1953, Winnifred looked after eighteen-month-old Frank for a week, and both she and Frank delighted in playing with him. While in Arizona some months later, Winnifred proudly displayed a photo of baby Elizabeth and joked, "This is how we breed children in Canada."[26]

Winnifred could hardly help making comparisons between the happy and productive life of her grandson, who took nothing from her, and Paul, an eternal drain. She told Paul, "Tim says, and so does Mary, they have no wish whatsoever to be rich or have too much money. . . . He could have come with our company at big salary, and he turned Frank down. Said he had been four years studying to be a mathematician and was not cut out to be an oil man. Oh Paul I wish you had one half of his common sense."[27]

Maurice wrote to Winnifred about their granddaughter growing up in New York, and Winnifred enjoyed receiving pictures, though she had seen her only twice. "She must be an exceptional kiddy," Winnifred told Paul. "She seems to be a solemn little pet. I daresay she is clever." She reminded him, "Always remember about Maurice and his wife that they did support and take care of your wife and child when you were unable to do so yourself." By now her view of the Finkelsteins had mellowed.[28]

Winnifred was now seventy-seven (though her children, to be sure, thought she was three years younger), with only two years left to live. Despite her sadness about her sons, she still enjoyed life. Her photographs at this period show her sparkle, her undiminished joie de vivre, and her companionable relationship with Frank. (When photographed together she would always stand a little behind him to "hide the fat.") They shopped and traveled and went visiting together, a contented elderly pair. Every winter they traveled to warmer climates—California, Arizona, and once, in 1950, to Hawaii.

By now Winnifred had fully accepted that her husband would never tolerate her alcoholic son in Calgary; they had made their peace and were comfortable together. In the summer of 1951, they took a cruise to Alaska. This was overshadowed by the fact that "Rose is dying of nephritis and dropsy in a New York hospital and Frank is having to pay for it all."[29] The mention of money was seldom absent from any letter Winnifred ever wrote.

There were still tensions in the household, as Winnifred remained a volatile personality, very different from quiet Frank and efficient Doris. Tim recollected that Winnifred (Winnie or Dommy, as he called her) "could be quite inconsiderate. She would put on a regal pose, want to be treated like a great lady, and order people to 'Get me this or that.' Doris wasn't having any, and told her what she thought." There was always some degree of friction between the two women. Mother and daughter loved each other, but they were polar opposites in temperament. Tim remembers Winnifred's humor, her dated slang ("You slay me!").[30] Doris, in contrast, was much concerned with things proper and ladylike. In later years, the Japanese housekeeper, Mary Moriyama ("Maryama"), who had been with the family since World War II, became a beloved friend to both women; yet Doris would eat in the dining room and Mary in the kitchen, as befitted women of different social status. Doris was not proud of her Asian ancestry. Once, she advised her daughter-in-law not to tell her children they were Chinese, for she remembered how hard it was for her and her brothers as children in New York: other kids had thrown stones at them because they looked different.

Winnifred never stopped worrying about Paul's ruined prospects, his life and attitudes so different from her own creed of hard work and independence. "Consider all the wasted years, and what have you got. From the age of 15 I had to work and work hard," she wrote. "I am afraid this letter is going to hurt you. Well, don't let it. Remember only that I love you and am behind you. But Time marches on and I can no longer see far ahead."[31]

Winnifred had given up expecting Paul ever to work. With an elderly woman's realistic, unsentimental assessment of her son, she told Doris, "Either he could not hold a job or he does not want to and is not equal to it. Fact is, I think he had better stick to his last and win or lose go on writing, poetry and what not. After all, money is not everything." This was Winnifred's mature philosophy talking.[32]

Bothered by her arthritis, refusing a hip operation with a plastic plate ("Not for me—I'm too old"), Winnifred, feeling blue, complained to Paul about her home, with which in an ordinary frame of mind she was satisfied. "I have to live where I loathe it, viz 9 months a year in Calgary. I have begged and pleaded with Frank to live in California. No dice. We keep on living in the same old dump and I hate it more than you hate New York."[33] Probably what she hated was not being in motion any more, as she always used to be.

In May 1953, Winnifred received the only letter ever sent her by her future biographer, then age seven: "I got Denny's dear letter and will write her in a day or two."[34]

Winnifred's once boundless energy was fading. "I don't write often because I am not well, and have an inclination to want to lie down and am always tired and drowsy," she told Paul. "Anyway I just don't feel like writing letters, and there really seems only one thing you are interested in." She sensed the end approaching. "Now in case anything happens to me. . . . You are well provided for in my will, but not too much, for I had to distribute my estate over so many. . . ."[35]

In November she told Paul despairingly, "Yes, I know it takes a long time to become a playwright or an author, but you have been at it for over forty years—I mean it's taken you that long to get down to writing." In April 1954, Paul wrote his last letter to his mother, which she never opened: "I am sorry I've been such an expensive son."[36]

Winnifred died very suddenly, without warning on April 8. She and Frank were returning from California by car and were in a hotel in Butte, Montana, when she became ill and started to cry and choke. She weepingly confessed that her blood sugar number had been wrong for days, and she was frightened about it. Frank called a doctor, but Winnifred suffered a heart attack and was dead within minutes. Grief-stricken and bewildered, Frank could only say, stunned, "I never knew anyone could die so fast."[37]

Paul showed up in Calgary for the funeral, his first visit to Calgary in many years, and if he ever hoped for help or sympathy from Frank, he ruined that chance by drinking heavily during his visit; five empty bottles of liquor were found in his room after he left, one for each day of his stay. Knowing well who held the purse strings now, he did his pathetic best to make amends, writing an apology: "I freely admit I drank considerably while in Canada. *It began when I saw mother's face,* in the Chapel."[38]

Paul and Doris wrote copiously to each other in the aftermath of Winnifred's death, but instead of being brought together by their grief, they devolved into a state of permanent recrimination. It was not possible to reconcile their two positions. Doris dutifully doled out good advice, to which he was deaf. She could never understand why he would not support himself and thought his drinking problems were of his own making. Paul, for his part, thought she had wormed herself into Frank's favor as sole heir to the Commonwealth Petroleum fortune, while poisoning Frank's mind against him. Paul was an artist; he should not have to work. With such a rich family, why could he not be supported in comfort? To Doris, Paul was a parasite; to Paul, Doris was cruel and treacherous.

One thing both brother and sister shared was their sorrow over the loss of their mother. As Paul expressed it, "More and more I realize how much I loved her; and how irreplaceable it all is. When I think how often I failed her expectations, and how bright and optimistic she always was, full of new hope, and backing her children in spite of anything."[39] After a sordid quarrel over who was to pay Paul's plane fare to the funeral, they agreed not to correspond, but there was no one but Doris to whom Paul could tell his feelings about his mother. "I have been thinking much of little mother, her poor tired worried and suddenly animated face," he wrote. "I think she was deeply depressed about her writing, feeling it dated—for she had the glorious story-tellers gift that Chekhov had, and Kipling. I did not reassure her enough, and now I cry about it, because this would have made her so happy."[40]

He remembered how Winnifred told him to "make every second count, or your inspiration would flicker out. Mine did." He grieved, "The trouble with my writing now is that the only one in the world whose opinion counted with me, was mother. I tried to get started the other day, and the pen fell out of my hand. I thought, What's the use? Mother will never see it. And if I have success mother won't hear of it."[41]

Paul and Doris in their grief exchanged many letters about their mother, some of which reopened old wounds. It was Paul their mother liked, he insisted: "Me, her writer son, as she was a writer too, with an extreme sense of beauty. It is a pity she isn't here to break up our quarrel, as she did when we were children," he said with perfect truth. But Winnifred lived on in her "*great* children, and in our own children, Timmy, and Denny—the most like her of any of her blood." Paul was debarred by the Finkelsteins from seeing Denny, whom he wistfully described to Doris as "a beauty and a genius. . . . If only Denny and Tim could meet, they would *worship* one another."[42]

Doris, vacationing in Jamaica, wrote to her brother, "Do you remember in Mamma's *Me* her vivid description of Kingston, the heat, the scavengers and the scorpions. . . . I want to see the Myrtle Bank Hotel where Mamma lived and worked. Of all her novels, I always liked *Me* best, for to me it was Mamma."[43]

They agreed about that. Later she wrote him sympathetically, sorry that he seemed so despairing and so lonely. But he could not accept her kindness and responded bitterly, "I have no gratitude toward you people. . . . You have an iron conception of life. I understand that conception, but can see too that life is more than just iron—it also has texture, and richness, and mother's rich, rather wild, and exotic personality should have taught you that, for you both loved her." Paul summed up his basic disagreement with Doris: "What you say about a middle-aged man begging his sister, who works, for money, making you ill, I can only answer this way: I am a writer and poet, Doris, and things that you see clearly are absolutely blank walls of mystification to me. . . . Things that are as clear as day to you to me will always be towering mysteries."[44]

But in a lucid and humorous moment, he ruefully wrote, "If any child of mine even looked as though it were about to write a poem, I assure you I'd smack that poem out of the child's hands so fast it wouldn't know what had happened."[45]

In 1956 Frank had cancer surgery. "I will not speak of my own feelings. I feel as if my whole life is being uprooted," said Doris.[46] Paul replied, "I hate to think of my old range companion having pain. . . . I love Frank almost as much as our mama."[47]

Frank died that May, and Paul was anxiously interested in his will. "Since with my mother I was instrumental in founding Frank's fortune, please keep me informed," he wrote.[48] He feared being cut off and begged Doris not to keep him dangling for the news. It came soon enough: he was indeed cut out of Frank's will. His disappointment was grievous. "Gather in the lucre, Doris, hand it over to Tim," he wrote bitterly.[49] With the vast, tragic unwisdom of the self-destructive, he failed to recognize that Doris had been Frank's right hand for decades and that Frank was not the man to entrust a fortune to an alcoholic stepson. In spite of these facts, another truth rankled: Doris was wealthy, Paul was not.

He was often on the streets, and his health rapidly deteriorated. The Finkelsteins were dead, and Bunny was in a hospital, having "cracked up completely after her father's and mother's deaths," Paul told Doris. Denny was being looked after by Bunny's brother, a young psychiatrist who kept Paul from seeing her "as much as Maurice did."[50] When Bunny got out of the hospital, she saw Paul, and she wrote to Doris, "There is nothing that I know of that anyone can do for him. . . . His life must be a constant struggle to remain alive."[51]

Paul spent most of his time at the Marshall Chess Club, where Doris paid his dues and he could have a hot meal. But communications again broke down when he instigated a lawsuit against her, in an attempt to increase his inheritance. She had not heard from him in many months when she received his last letter, a wild pencilled scrawl on the back of an envelope: "You must surely have known by now my lawsuit was not brought against you, but to protect the interests of my daughter, who is as dear to me as Tim is to you. I am ill and tired—and would like to think my closest living relative is still my big sister and my friend. In short, Doris, I toss in the sponge. You've won."[52]

Weeks later, in November 1961, Doris received a cable from Bunny's brother that Paul had been found dead at his rooming house. Doris came to New York to bury him and consulted with his writer friend Robert Clairmont about trying to get his poetry published. "His work is of the kind called *difficult*," said Clairmont. "I wonder if Denny is literary—do you know?" Doris had no way of knowing whether Denny was literary; she replied that her niece had taken her father's death hard and had "built up an image of him that really does not fit him at all. She is only 16 of course and had not been in touch with Paul for years. When I saw her, I did not in any way try to tear down her image of her father—it would only hurt her."[53]

Doris grieved for her brother's wasted life and also for Perry, who died, still institutionalized, three years later. With Paul, at least, she had been able to share memories of their mother. In one of his last, rare, friendly letters to his sister, Paul remembered Winnifred: "Mama would bring out the best in one; she could make one rage, at times, but she was Mama, magical, wonderful, and great."[54]

Epilogue: Inheritance

"God had planted in *me* the fairy germs; that I knew."
—[Winnifred Eaton,] *Me*

I WAS SIXTEEN when I attended my father's funeral. I remembered seeing him only two or three times in my life—the last time when my "good grandmother" Naomi died, and he was allowed to pay me a brief visit while we were sitting shiva. He was a tall, sandy-haired, soft-spoken man who had seen better days, and he came and stood uneasily at my bedside—I was ten, reading in bed—and muttered a few words of condolence. He was worried that I wore glasses and diffidently asked if I read a lot. I must be sure to keep the light behind me when I read—it was very important. That is the sole piece of advice I ever remember receiving from my father.

A few years later, I happened to answer the telephone on one of the rare occasions when he called—he may have called more often, but I had never been allowed to speak to him. The uncle and aunt with whom I lived, a psychiatrist and his wife, were timid souls, with no inclination for visits from any drunken poet, and the established policy of keeping my father away from me seemed the wisest. I was used to it, but the result was that I grew up in the same city with my father and never knew him.

In the hesitant manner I remembered, he said he would like to see me sometime; would I like that? I would, but I was afraid. I had so often been told that it would be "bad" for me, in some ill-defined, mysteriously psychological way, to see him. "If Uncle Jim says so, I would like to," I hedged cautiously, trying not to sound discouraging. Maybe sometime. But no meeting ever happened, and the next I heard, he was dead. I cried, for now I would never know my mysterious poet father.

My mother was in and out of mental hospitals. I despised her mental weakness and sadly missed my grandparents, who had been like parents to me but were now dead. I was not happy with my uncle and aunt and felt that I had no one in the world left of my own.

So when my father died, I put on a black dress, which my aunt thought excessive, like my grief. The funeral was sparsely attended. My aunt Doris had come from Canada with her son, Tim, and arranged the funeral, but the only other people present were me, my uncle Jim, my father's friend Robert Clairmont, his spidery wife, and two tiny, teary, elderly, Chinese-looking ladies, in very old-fashioned, long black dresses and hats with veils. They were no taller than I was and peered at me with intense curiosity. They were introduced to me as my father's aunts. There seemed no way to have any connection with them; I had never known my father had any relatives at all, and they were completely outside my knowledge and experience. "You didn't even know Paul had any aunts, did you?" they asked smilingly, and all I could do was smile back and admit it, at a loss for words. They were Florence and Beryl, Winnifred's younger sisters.

In spite of this meeting, I did not really comprehend that I was part Chinese until long after I grew up. My parents had been separated as long as I could remember, and all I knew about my father, Paul Eaton Reeve, was that my maternal grandparents disapproved of him because he was a drunk, a poet, and a bum, who never worked. Worst of all, he was not Jewish but Christian. Any suggestion that he might be invited to the house to see me brought fit of hysterics to my volatile mother.

In the spirit of fairness, my grandfather Maurice used to tell me, "You are only half Jewish; your father is Christian. When you have attained the age of reason, you will be able to choose for yourself which you want to be." But when he jocularly put the question to me on my seventh birthday, I, in a characteristic contrarian spirit, answered, "Well, then, I'd like to be Christian." I was promptly told that it was out of the question. But I grew up to feel neither Jewish nor Christian—just nothing. Half and half; either or neither? Although I never encountered any anti-Semitism growing up in New York (and was startled to find evidences of it in Winnifred's letters), I could later divine, in a small way, what it meant to be racially divided, as she was. It meant that you could not be easily defined.

Once, my father left a battered old suitcase in the house, and my grandfather, who had sympathy for him, said, "Paul has nothing; he is so poor, he lives alone in a terrible little room. Maybe we should buy him a better suitcase. Would you like to, Denny?" "Oh, *yes,*" I said enthusiastically; but when my mother heard about it, she screamed and cried so that my grandfather quickly backed off.

If there was little contact with my father, there was still less with his family. All I knew about Winnifred was that she was quite a character (this was said with a rolling of eyes). She was an author and had published—oh, dozens of books. I had one Doris had given me: a crudely orange-covered book entitled *Cattle*. I tried to read it as a child and gave up in boredom. It was about cattle, all right. There was nothing for a young New York girl to relate to at all. Later, we found a fanciful Japanese romance with a ludicrous title, *The Heart of Hyacinth*—equally impenetrable. My poet father, I was told, considered these books "junk." There was also an odd photograph of Winnifred in a kimono, of all things; she wrote a lot of Japanese novels, under a weird pen name, Onoto Watanna. Japanese? It made no sense. I knew I had been named Winifred after her, but I didn't like it and had it changed.

I was also told she was very rich—Frank Reeve had seven million dollars, it was said. But she only sent my father a little money every week out of her household allowance—Frank would not let her send more—and that was all my father lived on. No wonder he was so shabby! And I was led to believe Winnifred was a famous liar—she said that she was half-Chinese, that her family was descended from Sir Isaac Newton, and that her great-grandpapa had been knighted. Those were the kind of wild stories she told.

Outlandish as these stories were, they actually did not make much impression on me. Winnifred lived thousands of miles away, in Canada, a land of ice and snow. My view of the world was very much the one of the famous *New Yorker* cover, the drawing of Manhattan and the rest of the world outside Manhattan petering out after Tenth Avenue. Winnifred died in 1954. I was eight and unmoved. "Should we tell her?—it might upset her," my grandmother Naomi wondered. "She didn't know her at all," my mother shrugged. "So that's good." Subject closed.

When Winnifred's widower, Frank Reeve, and my aunt Doris came to town on their way around the world, they stayed at the glamorous Plaza Hotel and took us to dinner there. Frank was a Calgary oilman whom I remember as wearing a white suit and an enormous Texas-style hat (though I have since been told he never wore either). Still, it is hard to convey, years later, in a world where people dress in any way they can think of, how outlandishly out of place he seemed in 1950s Manhattan. He was, however, a good-natured man, who enjoyed showing me the way his Cadillac's power windows rolled down. It was the first car I ever saw that did that, and it proved he really *was* rich. Aunt Doris seemed a dour, rather sad lady—thin, with a melancholy face. Occasionally she wrote me rather dry, stiff, properly auntly letters, inviting me to Calgary to see the Stampede. I was an art student at the High School of Music and Art in New York City, the bohemian daughter of a bohemian father, given to black turtleneck sweaters, black eyeliner, white lipstick, dangling earrings, and long cigarette holders; it was as likely that I would ever go to a stampede or rodeo in Canada as that I might go to the moon. People traveled less readily in those days, and it never once occurred to me as possible.

Having no real family, I did what teenage girls longing for love have eternally been known to do—got pregnant, got married, and gave birth to my son, whom I named Paul. Quickly divorced, I put myself through City College of New York as a history major and in the 1970s moved to Los Angeles with my second husband, Peter—a poet too, perhaps not entirely coincidentally. I knew I wanted to be a writer; it had lodged in my mind somehow that I was the granddaughter and daughter of writers.

In one of her occasional letters, Aunt Doris suggested that if I was going to Hollywood, I should look up my grandmother's old literary agent Ben Medford, who was still out there: he might help me get a start. He did. A genial, dapper little red-headed man then in his seventies, he suggested that I try working as a reader. I had never heard of such a job before, and it sounded pretty good after the depressing office jobs that were all that seemed open to me. He gave me a few scripts to read and paid for my "coverage" of them by taking me to lunch. Once I had samples of my work, I phoned every literary agency in the Yellow Pages, and before long I had a job. Eventually, I became a story analyst at a movie studio and spent all my time either reading or writing novels, mostly about Jane Austen, whose created universe seemed so much more orderly and understandable than my own had been. I was happily busy with my family and my work and never thought at all about my relatives in Canada, who after all had played little part in my life. Winnifred was only a faint, unimportant memory. Only much later, when my son followed me in working for a studio story department, did I realize there was an unbroken connection of sorts: dating back as far as 1915, in the early days of movies, from my grandmother and my father, to me and my son, a member of each generation had spent at least some time working in movie studio story departments—an odd circumstance, yet it was not an intentional matter of descendants' following in the family footsteps; it just happened that way.

In 1977, Aunt Doris died, and I flew to Calgary for her funeral. I spent a few days getting to know her son, Tim, my first cousin, a mathematics professor with five children. They were curious about me, and I was curious about them. They brought out all the family albums and books, and to my astonishment, I learned that the vague stories I had heard about my grandmother were true. Winnifred Eaton Reeve really was a fascinating woman.

She had not written dozens of novels, but she had written over a dozen, and there they were, palpable and real. Tim had them all, and I promptly sat down and read *Me.*

Imagine the effect of finding out that the plucky, self-involved, natural writer who was the heroine of *Me* was my grandmother! I identified. Why, I was a writer, too, and plucky—I had survived to become normal and happy and successful after a Gothic childhood. Could I have inherited some of her gifts? It was a pleasant surprise to find that Winnifred did not only write novels about cows or fanciful Japanese ones I could not relate to at all: *Me* was a genuinely riveting, page-turning, compelling narrative. As a very poor young girl, she had left her parents and thirteen brothers and sisters in Montreal and gone all the way to Jamaica to be a reporter. What spunk!

Not only that, she *was* Chinese! To be exact, half—just as racially Chinese as I was Jewish. It had never occurred to me that even if the story about her being Chinese was true, there could be any proof of it; but Tim showed me a photograph of Winnifred's mother. There was the proof: my great-grandmother, Grace Trefusius Eaton, was, beyond a doubt, a true-enough Chinese lady—wearing a proper high-necked Victorian dress and having quite a strong family resemblance to me. (My son was much less charmed to discover later that he is the image of Bertrand Babcock.)

It seemed improbable, fantastic, sitting in Calgary among my Canadian cousins, that we could have Chinese ancestors or be related to such a woman as Sui Sin Far—my great-aunt—who had written, "Behold, how great and glorious and noble are the Chinese people!" But it was so.

Glad to have become acquainted with my cousins and to have learned a little about such a fascinating heritage, I went home to Los Angeles and began acquiring books by Winnifred. They were in secondhand bookshops for ten or fifteen dollars, and in a few years, I had them all, even her rare cookbook. In most of them, I saw the raw gift for narrative that was her distinctive voice: a talent that, however unpolished or unliterary the style might be, made you want to know *what would happen next*—that gift which, after some years as a professional reader, I had learned to prize more highly than rubies.

Having inherited from this unknown fairy grandmother some bad gifts along with the good, I like to think a few of her qualities (the fairy germs, she called them) must have come down to me, by some peculiar spiritual route. Like her, I'm vain, egotistical, pushy, vivacious, extremely enthusiastic about life, impulsive, quick, unbusinesslike, possessed of a strong writing vocation, short, dark, and fond of men. However, unlike Winnifred, my life has mostly been quietly spent reading and writing, not adventurously "doing" as she did: she was infinitely more flamboyant, and I have often thought it's a lucky thing for the reader that I am writing about Winnifred rather than her writing about me.

The adventure, as travelers say, was truly in the journey: as fact after fact was uncovered and the story hammered home, I had the satisfying feeling of a circle being closed in my life. Tantalizing and unexplained parts of the picture had always been visible, but now I was seeing it whole. To be able to share what I have learned with others is a privilege and a joy. Has not this journey been an enviable inheritance in itself?

Notes

Introduction

1. [Winnifred Eaton Babcock,] *Me: A Book of Remembrance* (New York: Century, 1915), 76 (hereafter simply *Me*).

2. Ibid., 115.

3. Sui Sin Far, "Leaves from the Mental Portfolio of an Eurasian," *Independent*, January 21, 1909, reprinted in Sui Sin Far, *Mrs. Spring Fragrance and Other Writings*, ed. Amy Ling and Annette White-Parks (Urbana: University of Illinois Press, 1995), 222.

4. [Winnifred Eaton Babcock,] *Marion: The Story of an Artist's Model* (New York: W. J. Watt, 1916), 14 (hereafter simply *Marion*).

5. Sui Sin Far, "Leaves," 222.

6. *Me*, 153.

7. Phelps Decker, memo, March 9, 1925, box 3, Winnifred Eaton Reeve Fonds, Special Collections, University of Calgary Library, Calgary, Albert, Canada (hereafter referred to as Calgary Archives).

8. Amy Ling, "Revelation and Mask: Autobiographies of the Eaton Sisters," *a/b Auto/Biography Studies* 3 (Summer 1987): 50.

9. Amy Ling, *Between Worlds: Women Writers of Chinese Ancestry* (New York: Pergamon, 1990), 21.

10. Amy Ling, "Winnifred Eaton: Ethnic Chameleon and Popular Success," *MELUS* 11 (Fall 1984): 13.

11. Samina Najmi, introduction to *The Heart of Hyacinth*, by Onoto Watanna (1903; reprint, Seattle: University of Washington Press, 2000), xxxiii.

12. Eve Oishi, introduction to *Miss Numè of Japan*, by Onoto Watanna (1899; reprint, Baltimore: Johns Hopkins University Press, 1999), xi.

13. *Me*, 85.

14. Ling, "Winnifred Eaton," 5–15.

15. Paul G. Rooney, interview with author, Toronto, 1998.

Chapter 1: A Half-Caste Child

1. Winnie Eaton, "A Poor Devil," *Metropolitan Magazine*, n.d., box 14, Calgary Archives.

2. Sui Sin Far, "Leaves," 222.

3. *Marion*, 2.

4. Recounted by Paul G. Rooney, interview with author, Toronto, 1998.

5. Cari Beauchamp, *Without Lying Down: A Biography of Frances Marion* (New York: Scribners, 1997), 381.

6. Ling, *Between Worlds*, 33.

7. For instance, E. K. Brown and Leon Edel, *Willa Cather: A Critical Biography* (New York: Alfred A. Knopf, 1953), comment that "Cather began to give 1876 as the year of her birth when she was on the staff of *McClure's Magazine* . . . because S. S. McClure advised her to subtract two or three years from her age" (13).

8. Annette White-Parks, *Sui Sin Far/Edith Maude Eaton: A Literary Biography* (Urbana: University of Illinois Press, 1995), 23.

9. Marriage certificate, Shanghai.

10. Macclesfield historian [signature unreadable] to Rose Lewis, January 11, 1968, in author's possession. In 1860, Edward Eaton went into the chemical business, taking over from Edward Marsden a business founded in 1830. Local trade directories list him as engaged in chemical manufacture in Fountain Street, Macclesfield, as late as 1896. The family moved to "a very fine house," Lower Beech House, in 1872. It was demolished in the 1960s. Ibid.

11. Census records, District of Macclesfield, Subdistrict of Prestbury, County of Chester, England, 1861, 1871, 1881.

12. Winnifred Reeve to Paul Reeve, n.d., in author's possession.

13. *Me*, 113.

14. Sui Sin Far, "Leaves," 222.

15. Florence Winkelman to Elizabeth Rooney, 1979, copy in author's possession.

16. Kenneth Scott Latourette, *A History of Christian Missions in China* (New York: Macmillan, 1929), 231n.

17. John Mann, *Highbury Fields: The Most Interesting School in London* (Winchester, England: Edgeley Publications, 1994), 40–60.

18. Sui Sin Far, "Leaves," 221.

19. Grace Eaton Obituary, *Montreal Gazette*, May 8, 1922.

20. Doris Rooney to Yoshiro Ando, November 28, 1969, box 2, Calgary Archives.

21. Onoto Watanna, "A Neighbor's Garden, My Own, and a Dream One," *Good Housekeeping*, April 1908, 347.

22. "Edward Eaton's Unusual Career Comes to an End," undated clipping of his obituary, box 14, Calgary Archives.

23. "Death Closes Varied Career," undated clipping of Edward Eaton's obituary, box 14, Calgary Archives.

24. Quoted in Elizabeth Bailey Price, "Onoto Watanna, an Amazing Author," *MacLean's Magazine*, October 15, 1922, 64.

25. "Death Closes Varied Career."

26. Price, "Onoto Watanna, an Amazing Author," 64.

27. White-Parks, *Sui Sin Far*, 14.

28. "Onoto Watanna, the Japanese Woman Writer," *Current Literature,* October 1897, 306.

29. Paul Rooney, interview with author, Toronto, 1998.

30. Birth certificate, District of Macclesfield, Subdistrict of Prestbury, County of Chester, England.

31. White-Parks, *Sui Sin Far,* 15.

32. The children of Edward and Grace Eaton were Edward Charles, 1864–1906; Edith Maude, 1865–1914; Grace Helen, 1867–1957; Sara, 1868–1940; Ernest George, 1869–1974; Christina Agnes, 1870–1927; May Darling, 1874–1967; Winnifred, 1875–1954; George, 1879–1941; Hubert, 1879–1902; Rose, 1881–1957; Laurence, 1882–1884; Florence, 1885–1963; and Beryl, 1887–1968.

33. White-Parks, *Sui Sin Far,* 23.

34. Réjean Charbonneau, Aline Charles, Andre Cousineau, and Carmen Soucy-Roy, *De fil en aiguille: Chronique ouvrière d'une filature de coton à Hochelaga in 1880* (Montreal: Société Saint-Jean-Baptiste [section Maissonneuve] in collaboration with l'Atelier d'Histoire Hochelaga-Maisonneuve, 1985), 82, lists Joseph Thibault at 288 St. Mary Street.

35. White-Parks, *Sui Sin Far,* 25.

36. Ibid., 19.

37. Ibid., 20. "In 1877 the Eatons' address was 62 Moreau; in 1878 it was 17 Marlborough; and during 1880–82 it became 42 Seaver and then 32 Seaver" (ibid.).

38. Ibid., 21.

39. Ibid.

40. Sui Sin Far, "Leaves," 221.

41. Ibid., 222.

42. Ibid.

43. Sui Sin Far, "Sui Sin Far, the Half Chinese Writer, Tells of Her Career," *Boston Globe,* May 5, 1912, reprinted in *Mrs. Spring Fragrance and Other Writings,* ed. Ling and White-Parks, 290.

44. Winnifred Eaton to Paul Eaton Reeve, n.d., in author's possession.

45. Recounted by Paul G. Rooney, interview with author, Toronto, 1997.

46. Sui Sin Far, "Leaves," 222.

47. Suggested by Dominika Ferens.

48. Sui Sin Far, "Sui Sin Far, the Half Chinese Writer," 291.

49. *Me,* 29.

50. Winnifred Reeve, "Memories," undated clipping, box 14, Calgary Archives.

51. Michel Lessard, *Montréal, métropole du Québec: Images oubliées de la vie quotidienne, 1852–1910* (Montreal: Les Éditions de l'Homme, une division du groupe Sogides, 1992), photograph 149, Studio Notman et Eugene L'Africain, Le Mikado, en 1886, Collection Archives Notman.

52. Sui Sin Far, "Sui Sin Far, the Half Chinese Writer," 291.

53. *Marion,* 41

54. White-Parks, *Sui Sin Far,* 63

55. Ibid., 28.

56. "Will Montreal Have a Chinatown?" *Montreal Daily Star,* December 14, 1895.

57. Ibid.

58. Sui Sin Far, "Sui Sin Far, the Half Chinese Writer," 292.

59. Sui Sin Far, "Leaves," 227.

60. Winnifred Reeve to Paul Eaton Reeve, n.d., in author's possession.

61. L. Charles Laferrière, interview with author, April 1997.

62. Walter Blackburn Harte, "Bubble and Squeak," *Lotus,* May 1897, 160–67.

63. Walter Blackburn Harte, "Lucky Richard's Manual on How to Spend Money," *Fly Leaf,* March 1896, 6.

64. Harte, "Bubble and Squeak," 160.

65. Edith Eaton, "The Gamblers," *Fly Leaf,* February 1896, 14–18. See "The Story of Iso," *Lotus,* August 1896, 117–19; and "A Love Story of the Orient," *Lotus,* October 1896, 203–7. For Harte quote, see "Bubble and Squeak," *Lotus,* October 1896, 217.

66. Grace H. Harte, "The Battle for the Right of Women to Practice Law," *Women Lawyers' Journal* 33 (Summer 1947): 144, 148.

67. James Doyle, "Law, Legislation, and Literature: The Life of Grace H. Harte," *Biography* 17 (Fall 1994): 377 (first quote), 378 (second quote quote), 381 (third quote).

68. Grace Harte to A. S. Cody, September 6, 1900, A. S. Cody Collection, Amherst College. Courtesy of James Doyle.

69. Morrill Cody, excerpt from a note included with a donation of his father's papers to Amherst College Library, August 14, 1965. Courtesy of James Doyle.

Chapter 2: Jamaican Adventure

1. Winnifred Eaton, "Sneer Not," *Gall's News Letter,* March 10, 1896, n.p.

2. Quoted in White-Parks, *Sui Sin Far,* 33.

3. Frank Fonda Taylor, *To Hell with Paradise: A History of the Jamaican Tourist Industry* (Pittsburgh: University of Pittsburgh Press, 1993), 82.

4. Ibid., 63.

5. Editorial, *Jamaica Post,* February 22, 1899.

6. Taylor, *To Hell with Paradise,* 89–91.

7. Edith Eaton [A Canadian Firefly, pseud.], "The Girl of the Period: A Veracious Chronicle of Opinion," *Gall's News Letter,* February 8, 1897, n.p.

8. Clinton V. Black, *History of Jamaica* (1973; reprint, London: Collins Sangster, 1979), 188.

9. Taylor, *To Hell with Paradise,* 104.

10. Ibid., 107.

11. Ibid., quoting Presson Slosson, *The Great Crusade and After, 1914–1928* (New York: Macmillan, 1930), 249.

12. "A Japanese Girl and an Author," *Seattle Post-Intelligencer,* May 17, 1899, clipping, box 14, Calgary Archives.

13. Linda Trinh Moser has written extensively on this subject in her dissertation, "Chinese Prostitutes, Japanese Geishas, and Working Women: Images of Race, Class and Gender in the Work of Edith Eaton/Sui Sin Far and Winnifred Eaton/Onoto Watanna" (Ph.D. diss., University of California at Davis, 1997).

14. Sui Sin Far, "Sui Sin Far, the Half Chinese Writer," 292.

15. Sui Sin Far, "Leaves," 226.

16. Ibid.

17. A family legend exists that Grace Eaton was known as Lotus Blossom, and White-

Parks thus refers to that name in *Sui Sin Far;* I do not to use the name because there is no solid evidence for it.

18. White-Parks, *Sui Sin Far,* 33.

19. Sui Sin Far, "Sui Sin Far, the Half Chinese Writer," 293.

20. Advertisement, *Gall's News Letter,* December 16, 1896, n.p.

Chapter 3: Chicago

1. "A Japanese Girl and an Author," *Seattle Post-Intelligencer,* May 17, 1899, clipping, box 14, Calgary Archives.

2. Joanne Meyerowitz, "Sexual Geography and Gender Economy: The Furnished-Room Districts of Chicago, 1890–1930," in *Unequal Sisters: A Multicultural Reader in U.S. Women's History,* 2d ed., ed. Vicki Ruiz and Ellen DuBois (New York: Routledge, 1994), 189.

3. Ibid., 190.

4. Ibid., 191.

5. Onoto Watanna, "Starving and Writing in New York," *MacLean's Magazine,* October 15, 1922, 66.

6. Undated clipping, box 14, Calgary Archives. The remains of this scrapbook are in the Calgary Archives.

7. Undated clipping, box 14, Calgary Archives.

8. "Onoto Watanna, the Japanese Woman Writer," 306.

9. Scrapbook, box 14, Calgary Archives.

10. "Onoto Watanna," *Harper's Weekly,* December 5, 1903, 1959.

11. "Onoto Watanna," *Frank Leslie's Popular Monthly,* September 1899, 553–54.

12. "A Japanese Girl and an Author," *Seattle Post-Intelligencer,* May 17, 1899, clipping, box 14, Calgary Archives.

13. "Tale of a Sonnet," February 20, 1904, clipping, box 14, Calgary Archives.

14. Frank Putnam, *Love Lyrics* (Chicago: Blakely, 1898).

15. Ibid., 7.

16. Ibid., 27.

17. Yuko Matsukawa, "Cross-Dressing and Cross-Naming: Decoding Onoto Watanna," in *Tricksterism in Turn-of-the-Century American Literature: A Multicultural Perspective,* ed. Elizabeth Ammons and Annette White-Parks (Hanover, N.H.: University Press of New England, 1994), 113.

18. Yone Noguchi to Frank Putnam, February 15, 1899, Yone Noguchi Papers, Bancroft Library, University of California at Berkeley.

19. Yone Noguchi to Charles W. Stoddard, June 19, 1900, in *Yone Noguchi Collected English Letters,* ed. Ikuko Atsumi (Tokyo: Yone Noguchi Society, 1975), 44.

20. Undated clipping, box 14, Calgary Archives.

21. Winnifred to Frank Reeve, December 27, 1917, box 1, Calgary Archives.

22. Moser, "Chinese Prostitutes, Japanese Geishas, and Working Women," 73.

Chapter 4: Becoming Japanese

1. J. D. MacBurnie, letter to the editor, *Montreal Star,* January 4, 1895; "The Chinese Land of Promise," *Montreal Star,* June 23, 1895.

2. "Massacre at Port Arthur," *Montreal Star,* January 8, 1895.

3. Ling, "Winnifred Eaton," 5.

4. Among Winnifred's papers in the Calgary Archives is the flyleaf of a book entitled *The Mikado's Empire* by William Elliot Griffis, dated 1902. This volume of personal experiences in Japan is an indication of the kind of material Winnifred and her husband were reading at that time.

5. Alice Mabel Bacon, *Japanese Girls and Women* (Boston: Houghton Mifflin, 1891) and *A Japanese Interior* (Boston: Houghton Mifflin, 1883); Isabella Bird Bishop, *Unbeaten Tracks in Japan* (New York: Putnam, 1881); Mrs. Hugh Fraser, *Letters from Japan* (New York: Macmillan, 1899) and *Custom of the Country* (New York: Macmillan, 1899).

6. Onoto Watanna, "Every-Day Life in Japan," *Harper's Weekly,* October 20, 1904, 500–528; "The Japanese Drama and the Actor," *Critic,* September 1902, 231–37; "The Marvelous Miniature Trees of Japan," *Woman's Home Companion,* June 1904, 16–17; and "The Life of a Japanese Girl," *Ladies' Home Journal,* April 1899, 165.

7. Doris Rooney to Yoshiro Ando, November 28, 1969, box 2, Calgary Archives.

8. John Luther Long, *Miss Cherry-Blossom of Tokyo* (Philadelphia: J. B. Lippencott, 1895); John Luther Long, *Madame Butterfly* (1898 reprint, New York: Century, 1903).

9. Pierre Loti, *Madame Chrysanthemum,* trans. Laura Ensor (1888; reprint, London: KPI, 1985), 167.

10. Dominika Ferens, "Edith and Winnifred Eaton: The Uses of Ethnography in Turn-of-the-Century Asian American Literature" (Ph.D. diss., University of California at Los Angeles, 1998), 172.

11. "Japanese-American Romance," *Chicago Tribune,* undated clipping, Scrapbook, box 14, Calgary Archives.

12. Matsukawa, "Cross-Dressing and Cross-Naming," 107.

13. Ibid., 109.

14. Doris Rooney to Yoshiro Ando, November 28, 1969, box 2, Calgary Archives.

15. Matsukawa, "Cross-Dressing and Cross-Naming," 107.

16. Ibid., 116.

17. James Doyle, "Sui Sin Far and Onoto Watanna: Two Early Chinese-Canadian Authors," *Canadian Literature* 140 (Spring 1994): 54.

18. Onoto Watanna, "A Half Caste," *Frank Leslie's Popular Monthly,* September 1899, 496.

19. Ferens, "Edith and Winnifred Eaton," 170.

20. Matsukawa, "Cross-Dressing and Cross-Naming," 122.

21. "Onoto Watanna," *Harper's Weekly,* December 5, 1903, 1959.

22. Ferens, "Edith and Winnifred Eaton," 171.

23. Ibid., 172.

24. Winnifred wrote that she "knew him well in Chicago . . . when he was about 22 years old." Winnifred to Paul Eaton Reeve, n.d., in author's possession.

25. Ling, *Between Worlds,* 52.

26. Amy Ling, "Oak and Bamboo: The Eaton Sisters," unpublished manuscript, n.d., 65, in author's possession.

27. Ling, *Between Worlds,* 51.

28. "A Charming Japanese Tale," *New York Times Book Review,* August 19, 1899, 559.

29. *Brooklyn Eagle,* undated clipping, Scrapbook, box 14, Calgary Archives.

30. Ling, "Oak and Bamboo," 61.
31. Sui Sin Far, "Leaves," 230.
32. Ibid.

Chapter 5: The Lady of the Lavender Books

1. "Onoto Watanna," *Harper's Weekly,* December 5, 1903, 1959.
2. Yone Noguchi to Frank Putnam, n.d. [1901], Yone Noguchi Papers, Bancroft Library, University of California at Berkeley.
3. Stephen Babcock, *Babcock Genealogy* (New York: Eaton and Mains, 1903), x.
4. "Alumniana," *Hamilton Literary Magazine,* March 1899, n.p.; *Hamilton Literary Magazine,* June 1904, 32.
5. "Class Statistics," *Hamilton Literary Magazine,* May 1898, n.p.
6. Bertrand Babcock, *A Syndicated Prince,* serialized in *Eclectic Magazine,* May, 377–84, June, 544–50, July, 73–80, August, 171–84, September, 248–60, October, 369–75, November, 467–73, and December 1906, 549–55.
7. Bertrand W. Babcock, "The Psychological Investigator," *Eclectic Magazine,* April 1907, 368.
8. Bertrand W. Babcock, "Horses in the Big War," *Outing Magazine,* May 1919, 77.
9. Babcock, *A Syndicated Prince,* June, 547.
10. Ibid., 548.
11. Bertrand W. Babcock, "The Deadhead, and What He Costs the Theatre," *Theater Magazine,* July–December 1910, 95+.
12. Elizabeth Bailey Price, undated interview, *Vancouver Daily Province,* box 2, Calgary Archives.
13. Deed, April 22, 1905, City of Mount Vernon, New York County of Westchester, New York.
14. The house was sold to William Bohmert for $6,000. Information courtesy of Eileen Lewis, a family member.
15. Onoto Watanna, "Two Converts," *Harper's Monthly,* September 1901, 589.
16. Yone Noguchi, "The American Diary of a Japanese Girl," *Frank Leslie's Magazine,* December 1901, 198.
17. Wing Sing [Sui Sin Far], "Wing Sing of Los Angeles on His Travels," *Los Angeles Express,* February 4, 1904, and March 9, 1904.
18. Sui Sin Far, "Sui Sin Far, the Half Chinese Writer," 294 (first two quotes), 295 (third quote).
19. Quoted in White-Parks, *Sui Sin Far,* 46.
20. Ling, *Between Worlds,* 29. See Onoto Watanna, *A Japanese Nightingale* (New York: Harper and Brothers, 1901; reprint, New Brunswick, N.J.: Rutgers University Press, 2001).
21. Susan G. Larkin, "Genjiro Yeto: Between Japan and Japanism," *Greenwich History: The Journal of the Historical Society of the Town of Greenwich* 5 (2000): 8–31.
22. William Dean Howells, "A Psychological Counter-Current in Recent Fiction," *North American Review,* December 1901, 56.
23. "A Japanese Girl's Novel," *New York Times Book Review,* November 9, 1901, 819.
24. "Notes of a Bookman," *Harper's Weekly,* December 21, 1901, 1300.

25. *New York Herald Tribune,* April 19, 1902, 9.

26. Onoto Watanna, *The Wooing of Wistaria* (New York: Harper and Brothers, 1902).

27. Ling, "Oak and Bamboo," 82.

28. Onoto Watanna and Bertrand W. Babcock, "Eyes That Saw Not," *Harper's Monthly,* June 1902, 36.

29. "Onoto Watanna," *Harper's Magazine,* December 5, 1903, 1959.

30. "The Book-Buyer's Guide," *Critic,* December 1902, 585.

31. "Onoto Watanna Arrested," *New York Herald Tribune,* December 3, 1902.

32. Craig Timberlake, *The Bishop of Broadway: The Life and Work of David Belasco* (New York: Library Publishers, 1954), 22.

33. Ibid. He plagiarized articles in *Booklovers Magazine* on acting.

34. "Belasco Fights the Trust," *New York Herald Tribune,* December 3, 1902.

35. "Onoto Watanna Surrenders," *New York Herald Tribune,* December 4, 1902.

36. "Vacates Order of Arrest," *New York Herald Tribune,* February 7, 1903.

37. "Mrs. Babcock Wins the Belasco Suit," *New York News,* February 7, 1903.

38. Winnifred's notes summarizing the situation, n.d., box 14, Calgary Archives.

39. Quoted in Timberlake, *The Bishop of Broadway,* 227.

40. Alan Dale, "A Japanese Nightingale Is Drury Lane Melodrama Set to Light of Lanterns," *New York American,* November 21, 1903, 11.

41. "A Japanese Nightingale Suffers from Locomotor Ataxea and Influenza," November 21, 1903, clipping, box 14, Calgary Archives.

42. "A Japanese Nightingale: Dramaticized Novel at Daly's Has Rich Trimmings," *New York Times,* November 20, 1903.

43. "A Japanese Nightingale," *Theater Magazine,* January 1904, 4.

44. *New York Post,* November 20, 1903, clipping, box 14, Calgary Arhives.

45. "Mediocrity Once More," *New York News,* n.d., clipping, box 14, Calgary Archives.

46. Yone Noguchi to Frank Putnam, [December 1903], Yone Noguchi Papers, Bancroft Library, University of California at Berkeley.

47. Winnifred Babcock, 171 West Seventy-third Street, N.Y.C., to Harper and Brothers, April 1, 1915, box 1, Calgary Archives.

48. "Jap Artist Sees 'A Japanese Nightingale,'" *Sunday Telgram,* November 29, 1903.

49. "Onoto Watanna," *Harper's Weekly,* December 5, 1903, 1959–60.

50. Peter Collier and David Horowitz, *The Fords: An American Epic* (New York: Summit Books, 1987), 50.

51. Ferens, "Edith and Winnifred Eaton," 108.

52. Onoto Watanna, "The Loves of Sakura Jiro and the Three Headed Maid," *Century Magazine,* March 1903, 760.

53. Onoto Watanna, *The Heart of Hyacinth* (New York: Harper and Brothers, 1903).

54. "The Heart of Hyacinth," *New York Times Book Review,* October 3, 1903, 685.

55. "Tale of a Sonnet: Dispute about the Origin of a Certain Descriptive Passage in Onoto Watanna's Book, 'A Japanese Nightingale,'" *New York Times Book Review,* February 20, 1904, 116.

56. Genevieve Farnell, "A Japanese Nightingale," letter, *New York Times Book Review,* January 16, 1904, 42.

57. Quoted in "Tale of a Sonnet," 116.

58. Ibid.

59. Ibid.

60. Ibid.

61. Ibid.

62. L. C. Willcox, "Onoto Watanna and the Sonnet," *New York Times Book Review*, January 30, 1904, 74.

Chapter 6: A Book and a Baby a Year

1. Macmillan Company to Bertrand Babcock, February 25, 1904, box 2, Calgary Archives.

2. "Love in Japan: Daughters of Nijo," *New York Times Book Review*, April 30, 1904, 301.

3. "Daughters of Nijo," *Out West Magazine*, June 1904, clipping, box 16, Calgary Archives.

4. "Natural Fighters, She Says of Japs," *Evening Telegraph*, February 12, 1904.

5. "The Love of Azalea," *New York Times Book Review*, October 29, 1904, 734.

6. "The Love of Azalea," *Independent*, undated clipping, Calgary Archives.

7. Elizabeth Bailey Price, "Onoto Watanna, Famous in Literary World, Resides in Calgary to Write," undated typescript [probably 1922], box 14, Calgary Archives.

8. "Children of Two Worlds: A Japanese Blossom," *New York Times Book Review*, January 12, 1907, 17.

9. Yone Noguchi, "Onoto Watanna and Her Japanese Work," *Taiyou* 13 (July 1907): 19–21.

10. Onoto Watanna, "The Wrench of Chance," *Harper's Weekly*, October 20, 1906, 1494–96.

11. Onoto Watanna, *The Diary of Delia: Being a Veracious Chronicle of the Kitchen, with Some Side-Lights on the Parlour* (New York: Doubleday, Page, 1907).

12. "The Diary of Delia," *New York Times Book Review*, June 15, 1907, n.p.

13. "The Diary of Delia," *New York Times Book Review*, June 29, 1907, 418.

14. Winnifred Reeve to Colonel Selig, October 8, 1934, box 2, Calgary Archives.

15. Onoto Watanna, "Delia Dissents," *Saturday Evening Post*, August 22, 1908, 22–23.

16. Onoto Watanna, "A Neighbor's Garden, My Own, and a Dream One," *Good Housekeeping*, April 1908, 348.

17. Price, "Onoto Watanna, Famous in Literary World, Resides in Calgary to Write."

18. Onoto Watanna, *Tama* (New York: Harper and Brothers, 1910).

19. Doris Rooney to Herman Finkelstein, October 6, 1964, in author's possession.

20. Winnifred Reeve, "Other People's Troubles: An Antidote to Your Own," *Farm and Ranch Review*, February 5, 1919, 138.

21. Introduction to "Other People's Troubles," unpublished manuscript, box 3, Calgary Archives.

22. Recounted by Paul G. Rooney, interview with author, Toronto, 1998.

23. "Tama," *New York Times Book Review*, January 14, 1911, 16.

24. Onoto Watanna, *The Honorable Miss Moonlight* (New York: Harper and Brothers, 1912).

25. "A Japanese Story: The Honorable Miss Moonlight," *New York Times Book Review*, October 27, 1912, 628.

26. "French Successes to Be Shown Here," *Theater Magazine*, October 1912, 120.

27. Publishing figures courtesy of Jean Lee Cole.

28. Information courtesy of Jean Lee Cole.

29. Sara Bosse, "Cooking and Serving a Chinese Dinner in America," *Harper's Bazaar,* January 1913, 27, 29+.

30. Sara Bosse, "Giving a Chinese Luncheon Party," *Harper's Bazaar,* March 1913, 135, 146.

31. Sara Bosse, "Giving a Chinese Tea in America," *Harper's Bazaar,* April 1913, 201.

32. Sara Bosse, "A New Dinner for Churches and Clubs," *Ladies' Home Journal,* October 1913, 113.

Chapter 7: Divorce

1. "Bullet Wound near His Heart," obituary of E. C. Eaton, undated clipping, box 14, Calgary Archives.

2. Doris Rooney to Yoshiro Ando, November 28, 1969, box 2, Calgary Archives.

3. "Sun Yat Sen Paid Visit to Montreal," undated clipping, box 14, Calgary Archives.

4. Doris Rooney to Paul G. Rooney, December 11, 1971, in posession of Paul G. Rooney.

5. Sui Sin Far, "Sui Sin Far, the Half Chinese Writer," 288, 296.

6. White-Parks, *Sui Sin Far,* 48.

7. "A New Note in Fiction," *New York Times,* July 7, 1912.

8. Sui Sin Far, "Leaves," 230.

9. "Well-Known Author of Chinese Stories Who Died Yesterday," *Montreal Daily Star,* April 8, 1914.

10. "Edith Eaton Dead: Author of Chinese Stories under the Name of Sui Sin Far," *New York Times,* April 9, 1914.

11. Quoted in White-Parks, *Sui Sin Far,* 50.

12. Ibid., 62.

13. Quoted in Winnifred Babcock to Ethelyn McKinney, July 14, 1916, Special Collections Department, Vassar College Library, Poughkeepsie, N.Y. Thanks to Lisa Botshon for finding this material.

14. Material about Jean Webster is from her biography, *Jean Webster, Storyteller,* by Alan Simpson and Mary Simpson, with Ralph Connor ([Poughkeepsie, N.Y.:] Tymor Associates, 1984).

15. "Calgary Woman Finds Success as Scenarist," *Edmonton Bulletin,* September 1, 1933, clipping, box 14, Calgary Archives.

16. Simpson and Simpson, *Jean Webster,* 199.

17. Winnifred Eaton Reeve (Onoto Watanna), "You Can't Run Away from Yourself," unpublished manuscript, box 3, Calgary Archives.

18. Doris Rooney, "Souvenirs of the Past," *Field, Horse and Rodeo,* June 1963, 46.

19. "Me: A Remembrance," *Literary Digest,* October 15, 1915, 852.

20. "Me," *New York Times Book Review,* August 22, 1915, 302.

21. "Me: A Rembrance," *Nation,* September 16, 1915, 359–60.

22. "Is Onoto Watanna Author of the Anonymous Novel *Me?*" *New York Times Book Review,* October 10, 1915, 869+.

23. Diary, May 1915, in author's possession.

24. They were newspapermen based in Chicago. J. Medill Patterson's family had founded the *Chicago Tribune,* and he was the coeditor in 1915. Max Annenberg also worked for the *Tribune,* and when Patterson founded the *Daily News* in 1927, Annenberg became his circulating editor. Their venture into the movie business was brief. Information from the *Columbia Encyclopedia,* 6th ed., 2000, online version.

25. "Onoto Watanna Writes for Farm and Ranch," *Farm and Ranch Review,* January 20, 1919, 83.

26. "Gloria's Romance," *New York Times,* June 16, 1916.

27. Anne Moey, "Have You the Power? The Palmer Photoplay Corporation and the Film Viewer/Author in the 1920s," *Film History* 9, no. 3 (1997): 300.

28. Paul Reynolds to Winnifred, October 14, 1915, box 1, Calgary Archives.

29. Winnifred Babcock to Ethelyn McKinney, July 14, 1916, Special Collections Department, Vassar Collage Library, Poughkeepsie, N.Y.

Chapter 8: Calgary Writer

1. Leslie Curtis, *Reno Reveries* (Reno: Distributed by Armanko Stationery, 1924), 22.

2. Ibid., 24.

3. Ibid., 95.

4. Winnifred Eaton Reeve (Onoto Watanna), "You Can't Run Away from Yourself," unpublished manuscript, box 3, Calgary Archives.

5. Winnifred Babcock to Frank Reeve, January 27, 1917, box 1, Calgary Archives.

6. Frank Reeve to Winifred Babcock, February 26, 1917, box 1, Calgary Archives.

7. Paul G. Rooney, interview with author, Toronto, 1998.

8. Onoto Watanna, "Lend Me Your Title," *MacLean's Magazine,* March 1919, 67 (rat quote), 69 (Count Toodle quote).

9. "Onoto Watanna Writes for Farm and Ranch," 83.

10. H. L. Amster to Winnifred Reeve, Boston, June 6, 1922, box 1, Calgary Archives: "I am sincerely sorry that you were called back home on such a sad mission as that of taking the remains of your good mother to Montreal."

11. "Anglo-Chinese Woman's Career," obituary of Grace Eaton, *Montreal Gazette,* May 8, 1922, box 1, Calgary Archives.

12. Onoto Watanna, *Sunny-San* (Toronto: McClelland and Stewart; New York: George H. Doran, 1922).

13. Moser, "Chinese Prostitutes, Japanese Geishas, and Working Women," 87.

14. H. L. Amster to Winnifred, June 29, 1922, box 1, Calgary Archives.

15. Ibid.

16. Ibid., December 22, 1922.

17. "Calgary's Little Theatre," *Canadian Bookman,* March 1924, 72.

18. Elizabeth Bailey Price, undated article, *Vancouver Daily Province,* box 14, Calgary Archives.

19. Winnifred Eaton Reeve (Onoto Watanna), "You Can't Run Away from Yourself," unpublished manuscript, box 3, Calgary Archives.

20. Winnifred Eaton Reeve, "Royal and Titled Ranchers in Alberta," *Montreal Daily Star,* August 30, 1924.

21. Winnifred Reeve (Onoto Watanna), "Motor Hoboes," undated clipping [1920s], box 14, Calgary Archives.

22. Doris Rooney to Yoshiro Ando, November 28, 1969, box 2, Calgary Archives.

23. Quoted in Elizabeth Bailey Price, "Onoto Watanna Has Written a New Book," *Canadian Bookman,* April 1922, 123.

24. Charlotte Gordon, "Mrs. Francis Reeve: Onoto Watanna," undated clipping, box 14, Calgary Archives.

25. Elizabeth Bailey Price, "Onoto Watanna, Famous in Literary World, Resides in Calgary to Write," 5, undated typescript [1920s], box 14, Calgary Arhives.

26. Onoto Watanna, "Elspeth," *Quill,* January 1923, 23–32.

27. Winnifred Eaton Reeve (Onoto Watanna), "You Can't Run Away from Yourself," unpublished manuscript, box 3, Calgary Archives.

28. "Calgary Woman Finds Success as a Scenarist," *Edmonton Bulletin,* September 1, 1933, box 14, Calgary Archives.

29. Winnifred Eaton, *Cattle* (New York: W. J. Watt, 1924).

30. "Vigorous Novel of Alberta," *Saturday Night Magazine,* February 2, 1924, 9.

31. Stephen Leacock, review of *Cattle, Goblin,* February 1924.

32. Paramount Pictures to Winnifred Reeve, July 6, 1920, box 1, Calgary Archives.

33. Winnifred Eaton Reeve, "Elmer Clifton," undated newspaper clipping [1920s], box 14, Calgary Archives.

34. Norman Zierold, *The Moguls* (New York: Coward-McCann, 1969), 108.

35. Max Foran, with Nonie Houlton, *Roland Gissing: The People's Painter* (Calgary: University of Calgary Press, 1988), 24.

36. Frank Putnam to Winnifred Reeve, October 5, 1922, box 1, Calgary Archives.

37. Ibid., December 17, 1923.

38. Ibid.

39. Ibid., February 16, 1924.

40. Ibid., April 25, 1924.

41. Ibid.

42. Ibid., May 26, 1924.

43. Winnifred Reeve to Frank Reeve, November 6, 1924, box 1, Calgary Archives.

44. Ibid.

Chapter 9: Hollywood Screenwriter

1. "Scenario Editor Finds Future Star Serving Coffee," *Universal Weekly,* August 29, 1925, 12.

2. Bernard F. Dick, *City of Dreams: The Making and Unmaking of Universal Pictures* (Lexington: University Press of Kentucky, 1997), 72.

3. Carl Laemmle Sr., memo, box 1, Calgary Archives.

4. "Universal Has Great Story Line-Up for 1926–27 Production," *Universal Weekly,* September 12, 1925, 18.

5. Edward Montagne to Winnifred Reeve, October 12, 1925, box 1, Calgary Archives.

6. Ibid.

7. Eda Galantiere to Winnifred Reeve, October 28, 1925, box 1, Calgary Archives.

8. Phelps Decker to Winnifred Reeve, October 28, 1925, box 1, Calgary Archives.

9. Ibid., December 4, 1925.

10. Ibid.

11. Eda Galantiere to Winnifred Reeve, February 17, 1928, box 1, Calgary Archives.

12. Beauchamp, *Without Lying Down*, 199.

13. Marsha McCreadie, *The Women Who Write the Movies: From Frances Marion to Nora Ephron* (New York: Birch Lane, 1994).

14. Larry Ceplair, *A Great Lady: A Life of the Screenwriter Sonya Levien* (Lanham, Md.: Scarecrow, 1996), 1.

15. Quoted in Benjamin B. Hampton, *A History of the American Film Industry from Its Beginnings to 1931* (New York: Dover, 1971), 49.

16. McCreadie, *The Women Who Write the Movies.*

17. Wendy Holliday, "Hollywood's Modern Women: Screenwriting, World Culture, and Feminism" (Ph.D. diss., New York University, 1995), 114.

18. Ibid., 40.

19. Ibid., 100.

20. Ibid., 98.

21. Donald Ogden Stuart, quoted in ibid., 40.

22. William Ludwig, quoted in Hampton, *A History of the American Film Industry*, 47.

23. Holliday, "Hollywood's Modern Women," 112.

24. Ibid., 114.

25. Ibid., 46.

26. Frances Marion, *"Off with Their Heads!"* (New York: Mamcillan, 1972), 83.

27. Hampton, *A History of the American Film Industry*, 43.

28. Ibid., 40.

29. Ibid., 29.

30. Winnifred Reeve, unpublished untitled poem, box 3, Calgary Archives.

31. Alfred A. Cohn to Winnifred Reeve, May 11, 1925, box 1, Calgary Archives.

32. Winnifred Reeve to Carl Laemmle Sr., memo, November 12, 1926, box 2, Calgary Archives.

33. Winnifred Reeve to Carl Laemmle Sr., memo, December 7, 1926, box 1, Calgary Archives.

34. Frederica Sagor Maas, *The Shocking Miss Pilgrim: A Writer in Early Hollywood* (Lexington: University Press of Kentucky, 1999), 48–49.

35. Frederica Sagor Maas, interview with author, September 21, 2000. Bringing this ironic story full circle, I read Maas's book as a story analyst at Warner Bros. seventy-five years after her encounter with my grandmother, which she remembered vividly.

36. Eda Galantiere to Winnifred Reeve, December 31, 1926, box 1, Calgary Archives.

37. Winnifred Reeve to William Selig, November 12, 1934, box 2, Calgary Archives.

38. Winnifred Reeve to Louis Whicher, September 20, 1933, box 2, Calgary Archives.

39. Paul G. Rooney, interview with author, Toronto, 1998.

40. Winnifred Reeve to Samuel Reat, September 14, 1929, box 1, Calgary Archives.

41. Doris Rooney to Herman Finkelstein, October 6, 1964, in author's possession.

42. Paul G. Rooney, interview with author, Toronto, 1998.

43. Perry Reeve to Winnifred Reeve, n.d., and to Doris Rooney, n.d., in author's possession.

44. "Movie Relatives," unpublished manuscript, box 13, Calgary Archives.

45. Winnifred Reeve, "I Could Get Any Woman's Husband," *Motion Picture Classics Magazine,* March 1929.

46. Winnifred Reeve, "How Frenchmen Make Love," *Motion Picture Magazine,* June 1929.

47. Onoto Watanna, "What Happened to Hayakawa? The Japanese Gentleman Reveals Why He Forsook the American Screen," *Motion Picture Magazine,* January 1929.

48. Onoto Watanna, "Honorable Movie Takee Sojin," *Motion Picture Classics Magazine,* March 1928.

49. *Movie Madness,* 205-page manuscript serialized in *Screen Secrets,* n.d. [1920s], box 15, Calgary Archives.

50. "Hollywood Melody," 232-page unpublished novel, n.d. [1920s], box 12, Calgary Archives.

51. Frank Reeve to Winnifred Reeve, February 3, 1927, box 1, Calgary Archives.

52. Rose de Rouville to Winnifred Reeve, n.d. [1920s], box 1, Calgary Archives.

53. Ibid.

54. Ibid.

55. Winnifred Reeve to Samuel Reat, September 14, 1929, box 1, Calgary Archives.

56. "The Mississippi Gambler," *New York Times,* October 28, 1929.

57. "East Is West," *New York Times,* November 4, 1930.

58. Winnifred Reeve to C. Gardner Sullivan, November 26, 1929, box 1, Calgary Archives.

59. Ibid. Jean Lee Cole, "On the Clock: Writing in Hollywood" (chapter from diss. in progress, University of Texas, Austin), has traced the contribution Winnifred's early screenplay made to the final film version of *Barbary Coast* (1935), on which Edward Chodorov and Ben Hecht are the credited screenwriters.

60. Winnifred Reeve to Carl Laemmle Jr., November 26, 1929, box 1, Calgary Archives.

61. W. L. Stern, business manager of Universal, to Winnifred Reeve, January 16, 1930, box 2, Calgary Archives.

62. W. L. Stern to Winnifred Reeve, memo, February 25, 1930, box 2, Calgary Archives.

63. Winnifred Reeve to Carl Laemmle Jr., memo, February 25, 1930, box 2, Calgary Archives.

64. Carl Laemmle Jr. to Winnifred Reeve, memo, February 28, 1930, box 2, Calgary Archives.

65. Winnifred Reeve to Carl Laemmle Jr, March 5, 1930, box 2, Calgary Archives.

66. H. L. Amster to Winnifred Reeve, February 26, 1930, box 2, Calgary Archives.

67. Frank Reeve to Winnifred Reeve, February 10, 1930, box 1, Calgary Archives.

68. Winnifred Reeve to Frank Reeve, February 14, 1930, box 1, Calgary Archives.

69. Winnifred Reeve to Henry Henigson, June 7, 1930, box 2, Calgary Archives.

70. Rose de Rouville to Winnifred Reeve, October 27, 1930, box 1, Calgary Archives.

71. Griesbach, O'Connor, solicitors, to Winnifred Reeve, May 9, 1931, box 1, Calgary Archives.

72. Frank Reeve to Winnifred Reeve, May 22, 1931, box 1, Calgary Archives.

73. Winnifred Reeve to Ben Medford, May 31, 1946, box 2, Calgary Archives.

74. Undated clipping [1930s?], box 14, Calgary Archives.

75. H. N. Swanson to Winnifred Reeve, April 2, 1938, Margaret Herrick Library, Center for Motion Picture Study, Academy of Motion Picture Arts and Sciences, Los Angeles. In 1972, the gentlemanly Swanson (whose name I picked out of a phone book), then nearly eighty, was my own first movie business employer.

76. Winnifred Reeve to William Selig, Ocotber 24, 1934, box 2, Calgary Archives.

77. Elizabeth Bailey Price, undated interview, *Vancouver Daily Province*, box 2, Calgary Archives.

Chapter 10: Vanquishing Mrs. Hill

1. Winnifred Reeve to Rose de Rouville, July 14, 1931, box 1, Calgary Archives.
2. Rose de Rouville to Winnifred Reeve, July 20, 1931, box 1, Calgary Archives.
3. Winnifred Reeve to Rose de Rouville, n.d. [1931], box 1, Calgary Archives.
4. Ibid.
5. Ibid.
6. Ibid.
7. Ibid.
8. Elizabeth Bailey Price to "Flos Beloved," August 20, 1931, box 1, Calgary Archives.
9. Winnifred Reeve, diary, n.d., box 1, Calgary Archives.
10. "Because We Were Lonely," *True Story*, April 1933, 28–30, 92–96.
11. Winnifred Reeve to J. McKinley Cameron, January 12, 1932, box 1, Calgary Archives.
12. J. McKinley Cameron to Winnifred Reeve, January 14, 1932, box 1, Calgary Archives.
13. Winnifred Reeve to J. McKinley Cameron, January 15, 1932, box 1, Calgary Archives.
14. Winnifred Reeve, "Second Honeymoon," unpublished manuscript, n.d., [1932], box 10, Calgary Archives.
15. Mentioned in Winnifred Reeve to Paul Reeve, n.d., in author's possession.
16. L. E. Whicher to Winnifred Reeve, February 16, 1933, box 2, Calgary Archives.
17. Winnifred Reeve to L. E. Whicher, February 22, 1933, box 2, Calgary Archives.
18. Winnifred Reeve to William Selig, September 6, 1934, box 2, Calgary Archives.
19. Grace Harte to Winnifred Reeve, December 27, 1938, box 2, Calgary Archives.

Chapter 11: Poetic Ends

1. Paul Reeve to Winnifred Reeve, n.d. [1929], in author's possession. Except where noted, the letters in this chapter are in the author's possession. Few have dates; Winnifred and Paul almost never dated their letters to each other. Doris, however, kept them filed in fairly good chronological order, and her own letters are dated.
2. Ibid.
3. Paul to Winnifred, [1942].
4. Winnifred to Paul, [1940s].
5. Ibid.
6. Ibid., June 1944.
7. Winnifred to Paul and Helen Reeve, [1940s].
8. Winnifred to Paul, [summer 1945].
9. Maurice Finkelstein to Winnifred Reeve, January 1948.

10. Winnifred to Doris, 1948, box 1, Calgary Archives.
11. Ibid.
12. Ibid.
13. Ibid.
14. Doris Rooney to Maurice Finkelstein, March 1, 1948.
15. Doris Rooney to Helen Reeve, March 1, 1948.
16. Maurice Finkelstein to Doris Rooney, March 4, 1948.
17. Doris Rooney to Maurice Finkelstein, March 7, 1948.
18. Paul Reeve to Winnifred Reeve, [1940s].
19. Winnifred Reeve to Doris Rooney, 1948, box 1, Calgary Archives.
20. "Portrait of a Poet," unpubished verse, n.d. [1940s], box 1, Calgary Archives.
21. Winnifred to Paul, [1940s].
22. Doris to Paul, [1950s].
23. Winnifred to Paul, [1950s].
24. Winnifred to Doris, [1949].
25. Winnifred to Paul, [1950s].
26. Recounted by Paul G. Rooney, interview with author, Toronto, 1998.
27. Winnifred to Paul, [1950s].
28. Ibid.
29. Ibid.
30. Paul G. Rooney, interview with author, Toronto, 1998.
31. Winnifred to Paul, [1950s].
32. Winnifred to Doris, [1950s].
33. Winnifred to Paul, [1950s].
34. Ibid., May 1953.
35. Ibid., [1950s].
36. Winnifred to Paul, November 1953; Paul to Winnifred, April 1954.
37. Recounted by Paul G. Rooney, interview with author, Toronto, 1998.
38. Paul to Doris, [1954].
39. Ibid.
40. Ibid.
41. Ibid.
42. Ibid.
43. Doris to Paul, February 5, 1955.
44. Paul to Doris, [1950s].
45. Ibid.
46. Doris to Paul, April 22, 1956.
47. Paul to Doris, [1956].
48. Ibid.
49. Ibid.
50. Ibid.
51. Helen Reeve to Doris, March 18, 1959.
52. Paul to Doris, [1961].
53. Robert Clairmont to Doris, received June 10, 1962.
54. Paul to Doris, [1961].

Bibliography

Winnifred Eaton's Works (Listed Chronologically)

NOVELS

Miss Numè of Japan. Chicago: Rand McNally, 1899; reprint, Baltimore: Johns Hopkins University Press, 1999.

A Japanese Nightingale. New York: Harper and Brothers, 1901; reprint, New Brunswick, N.J.: Rutgers Unversity Press, 2001.

The Wooing of Wistaria. New York: Harper and Brothers, 1902.

The Heart of Hyacinth. New York: Harper and Brothers, 1903; reprint, Seattle: University of Washington Press, 2000.

The Love of Azalea. New York: Dodd, Mead, 1904.

Daughters of Nijo: A Romance of Japan. New York: Macmillan, 1904.

A Japanese Blossom. New York: Harper and Brothers, 1906.

The Diary of Delia: Being a Veracious Chronicle of the Kitchen with Some Side-Lights on the Parlour. New York: Doubleday, Page, 1907.

Tama. New York: Harper and Brothers, 1910.

The Honorable Miss Moonlight. New York: Harper and Brothers, 1912.

Me: A Book of Remembrance. New York: Century, 1915; reprint, Jackson: University Press of Mississippi, 1997.

Marion: The Story of an Artist's Model. New York: W. J. Watt, 1916.

Movie Madness. Novel serialized in *Screen Secrets,* n.d. [1920s]. Box 15, Winnifred Eaton Reeve Fonds, Special Collections, University of Calgary Library, Calgary, Alberta, Canada.

"Hollywood Melody." Unpublished novel, n.d. [1920s]. Box 12, Winnifred Eaton Reeve Fonds, Special Collections, University of Calgary Library, Calgary, Alberta, Canada.

Sunny-San. Toronto: McClelland and Stewart; New York: George H. Doran, 1922.

Cattle. New York: W. J. Watt, 1924.

His Royal Nibs. New York: W. J. Watt, 1925.

SHORT FICTION

"A Poor Devil." *Metropolitan Magazine,* clipping, n.d. Box 14, Winnifred Eaton Reeve Fonds, Special Collections, University of Calgary Library, Calgary, Alberta, Canada.

"A Half Caste." *Frank Leslie's Popular Monthly,* September 1899, 489–96.

"Two Converts." *Harper's Monthly,* September 1901, 585–89. Reprinted in *Nineteenth-Century American Women Writers: An Anthology,* edited by Karen L. Kilcup (Cambridge, Mass.: Blackwell, 1997), 571–76.

"Kirishima-San." *Idler,* November 1901, 315–21.

"Margot." *Frank Leslie's Popular Monthly,* December 1901, 203–9.

"The Love of a Geisha Girl." Clipping, n.d. Box 14, Winnifred Eaton Reeve Fonds, Special Collections, University of Calgary Library, Calgary, Alberta, Canada.

"Tokiwa." *Red Book Magazine,* n.d., 49–57. Box 13, Winnifred Eaton Babcock Reeve Collection, Special Collections, University of Calgary Library, Calgary, Alberta, Canada.

"Eyes That Saw Not" (with Bertrand W. Babcock). *Harper's Monthly,* June 1902, 30–38.

"A Contract." *Frank Leslie's Popular Monthly,* August 1902, 370–79.

"The Loves of Sakura Jiro and the Three Headed Maid." *Century Magazine,* March 1903, 755–60. Reprinted in *Nineteenth-Century American Women Writers: An Anthology,* edited by Karen L. Kilcup (Cambridge, Mass.: Blackwell, 1997), 576–81.

"Miss Lily and Miss Chrysanthemum." *Ladies' Home Journal,* August 1903, 11–12.

"The Wrench of Chance." *Harper's Weekly,* October 20, 1906, 1494–96, 1505, 1531.

"The Manoeuvers of O-Yasu-san." *Saturday Evening Post,* January 25, 1908, 9–11, 22.

"A Neighbor's Garden, My Own, and a Dream One." *Good Housekeeping,* April 1908, 347–53, and May 1908, 484–90.

"Delia Dissents." *Saturday Evening Post,* August 22, 1908, 22–23.

"An Unexpected Grandchild." *Lippincott's Monthly,* December 1909, 689–96.

"Lend Me Your Title." *MacLean's Magazine,* February 1919, 13, 14, 72–74, and March 1919, 16, 18–19, 66–69.

"Other People's Troubles: An Antidote to Your Own." *Farm and Ranch Review,* February 5, 138–40, February 20, n.p., March 20, 331–34, April 5, 406, April 21, n.p., May 5, n.p., June 5, 662, June 20, n.p., July 21, n.p., August 5, 889, 1919.

"Elspeth." *Quill,* January 1923, 23–30.

"Second Honeymoon." Unpublished manuscript, n.d. [1932]. Box 10, Winnifred Eaton Reeve Fonds, Special Collections, University of Calgary Library, Calgary, Alberta, Canada.

"Because We Were Lonely." *True Story,* April 1933, 28–30, 92–96.

NONFICTION

"Sneer Not." *Gall's News Letter* (Kingston, Jamaica), March 10, 1896, n.p.

"A Rhapsody on Japan." *American Home Journal,* n.d. [1890s]. Box 14, Winnifred Eaton Reeve Fonds, Special Collections, University of Calgary Library, Calgary, Alberta, Canada.

"The Half Caste." *Conkey's Home Journal,* November 1898. Box 14, Winnifred Eaton Reeve Fonds, Special Collections, University of Calgary Library, Calgary, Alberta, Canada.

"The Life of a Japanese Girl." *Ladies' Home Journal,* April 1899, 7.

"When the Young Look Forward to Old Age." *Ladies' Home Journal,* n.d. [1899?]. Box 14, Winnifred Eaton Reeve Fonds, Special Collections, University of Calgary Library, Calgary, Alberta, Canada.
"New Year's Day in Japan." *Frank Leslie's Popular Monthly,* January 1900, 283–86.
"The Japanese Drama and the Actor." *Critic,* September 1902, 231–37.
"The Marvelous Miniature Trees of Japan." *Woman's Home Companion,* June 1904, 16–17.
"Every-Day Life in Japan." *Harper's Weekly,* October 20, 1904, 500–503, 527–28.
"The Japanese in America." *Eclectic Magazine,* February 1907, 100–104.
Chinese-Japanese Cookbook (with Sara Bosse). Chicago: Rand McNally, 1914.
"Elmer Clifton." Undated article [1920s]. Box 14, Winnifred Eaton Reeve Fonds, Special Collections, University of Calgary Library, Calgary, Alberta, Canada.
"Motor Hoboes." Undated article [1920s]. Box 14, Winnifred Eaton Reeve Fonds, Special Collections, University of Calgary Library, Calgary, Alberta, Canada.
"Starving and Writing in New York." *MacLean's Magazine,* October 15, 1922, 66–67.
"The Canadian Spirit in Our Literature." *Calgary Daily Herald,* March 24, 1923.
"A Protest." *Canadian Bookman,* March 1924, 72.
"Statement by Mrs. Winnifred Reeve." *Canadian Bookman,* May 1924, 118.
"An Art Gallery for Calgary." Calgary newspaper, April 20, 1924. Box 14, Winnifred Eaton Reeve Fonds, Special Collections, University of Calgary Library, Calgary, Alberta, Canada.
"Royal and Titled Ranchers in Alberta." *Montreal Daily Star,* August 30, 1924.
"You Can't Run Away from Yourself." Unpublished manuscript. Box 3, Winnifred Eaton Reeve Fonds, Special Collections, University of Calgary Library, Calgary, Alberta, Canada.
"Honorable Movie Takee Sojin." *Motion Picture Classics Magazine,* March 1928.
"Movie Relatives." Unpublished manuscript, n.d. Box 14, Winnifred Eaton Reeve Fonds, Special Collections, University of Calgary Library, Calgary, Alberta, Canada.
"Butchering Brains: An Author in Hollywood Is as a Lamb in an Abattoir." *Motion Picture Magazine,* September 1928, 28–29, 110+.
"What Happened to Hayakawa? The Japanese Gentleman Reveals Why He Forsook the American Screen." *Motion Picture Magazine,* January 1929.
"I Could Get Any Woman's Husband!" *Motion Picture Classics Magazine,* March 1929.
"How Frenchmen Make Love." *Motion Picture Magazine,* June 1929.
"Memories." Undated article [1930s?]. Box 14, Winnifred Eaton Reeve Fonds, Special Collections, University of Calgary Library, Calgary, Alberta, Canada.
"Portrait of a Poet." Unpublished verse, n.d. [1940s]. Box 1, Winnifred Eaton Reeve Fonds, Special Collections, University of Calgary Library, Calgary, Alberta, Canada.

Reviews and Articles about Winnifred Eaton

"Author Plays a Great Part on World's Stage." Undated clipping [1922]. Box 14, Winnifred Eaton Reeve Fonds, Special Collections, University of Calgary Library, Calgary, Alberta, Canada.
"Belasco Fights the Trust." *New York Herald Tribune,* December 3, 1902.
"The Book-Buyer's Guide," *Critic,* December 1902, 585.

"Calgary Author Finds Hollywood World's Play City." Undated clipping [1920s]. Box 14, Winnifred Eaton Reeve Fonds, Special Collections, University of Calgary Library, Calgary, Alberta, Canada.

"Calgary's Little Theatre." *Canadian Bookman,* March 1924, clipping. Box 14, Winnifred Eaton Reeve Fonds, Special Collections, University of Calgary Library, Calgary, Alberta, Canada.

"Calgary Woman Finds Success as Scenarist." *Edmonton Bulletin,* September 1, 1933, clipping. Box 14, Winnifred Eaton Reeve Fonds, Special Collections, University of Calgary Library, Calgary, Alberta, Canada.

"A Charming Japanese Tale." *New York Times Book Review,* August 19, 1899, 559.

"Children of Two Worlds: A Japanese Blossom." *New York Times Book Review,* January 12, 1907, 17.

"Couple Enriched City's Culture." Calgary newspaper clipping, September 30, 1995. Box 14, Winnifred Eaton Reeve Fonds, Special Collections, University of Calgary Library, Calgary, Alberta, Canada.

Dale, Alan. "A Japanese Nightingale Is Drury Lane Melodrama Set to Light of Lanterns." *New York American,* November 21, 1903, 11.

"Daughters of Nijo." *Out West Magazine,* June 1904. Box 16, Winnifred Eaton Reeve Fonds, Special Collections, University of Calgary Library, Calgary, Alberta, Canada.

"The Diary of Delia." *New York Times Book Review,* June 15, 1907, n.p.

"The Diary of Delia." *New York Times Book Review,* June 29, 1907, 418.

Farnell, Genevieve. "A Japanese Nightingale" (letter). *New York Times Book Review,* January 16, 1904, 42.

Gordon, Charlotte. "Mrs. Francis Reeve: Onoto Watanna." Undated clipping. Box 14, Winnifred Eaton Reeve Fonds, Special Collections, University of Calgary Library, Calgary, Alberta, Canada.

"The Heart of Hyacinth." *New York Times Book Review,* October 3, 1903, 685.

"Is Onoto Watanna Author of the Anonymous Novel 'Me'?" *New York Times Book Review,* October 10, 1915, 869+.

"A Japanese Girl's Novel." *New York Times Book Review,* November 9, 1901, 819.

"A Japanese Nightingale." *Theater Magazine,* January 1904, 4.

"A Japanese Nightingale: Dramatized Novel at Daly's Has Rich Trimmings." *New York Times,* November 20, 1903.

"Japanese Nightingale Suffers from Locomotor Ataxia and Influenza." Newspaper clipping, November 21, 1903. Box 14, Winnifred Eaton Reeve Fonds, Special Collections, University of Calgary Library, Calgary, Alberta, Canada.

"A Japanese Story: The Honorable Miss Moonlight." *New York Times Book Review,* October 27, 1912, 628.

"Jap Artist Sees 'A Japanese Nightingale.'" *Sunday Telegraph,* November 29, 1903.

"The Kitchen's Viewpoint: The Diary of Delia." *New York Times Book Review,* June 15, 1907, clipping. Box 16, Winnifred Eaton Reeve Fonds, Special Collections, University of Calgary Library, Calgary, Alberta, Canada.

Lang, Naomi. "Alberta Women Who Make News Include Noted Novelist, Scenarist." *Calgary Herald,* September 6, 1941.

"Late Author's Books Coveted by Museums." *Albertan*, March 27, 1963.
"Love in Japan: Daughters of Nijo." *New York Times Book Review*, April 30, 1904, 301.
"The Love of Azalea." *Independent*, December 8, 1904, 1332.
"The Love of Azalea." *New York Times Book Review*, October 29, 1904, 734.
Marshall, Marguerite Mooers, "Onoto Watanna Decries 'Yellow Peril' in Talk on Women of East and West." Undated clipping [1930s]. Box 14, Winnifred Eaton Reeve Fonds, Special Collections, University of Calgary Library, Calgary, Alberta, Canada.
"Me." *New York Times Book Review*, August 22, 1915, 302.
"Me: A Rembrance." *Literary Digest*, October 15, 1915, 852.
"Me: A Remembrance." *Nation*, September 16, 1915, 359–60.
"'Movie Madness,' New Local Novel, Tells Life in Hollywood." Undated clipping [1920s]. Box 14, Winnifred Eaton Reeve Fonds, Special Collections, University of Calgary Library, Calgary, Alberta, Canada.
"Mrs. Babcock Wins the Belasco Suit." *New York News*, February 7, 1903.
"Mrs. F. F. Reeve, Author, 76, Dies." Undated clipping [1954]. Box 1, Winnifred Eaton Reeve Fonds, Special Collections, University of Calgary Library, Calgary, Alberta, Canada.
"Natural Fighters, She Says of Japs." *Evening Telegraph*, February 12, 1904.
"A New Note in Fiction." *New York Times*, July 7, 1912.
Noguchi, Yone. "Onoto Watanna and Her Japanese Work." *Taiyou* 13 (June 1907): 18–21; 13 (July 1907): 19–21.
"Noted Calgary Writer Dies." Undated clipping [1954]. Box 14, Winnifred Eaton Reeve Fonds, Special Collections, University of Calgary Library, Calgary, Alberta, Canada.
"Notes of a Bookman." *Harper's Weekly*, December 21, 1901, 1300.
"Novels, Japanese and Japanned." *Independent*, June 23, 1904.
"Onoto Watanna." *Frank Leslie's Popular Monthly*, August 1902.
"Onoto Watanna." *Frank Leslie's Popular Monthly*, September 1899, 553–54.
"Onoto Watanna." *Harper's Weekly*, December 5, 1903, 1959–60.
"Onoto Watanna Arrested." *New York Herald Tribune*, December 3, 1902.
"Onoto Watanna Surrenders." *New York Herald Tribune*, December 4, 1902.
"Onoto Watanna, the Japanese Woman Writer." *Current Literature*, October 1897, 306.
"Onoto Watanna Writes for Farm and Ranch." *Farm and Ranch Review*, January 20, 1919, 8.
Price, Elizabeth Bailey. "Onoto Watanna, Famous in Literary World, Resides in Calgary to Write." Undated typescript [1920s]. Box 14, Winnifred Eaton Reeve Fonds, Special Collections, University of Calgary Library, Calgary, Alberta, Canada.
———. "Onoto Watanna Has Written a New Book." *Canadian Bookman*, April 1922, 123–25.
———. "Onoto Watanna, an Amazing Author." *MacLean's Magazine*, October 15, 1922, 64–65.
Rooney, Doris. "Souvenir from the Past." *Field, Horse and Rodeo*, July 1963, 45–47.
"Scenario Editor Finds Future Star Serving Coffee." *Universal Weekly*, August 29, 1925, 12.
"Tale of a Sonnet: Dispute about the Origin of a Certain Descriptive Passage in Onoto Watanna's Book, 'A Japanese Nightingale.'" *New York Times Book Review*, February 20, 1904, 116.

"Tama." *New York Times Book Review,* January 14, 1911, 16.
"$313,000 Will Filed." Undated clipping [1954]. Box 14, Winnifred Eaton Reeve Fonds, Special Collections, University of Calgary Library, Calgary, Alberta, Canada.
"Universal Has Great Story Line-Up for 1926–27 Production." *Universal Weekly,* September 12, 1925, 18.
"Vacates Order of Arrest." *New York Herald Tribune,* February 7, 1903.
"Vigorous Novel of Alberta." *Saturday Night Magazine,* February 2, 1924, 9.
Willcox, L. C. "Onoto Watanna and the Sonnet." *New York Times Book Review,* January 30, 1904, 74.

Other Sources

ARCHIVAL

Babcock, Frank. Papers. Department of Special Collections, Hamilton College, Clinton, N.Y.
Gall's News Letter. Microfilm Collection, Library of Congress, Washington D.C.
Noguchi, Yone. Papers. Bancroft Library, University of California at Berkeley.
Reeve, Winnifred Eaton. Fonds. Special Collections, University of Calgary Library, Calgary, Alberta, Canada.
Webster, Jean. Papers. Special Collections Department, Vassar College Library, Poughkeepsie, N.Y.

BOOKS, ARTICLES, AND DISSERTATIONS

Arnold, Edwin. *Japonica.* New York: Charles Scribner's Sons, 1891.
———. *Seas and Lands.* London: Longmans, Green, 1894.
Babcock, Bertrand W. *A Syndicated Prince.* Serialized in *Eclectic Magazine,* May 1906, 377–84; June 1906, 544–50; July 1906, 73–80; August 1906, 171–84; September 1906, 248–60; October 1906, 369–75; November 1906, 467–73; December 1906, 549–55.
———. "The Psychological Investigator." *Eclectic Magazine,* April 1907, 368–70.
———. "The Deadhead, and What He Costs the Theatre." *Theater Magazine,* July–December 1910, 95–97+.
———. "Horses in the Big War." *Outing Magazine,* May 1919, 77–79.
Babcock, Stephen. *Babcock Genealogy.* New York: Eaton and Mains, 1903.
Beauchamp, Cari. *Without Lying Down: A Biography of Frances Marion.* New York: Scribners, 1997.
Belasco, David. "The Darling of the Gods" and "Madame Butterfly." In *Six Plays,* by David Belasco. Boston: Little, Brown, 1929.
Bird, Isabella L. *Unbeaten Tracks in Japan.* New York: G. P. Putnam, 1881.
Black, Clinton V. *History of Jamaica.* 1973. Reprint, London: Collins Sangster, 1979.
Blake, Nelson Manfred. *The Road to Reno: A History of Divorce in the United States.* New York: Macmillan, 1962.
Blanch, Lesley. *Pierre Loti, the Legendary Romantic.* New York: Harcourt Brace Jovanovich, 1983.
Bosse, Sara. "Cooking and Serving a Chinese Dinner in America." *Harper's Bazaar,* January 1913, 27, 29+.

———. "Giving a Chinese Luncheon Party." *Harper's Bazaar,* March 1913, 135, 146.

———. "Giving a Chinese Tea in America." *Harper's Bazaar,* April 1913, 192+.

———. "A New Dinner for Churches and Clubs." *Ladies' Home Journal,* October 1913, 113.

Botshon, Lisa. "Cautious Pluralism: Ethnic Women Writers and Early Twentieth-Century U.S. Popular Culture." Ph.D. diss., Columbia University, 1997.

Brown, E. K., and Leon Edel. *Willa Cather: A Critical Biography.* New York: Alfred A. Knopf, 1953.

Ceplair, Larry. *A Great Lady: A Life of the Screenwriter Sonya Levien.* Lanham, Md.: Scarecrow, 1996.

Chan, Sucheng. *Asian Americans: An Interpretive History.* Boston: Twayne, 1991.

Charbonneau, Réjean, Aline Charles, Andre Cousineau, and Carmen Soucy-Roy. *De fil en aiguille: Chronique ouvrière d'une filature de coton à Hochelaga in 1880.* Montreal: Societe Saint-Jean-Baptiste (section Maissonneuve) in collaboration with l'Atelier d'Histoire Hochelaga-Maissonneuve, 1985.

Clement, Ernest W. *A Handbook of Modern Japan.* Detroit: A. C. McClurg, 1904.

Cole, Jean Lee. "A Land of Sanctuary: Winnifred Eaton's Canadian Prairie" and "On the Clock: Writing in Hollywood." Chapters from diss. in progress, University of Texas, Austin.

Collier, Peter, and David Horowitz. *The Fords: An American Epic.* New York: Summit Books, 1987.

Con, Harry, Ronald J. Con, Graham Johnson, Edgar Wickberg, and William E. Willmott. *From China to Canada: A History of the Chinese Communities in Canada.* Edited by Edgar Wickberg. Toronto: McClelland and Stewart, 1982.

Curtis, Leslie. *Reno Reveries.* Reno: Distributed by Armanko Stationery, 1924.

Dempsey, Hugh A. *History in Their Blood: The Indian Portraits of Nicholas de Grandmaison.* New York: Hudson Hills, 1982.

Di Biase, Linda Popp. "The Alberta Years of Winnifred Eaton." *Alberta History* 39 (Spring 1991): 1–8.

Dick, Bernard F. *City of Dreams: The Making and Remaking of Universal Pictures.* Lexington: University Press of Kentucky, 1997.

Doyle, James. "Canadian Women Writers and the American Literary Milieu of the 1890s." In *Rediscovering Our Foremothers, Nineteenth-Century Canadian Women Writers,* edited by Lorraine McMullen. Ottawa: University of Ottawa Press, 1988.

———. "Sui Sin Far and Onoto Watanna: Two Early Chinese-Canadian Authors." *Canadian Literature,* Spring 1994, 50–58.

———. "Law, Legislation, and Literature: The Life of Grace H. Harte." *Biography* 17 (Fall 1994): 367–85.

———. *The Fin de Siècle Spirit: Walter Blackburn Harte and the American/Canadian Literary Milieu of the 1890s.* Toronto: ECW, 1995.

Dreiser, Theodore. *Sister Carrie.* New York: Doubleday, Page, 1900.

Drinkwater, John. *The Life and Adventures of Carl Laemmle.* New York: G. P. Putnam's Sons, 1931.

Ferens, Dominika. "Edith and Winnifred Eaton: The Uses of Ethnography in Turn-of-the-Century Asian American Literature." Ph.D. diss., University of California at Los Angeles, 1998.

Foran, Max, with Nonie Houlton. *Roland Gissing: The People's Painter.* Calgary: University of Calgary Press, 1988.

Francke, Lizzie. *Script Girls: Women Screenwriters in Hollywood.* London: British Film Institute, 1994.

Gissing, George. *New Grub Street.* 1891. Reprint, London: Penguin Classics Edition, 1985.

Glynn-Ward, H. *The Writing on the Wall.* Vancouver: Sun, 1921.

Hampton, Benjamin B. *A History of the American Film Industry from Its Beginnings to 1931.* New York: Dover, 1971.

Harte, Walter Blackburn. "Bubble and Squeak." *Fly Leaf,* December 1895, 26–31, March 1896, 20–32, and April 1896, 18–32; *Lotus,* October 1896, 212–18, and May 1897, 160–67.

———. "Lucky Richard's Manual on How to Spend Money." *Fly Leaf,* March 1896, 1–10.

Hearn, Lafcadio. *Glimpses of Unfamiliar Japan.* Boston: Houghton, Mifflin, 1894.

———. *Out of the East: Reveries and Studies in New Japan.* Boston: Houghton, Mifflin, 1895.

Helly, Denise. *Les chinois à Montreal, 1877–1951.* Montreal: Quebecois de recherche sur la culture, 1987.

Holliday, Wendy. "Hollywood's Modern Women: Screenwriting, World Culture, and Feminism, 1910–1940." Ph.D. diss., New York University, 1995.

Howells, William Dean. "A Psychological Counter-Current in Recent Fiction." *North American Review* 173 (December 1901): 872–88.

Kessler-Harris, Alice. *Out to Work: A History of Wage-Earning Women in the United States.* New York: Oxford University Press, 1982.

Larkin, Susan G. "Genjiro Yeto: Between Japan and Japanism." *Greenwich History: The Journal of the Historical Society of the Town of Greenwich* 5 (2000): 8–21.

Latourette, Kenneth Scott. *A History of Christian Missions in China.* New York: Macmillan, 1929.

Leacock, Stephen. Review of *Cattle. Goblin,* February 1924.

Lessard, Michel. *Montréal, métropole du Québec: Images oubliées de la vie quotidienne, 1852–1910.* Montreal: Les Éditions de l'Homme, une division du groupe Sogides, 1992.

L'Histoire du logement ouvrièr à Hochelaga-Maissonneuve. Montreal: l'Atelier d'Histoire Hochelaga-Maissonneuve, 1980.

Ling, Amy. "Winnifred Eaton: Ethnic Chameleon and Popular Success." *MELUS* 11 (Fall 1984): 4–15.

———. "Revelation and Mask: Autobiographies of the Eaton Sisters." *a/b Auto/Biography Studies* 3 (Summer 1987): 46–52.

———. *Between Worlds: Women Writers of Chinese Ancestry.* New York: Pergamon, 1990.

———. "Creating One's Own Self: The Eaton Sisters." In *Reading the Literatures of Asian America,* edited by Shirley Lim and Amy Ling. Philadelphia: Temple University Press, 1992.

———. "Gender Issues in Early Chinese American Autobiography." In *A Gathering of Voices on the Asian American Experience,* edited by Annette White-Parks. Fort Atkinson, Wis.: Highsmith, 1994.

———. "Oak and Bamboo: The Eaton Sisters." Unpublished manuscript, n.d.

Little, Frances. *The Lady of the Decoration.* Toronto: Musson, 1906.

Long, John Luther. *Miss Cherry Blossom of Tokyo.* Philadelphia: J. B. Lippincott, 1895.

———. *Madame Butterfly.* 1898. Reprint, New York: Century, 1903.

Loti, Pierre. *Madame Chrysanthemum.* 1888. Translated by Laura Ensor. Reprint, London: KPI, 1985.

Maas, Frederica Sagor. *The Shocking Miss Pilgrim: A Writer in Early Hollywood.* Lexington: University Press of Kentucky, 1999.

Mann, John. *Highbury Fields: The Most Interesting School in London.* Winchester, England: Edgeley Publications, 1994.

Marion, Frances. *Off with Their Heads!* New York: Macmillan, 1972.

Matsukawa, Yuko. "Cross-Dressing and Cross-Naming: Decoding Onoto Watanna." In *Tricksterism in Turn-of-the-Century American Literature: A Multicultural Perspective,* edited by Elizabeth Ammons and Annette White-Parks. Hanover, N.H.: University Press of New England, 1994.

McCourt, Edward A. *The Canadian West in Fiction.* Toronto: Ryerson, 1949.

McCreadie, Marsha. *The Women Who Write the Movies: From Frances Marion to Nora Ephron.* New York: Birch Lane, 1994.

Melnyk, George. *The Literary History of Alberta,* vol. 1, *From Writing-on-Stone to World War Two.* Edmonton: Edmonton University Press, 1998.

Meyerowitz, Joanne. "Sexual Geography and Gender Economy: The Furnished-Room Districts of Chicago, 1890–1930." In *Unequal Sisters: A Multicultural Reader in U.S. Women's History,* 2d ed., edited by Vicki Ruiz and Ellen DuBois. New York: Routledge, 1994.

Miner, Earl. *The Japanese Tradition in British and American Literature.* Princeton, N.J.: Princeton University Press, 1958.

Moey, Anne. "Have You the Power? The Palmer Photoplay Corporation and the Film Viewer/Author in the 1920s." *Film History* 9, no. 3 (1997): 300–319.

Moser, Linda Trinh. Afterword to *Me: A Book of Remembrance.* 1915. Reprint, Jackson: University Press of Mississippi, 1997.

———. "Chinese Prostitutes, Japanese Geishas, and Working Women: Images of Race, Class and Gender in the Work of Edith Eaton/Sui Sin Far and Winnifred Eaton/Onoto Watanna." Ph.D. diss., University of California at Davis, 1997.

Najmi, Samina. "Representations of White Women in Works by Selected African American and Asian American Authors." Ph.D. diss., Tufts University, 1997.

———. Introduction to *The Heart of Hyacinth,* by Onoto Watanna. 1903. Reprint, Seattle: University of Washington Press, 2000.

Noguchi, Yone. "The American Diary of a Japanese Girl." *Frank Leslie's Popular Monthly,* November 1901, 75–82, and December 1901, 192–201.

———. *Yone Noguchi Collected English Letters.* Edited by Ikuko Atsumi. Tokyo: Yone Noguchi Society, 1975.

Oishi, Eve. Introduction to *Miss Numè of Japan,* by Onoto Watanna. 1899. Reprint, Baltimore: Johns Hopkins University Press, 1999.

Price, Elizabeth Bailey. "City of Calgary." *MacLean's Magazine,* April 15, 1933, 26, 40, 42.

Putnam, Frank. *Love Lyrics.* Chicago: Blakely, 1898.

Radway, Janice A. *Reading the Romance: Women, Patriarchy, and Popular Literature.* Chapel Hill: University of North Carolina Press, 1984.

Reeve, Paul Eaton. "Auto-da-Fe." In *Designed for Reading: An Anthology Drawn from the*

Saturday Review of Literature, 1924–1934, edited by Henry Seidel Canby. New York: Macmillan, 1934.

———. "Succumbing" and "Lightning Puppet." In *Modern Things*, edited by Parker Tyler. New York: Galleon, 1934.

Salverson, Laura Goodman. *Confessions of an Immigrant's Daughter.* Toronto: Ryerson, 1939.

Saxton, Alexander. *The Indispensible Enemy: Labor and the Anti-Chinese Movement in California.* Berkeley: University of California Press, 1971.

Shea, Pat. "Winnifred Eaton and the Politics of Miscegenation in Popular Fiction (Popular Literature and Film)." *MELUS* 22 (Summer 1997): 19–35.

Simpson, Alan, and Mary Simpson, with Ralph Connor. *Jean Webster, Storyteller.* [Poughkeepsie, N.Y.:] Tymor Associates, 1984.

Solberg, S. E. "The Eaton Sisters: Sui Sin Far and Onoto Watanna." Paper presented at the Pacific Northwest Asian American Writer's Conference, Seattle, Wash., April 1976.

———. "Sui Sin Far/Edith Eaton: First Chinese American Fictionist." *MELUS* 8 (Spring 1981): 27–29.

Spaulding, Carol Vivian. "Blue-Eyed Asians: Eurasianism in the Work of Edith Eaton/Sui Sin Far, Winnifred Eaton/Onoto Watanna, and Diana Chang." Ph.D. diss., University of Iowa, 1996.

Stempel, Tom. *A History of Screenwriting in the American Film.* New York: Continuum, 1988.

Sui Sin Far [A Canadian Firefly, pseud.]. "The Girl of the Period: A Veracious Chronicle of Opinion." *Gall's News Letter,* February 8, 1897, n.p.

———. *Mrs. Spring Fragrance and Other Writings.* Edited by Amy Ling and Annette White-Parks. Urbana: University of Illinois Press, 1995.

"Sun Yat Sen Paid Visit to Montreal." Undated newspaper clipping. Box 14, Winnifred Eaton Reeve Fonds, Special Collections, University of Calgary Library, Calgary, Alberta, Canada.

Szyliowicz, Irene. *Pierre Loti and Oriental Women.* London: Macmillan, 1988.

Takaki, Ronald. *Strangers from a Different Shore: A History of Asian Americans.* New York: Penguin, 1989.

———. *A Different Mirror: A History of Multicultural America.* Boston: Little, Brown, 1993.

Taylor, Frank Fonda. *To Hell with Paradise: A History of the Jamaican Tourist Industry.* Pittsburgh: University of Pittsburgh Press, 1993.

Timberlake, Craig. *The Bishop of Broadway: The Life and Work of David Belasco.* New York: Library Publishers, 1954.

Tupper, Eleanor, and George E. McReynolds. *Japan in American Public Opinion.* New York: Macmillan, 1937.

Webster, Jean. *Daddy-Long-Legs.* New York: Century, 1912.

Weisberg, Gabriel P., and Phillip Cate. *Japonisme: Japanese Influence on French Art, 1854–1910.* Cleveland, Ohio: Cleveland Museum of Art, 1975.

White-Parks, Annette. *Sui Sin Far/Edith Maude Eaton: A Literary Biography.* Urbana: University of Illinois Press, 1995.

"Will Montreal Have a Chinatown?" *Montreal Daily Star,* December 14, 1895.

Wu, William F. *The Yellow Peril: Chinese Americans in American Fiction, 1850–1940*. Camden, Conn.: Archon Books, 1982.

Yung, Judy. *Unbound Feet: A Social History of Chinese Women in San Francisco.* Berkeley: University of California Press, 1995.

Zierold, Norman. *The Moguls.* New York: Coward-McCann, 1969.

Index

DIANA BIRCHALL, Winnifred Eaton Reeve's granddaughter, grew up in New York City and now lives in Santa Monica, California, where she is a story analyst at Warner Bros. She is the author of several Jane Austen sequels and has also written for newspapers.

The Asian American Experience

The Hood River Issei: An Oral History of Japanese Settlers in Oregon's Hood River Valley *Linda Tamura*

Americanization, Acculturation, and Ethnic Identity: The Nisei Generation in Hawaii *Eileen H. Tamura*

Sui Sin Far/Edith Maude Eaton: A Literary Biography *Annette White-Parks*

Mrs. Spring Fragrance and Other Writings *Sui Sin Far; edited by Amy Ling and Annette White-Parks*

The Golden Mountain: The Autobiography of a Korean Immigrant, 1895–1960 *Easurk Emsen Charr; edited and with an introduction by Wayne Patterson*

Race and Politics: Asian Americans, Latinos, and Whites in a Los Angeles Suburb *Leland T. Saito*

Achieving the Impossible Dream: How Japanese Americans Obtained Redress *Mitchell T. Maki, Harry H. L. Kitano, and S. Megan Berthold*

If They Don't Bring Their Women Here: Chinese Female Immigration before Exclusion *George Anthony Peffer*

Growing Up Nisei: Race, Generation, and Culture among Japanese Americans of California, 1924–49 *David K. Yoo*

Chinese American Literature since the 1850s *Xiao-huang Yin*

Pacific Pioneers: Japanese Journeys to America and Hawaii, 1850–80 *John E. Van Sant*

Holding Up More Than Half the Sky: Chinese Women Garment Workers in New York City, 1948–92 *Xiaolan Bao*

Onoto Watanna: The Story of Winnifred Eaton *Diana Birchall*

Typeset in 10.5/13 Minion
Composed by Celia Shapland
for the University of Illinois Press
Manufactured by Thomson-Shore, Inc.

University of Illinois Press
1325 South Oak Street
Champaign, IL 61820-6903
www.press.uillinois.edu